Local Government Budgeting

Local Government Budgeting

A Managerial Approach

Gerasimos A. Gianakis
and Clifford P. McCue

 PRAEGER

Westport, Connecticut
London

The Library of Congress has cataloged the hardcover edition as follows:

Gianakis, Gerasimos A.
    Local government budgeting : a managerial approach / Gerasimos A.
  Gianakis, Clifford P. McCue.
        p.   cm.
    Includes bibliographical references and index.
    ISBN 1–56720–006–0 (alk. paper)
    1. Local budgets—United States.   2. Local finance—United States.
  I. McCue, Clifford P.   II. Title.
  HJ9147.G5   1999
  352.4'8214'0973—dc21   98–24563

British Library Cataloguing in Publication Data is available.

A hardcover edition of *Local Government Budgeting* is available from
Quorum Books, an imprint of Greenwood Publishing Group, Inc.
(ISBN 1–56720–006–0).

Library of Congress Catalog Card Number: 98–24563
ISBN: 0–275–95272–X

First published in 1999

Praeger Publishers, 88 Post Road West, Westport, CT 06881
An imprint of Greenwood Publishing Group, Inc.

Printed in the United States of America

The paper used in this book complies with the
Permanent Paper Standard issued by the National
Information Standards Organization (Z39.48–1984).

11th, 12th, 13th, 14th, 15th, 16th

This book is formally and gratefully dedicated to our wives, Mary Gianakis and Jacki G. McCue, who have had to put up with what must have seemed quixotic career moves and poorly considered locational decisions. Without their emotional and not inconsiderable financial support, this book would not have been possible. But it is also dedicated to our former comrades on the front lines of public service delivery. We hope the book serves as support in the form of understanding and as a catalyst for better communication with academia. In our experience, both have been in short supply.

Contents

Preface

The 1989 Southeast Conference on Public Administration (SECOPA) was held in Clearwater Beach, Florida. Many members assumed that the location would make this SECOPA a big draw, and, not disappointing, many of the leaders of the American Society for Public Administration (ASPA) and many prominent thinkers in budgeting and other areas of public administration were featured participants. One of the authors of this book was at that time a budget manager with the city of St. Petersburg, Florida. He had been a member of ASPA for ten years and was working on his doctoral dissertation in public administration. His professional career and educative efforts had been guided by the idea that public administration theory should seek to inform practice, and he managed to convince the budget director to make SECOPA the primary training event for her six-person staff that year. At least two of the budget analysts attended each of the eleven conference panels that were related to some aspect of public budgeting. At the post-conference staff meeting, the budget analysts and the other budget managers were unanimous in their opinion that the papers presented had been largely irrelevant to their professional duties. The majority of the papers had focused on the politics of federal budgeting and the economic implications of alternative resource allocation schemes. The only paper cited with any enthusiasm was one that anguished over the irrelevancy of budget theory to budget practice. As the budget director began to anguish over the fate of her training budget, this book began to take shape.

The authors have amassed a collective eighteen years of experience in the practice of local government budgeting and financial management. As of this writing we have dedicated a combined total of ten years to academic pursuits. Much of that time has been spent discussing the issues that have become the substance of this book. We decided to get around to the actual business of writing before the sounds of the gunfire of practice were completely muffled by the ubiquitous and multifarious ivy of academia—kudzu here in the South. The nature of the book is also rooted in our experiences in the classroom, where we were hard pressed to find a text that would serve as a suitable frame for the "war stories" in which the students seemed to revel. We sought a text that appreciated the unique context of local government budgeting and financial management. Local government budgeting is not only different from state and federal budgeting, it is often quite different from other local government budgeting, and therein lies part of the difficulty of theorizing about it. This is one of the issues that we explore in the book, in which we seek to examine theoretical issues in the context of practice, to illuminate practical problems through the application of theory, and to explore the possibilities of a practice-based theory of local government budgeting that holds normative implications for practice.

In order to develop theory for practice it is necessary to approach budgeting as it is experienced by practitioners—hence our subtitle, "A Managerial Approach." For practicing public administrators, public budgeting manifests itself as the resource allocation process of an organization that happens to operate in a very political environment. Budgeting is experienced as an internal process of an organization whose boundaries are quite permeable, particularly during the formal budgetary process. The organizational dimensions of budgeting are most fully realized at the local government level, because it is there that the public organization most clearly interfaces with the formal budgetary process as something that can be characterized as a single, integrated organization. The management of the budgetary process, the role of the process in shaping the nature of the organization, and the organization as a limiting factor on the nature of the process are all salient elements for professional practitioners. Theory-building efforts in budgeting must focus on these elements in order to provide theory that illuminates practice for practitioners.

By approaching budgeting as the resource allocation process of a public organization, we are able to avoid the artificial distinction between budgeting and financial management. Research and pedagogy in public administration have been characterized by excessive compartmentalization. The field has focused on the various parts of public management, but has largely ignored the whole. We attempt to tie the resource allocation process to public management by approaching it in its organizational context. Obviously, public agencies participate in a formal budgeting process and the local government organization houses a range of professional financial-management functions, but theory building that takes budgeting and finance out of the context in which these are practiced can only produce descriptions of tools and instrumental theory. Descriptive and normative theories require a broader view, particularly ones that seek to illuminate the nature of practice. We approach budgeting and financial management under the umbrella concept of managing public resources to maximize the capacity of the public organization to respond to community needs.

We do not presume, however, to prescribe for local government budgeting—a hopeless task given the wide variety of contexts that must be addressed. We strive to provide a theoretical understanding of the salient contextual issues in order to allow public managers to decide what is best for their particular jurisdictions, although we may proffer general suggestions based on our own understanding. Nor do we shy away from the word "best" in the context of public budgeting. Our organizationally based approach to theory building allows us to explore a normative theory of budgeting rooted in the professional practice of financial management broadly defined. The finance professional is charged with monitoring and maintaining the long-term financial viability of the organization he or she serves. Although the determination of the optimal mix of services for any political jurisdiction is ultimately a problem for political philosophy, all schemes are limited if resources are not available. The core professional function of the finance practitioner makes him or her at least partly responsible for the efficacy of the process through which organizational resources are allocated, obligates the practitioner to inform decision makers of the potential long-term effects of short-term allocation schemes, and makes it necessary for him or her to participate in the process of identifying and delineating the ramifications of alternative futures for the organization. This is not to say that the process of selecting among these alternatives is not also fraught with value issues, only that the finance officer's professional expertise allows him or her to participate as something more than a political actor, and his or her professional responsibility mandates that participation. Of course, all professional public administrators seek to make decisions that are "best" for their jurisdictions, and we contend that the resource allocation system of the public organization can be used to enhance the capacity of the organization's managers to recognize and pursue optimal alternatives. This broadly defined finance function is, therefore, a basic element of all public management. These issues are more fully developed in the nine chapters that comprise the text.

We do seek to prescribe for theory, and we have tried to write as practitioners speaking to researchers. This book is essentially a polemic on budget theory. It is also designed to be used as a second text in graduate courses in public budgeting and financial management, particularly in M.P.A. programs that focus on local government management. It is not a comprehensive text on all aspects of public budgeting and financial management. We explore the traditional budgeting concepts in the context of local government budgeting, and we introduce additional issues that we believe are particularly important at the local level. The book can also serve as a reference for local government budgeting practitioners. Each chapter ends with a section on a significant management issue related to the subject matter of the chapter. These may reflect structural or procedural issues, implementation problems, analytical techniques, or managerial capacity–building programs. They are designed to illustrate theoretical issues, as well as to present practical advice—at least from our perspective.

In Chapter 1 we differentiate local government budgeting from federal and state budgeting, as well as from budgeting in private-sector firms. Theory-building efforts have been largely focused on federal budgeting. National budgeting is big and sexy, and a single locus makes the development of a grand, unifying theory more practical. The idea that government agencies can be approached as independent political actors has made federal budgeting more attractive to political scientists, and the economic implications of the federal budget have made it more attractive to economists. Local governments typically manifest a stronger executive function than the national government and most state governments. The number of elected executives at the state level and the powers of the governor are variables that make some state budgeting processes more or less like local government budgeting. Local government executives also oversee additional administrative processes with which the budget process must interface; these include strategic and comprehensive planning, capital improvement and economic development programs, and programs designed to enhance the overall management capacity of the local government organization. Chapter 1 describes the organizational and environmental factors that shape the nature of local government budgeting.

In Chapter 2 we describe alternative budget formats and how the implementation of each is constrained by the factors described in Chapter 1. The organizational and managerial ramifications of budget formats are explored, and the factors that may constrain the implementation of results-oriented, or ''entrepreneurial,'' budgeting are identified. The implications of the revenue constraint in local government budgeting are also established in Chapter 2. An organization's capacity to manage its resources becomes more salient in a revenue-driven budget system. As the possibility of a viable revenue constraint becomes more probable at the national level of government, where expenditures have historically been driven by political demands, organizational capacity and managerial processes will become increasingly important considerations. The organizational roles of the budget office are also reviewed here. The budget office can simply print the final budget after considerable cutting and pasting—thus playing the relatively minor role of the publisher of the budget document—or it can be a major player in the policy-making process. Relationships between the budget office and substantive service delivery systems, and the part that alternative budget formats may play in enhancing or limiting these relationships, are also examined.

The execution and control of the final budget are the topics of Chapter 3. We describe the traditional ''nuts and bolts'' of budget execution: the establishment of allotments and the monitoring of expenditures; the within-year supplemental appropriations process and the budgeting of discretionary funds; the structure of the purchasing process and of accounting systems; the budgeting of internal services, and issues related to the costing of public services. We also make the point that the allocation of resources within the local government organization is a continuous process that extends beyond the elements of the formal budget process and the ''nuts and bolts'' described here. The resource allocation process must be understood in the context of the entire organization. The formal execution and control mechanisms employed are a function of, and at the same time determinants of, the nature of the local government organization. Thus, they can be used to influence and develop the management capacity of the organization. Management capacity includes the capacity to make resource allocation decisions that are optimal for the jurisdiction as a whole—that is, responsive to short-range demands for services and supportive of the jurisdiction's long-range financial viability.

Chapter 4 focuses on the issue of public productivity improvement. Traditional budget processes generate disincentives to productive management. We examine issues in program performance measurement, and we describe how the design, development, and implementation of a results-oriented performance measurement system can enhance the managerial capacity of an organization in addition to enhancing the rationality of the resource allocation process. The local government organization is a highly differentiated one, and problems associated with integration can generate resource allocation schemes that are sub-optimal for the political jurisdiction. A formal performance measurement system can serve to expand the decision perspectives of substantive service delivery managers. Chapter 5 follows these issues with an examination of some analytical techniques that can be used to support productivity enhancement efforts, including revenue forecasting methods and benefit-cost analysis. The role of structured analysis in the resource allocation process is reviewed, and issues related to the organizational placement of a formal analytical capacity are examined.

Chapter 6 begins with an examination of issues associated with the structure of local government revenue systems, including issues of equity, adequacy, and efficiency, as well as revenue management issues. The movement toward fees for services and greater reliance on own-source revenues makes revenue management an increasingly important function in local government. Revenue structures are also closely linked to economic development programs; specific revenue portfolios provide incentives and disincentives for actors within and outside the jurisdiction who make investment decisions related to the economic health of the community. We examine the factors that influence financial condition and fiscal health. Short-term decisions regarding the bundle of revenues a jurisdiction uses to fuel its services have long-term implications through their relationship to long-term financial condition and short-term political responsiveness. The role of finance professionals is crucial here, and it points to a normative theory of budgeting rooted in their fiduciary responsibilities as stewards of the organization.

In Chapter 7 we further develop this argument, and the relationship between economic development and budgeting is made more manifest through an examination of the capital improvement planning and the capital budgeting processes. Chapters 7 and 8 are more technical in nature, as we attempt to describe some of the tools available to local government managers to pursue the ends of professional management we had outlined earlier. Chapter 8 focuses on debt management. We examine alternative ways of financing infrastructure improvements and economic development efforts. The relationship between debt management and the funding of current operations is explored. Once again, effective debt management is a crucial element in the long-term financial viability of the jurisdiction, and it can also increase the resources available to the annual budget process. The roles and functions of bond-rating agencies and investor organizations are reviewed.

The book closes with a summary of the major issues examined in the previous chapters. In an age of competitive, fend-for-yourself federalism, budgetary decisions have important ramifications for a jurisdiction's ability to attract human, physical, and fiscal capital. We examine the local government budget process in the context of the strategic implications of resource allocation decisions. This makes budgeting something more than a political process in which it is determined "who gets what," and calls on professional public managers to be something more than referees in this process. The ends described here require building the capacity of the local government organization to make decisions that are optimal for the jurisdiction as a whole. Public managers must do more than simply strive to maximize resources at the level of their individual programs. In one sense, we have attempted to address the elemental budgetary issue posited by V. O. Key: "[O]n what basis shall it be decided to allocate x dollars to activity A instead of activity B?" (1940: 1138). We contend that the optimal basis is the long-term economic viability of the jurisdiction, and this also requires public managers to meet immediate needs for services economically and efficiently, and to build knowledge of the jurisdiction into their organizational processes and structures. We also suggest that budget theorists must look beyond budget formats and formal budget processes in order to reconcile the responsibility of the professional manager to maximize efficiency and effectiveness in public resource allocation schemes with the demands of democracy for accountability and control.

The budget process is the single organizational process that can serve to integrate the highly differentiated service delivery systems that comprise the local government organization. It is only during the budget process that the individual service agencies need even acknowledge that they are components of a single organization. The budget process is the single most important tool available to build the managerial capacity required to serve the ends described above. This points to the need to develop budget theory that is sensitive to the organizational context of budgeting. The proposed marriage of organizational theory and budget theory is a potentially fertile one, because practitioners experience budgeting as a continuous organizational process. If public administration is to develop budget theory that is useful to practitioners, that theory must reflect this organizational reality. This approach also allows public administration to make a unique contribution to budgeting, rather than simply importing and reflecting on approaches utilized in political science or economics. Public administration is a multidisciplinary field that has been artificially and unnecessarily compartmentalized. The approach to theory building in budgeting described herein elevates the subject from a formal process that government undertakes to a central element in the functioning and management of the government organization. This approach allows the field to bring its other substantive areas—such as personnel, program evaluation, administrative behavior, and organizational development—to bear on the budget process. The public organization provides the common focus for theory building in public management necessary for the field of public administration to ultimately define itself as a unique discipline.

REFERENCE

Key, V. O. (1940). "The Lack of Budgetary Theory." *American Political Science Review*, 34 (2): 1137–1140.

Chapter 1

The Environment of
Local Government Budgeting

Most practical budgeting may take place in a twilight zone between politics
and efficiency.

Aaron Wildavsky (1961)

Budgeting is highly political, but it is not the same thing as politics in
general. It represents a special corner of politics, with many of its own
characteristics.

Irene S. Rubin (1993)

This book examines public budgeting from the perspective of local government
public administrators and in the context of the organizations in which they function. Theories that reflect this operational context will be more useful and accessible to local government public managers than those that budget researchers
have produced to date. The vectors that define the ''special corner'' of politics
described by Rubin above intersect in the public organization, which here refers
to the totality of the service delivery components of a particular political jurisdiction. The typical local government organization also constitutes a province
replete with the uncertainties, paradoxes and illusions that Wildavsky's imagery
conjures up. The authors contend that researchers in budgeting have provided
local government administrators with precious few signposts to help them wend
their way through the resource allocation process. For practicing public administrators, public budgeting manifests itself as the resource allocation process of
an organization that happens to operate within a very public and highly political
environment. It is experienced as an internal process of an organization whose
boundaries can be quite permeable, particularly during the formal budgetary
process. The theoretical approach outlined here focuses on the state and local

government levels, particularly the latter, because it is there that the public organization most clearly interfaces with the formal budgetary process as something that can be characterized as a single, integrated organization. This allows the budget process to be approached as something other than a political brawl among independent actors.

Revolt, devolution, debt and globalism have precipitated a reemphasis on research at the state and local government levels, where traditional budget theory has enjoyed limited relevance. Efforts to build theories of public budgeting have historically focused on the national level, and these efforts have simply not produced theories that have utility for local government practitioners. These efforts have focused on describing an evolving budget process in what has become a volatile political environment. This traditional focus has been rendered even less relevant to local government budgeting by the virtual collapse of the formal budget process of the federal government. Globalism and decentralization have limited the utility of the national budget as a tool of fiscal and economic policy, and studies of the economic role of the national budget have also been rendered less relevant.

This book calls for more than simply moving the focus of budget research from the politics of the formal budgetary process as a whole to the analytical techniques involved in the preparation of the executive budget. The executive budget summarizes potential budgetary outcomes for various political constituencies developed by the public organization for submission to the formal budget process. The separate consideration of the executive budget is a precipitate of the traditional focus on the national level, where the president is required to submit a budget to the Congress, and this is characterized as the first step in the annual budget "cycle." The distinction between the executive budget and the formal budget process is an artificial one that tends to underestimate both the political nature of the executive budget process and the potential for the application of structured analysis in the formal budget process. More importantly, neither the formal budget process nor the executive budget process captures the continuous nature of the resource allocation process within the public organization. The actual public resource allocation process is characterized by a continuous series of disaggregated and fragmented, but nevertheless interdependent, overlapping, and parallel decision sequences (Rubin, 1993). The formal budgetary process provides no more than a summary snapshot of the dynamic interrelationships of these several dimensions of the resource allocation process. The structure of the public organization and its internal and external environmental relationships, however, can provide a locus for centering these dimensions, for examining their interrelationships, and for developing theories that have relevance for those who deal with them. An exclusive focus on the executive budget would overlook ways in which the resource allocation process influences and is influenced by organizational structure and managerial processes. It may also miss the capacity of public managers to provide efficient and effective delivery of public services, and the very nature of the public organizations in which they function can directly affect the resource allocation mix.

This book outlines an approach to the development of budget theory that can yield theories that have utility for local government managers. As former local government finance professionals, the authors attempt to bridge public administration practice and academia. We seek to create a dialogue between finance professionals, public managers, and budget researchers. Our emphasis on the importance of context and on developing theories rooted in the experience of practitioners may be perceived as evidence of a methodological bias in social science research. We admit to no such bias. Our experiences in practice have taught us to push ontological and epistemological issues into the background so we can feel free to grasp at any useful straws. This is all to say that these issues will not be examined any further in this book, partly in order to make it more accessible to students and practitioners, and partly because we generally subscribe to a multimethods approach in any case. Nor do we seek to outline a single theory of local government budgeting, but rather to make a case for an organization-based approach to the development of local government budgeting theory.

FEDERAL, STATE AND LOCAL GOVERNMENT BUDGETING

The study of budgeting concerns the process through which resources are allocated to public programs. All levels of government engage in budgeting, but the process occurs in a variety of structural arrangements and environmental contexts. Sometimes these structures and environments are so different that the single term "budgeting" can refer to qualitatively different things. We contend that one of the variables that differentiate budgeting in local governments from the national process is the salience of the public organization—broadly defined to encompass the totality of service delivery systems housed in an identifiable umbrella organization under a single executive—in the budget processes of the former. The federal government is a vast, sprawling enterprise comprised of a variety of organizations that enjoy varying degrees of autonomy. These are usually treated as independent political actors in traditional budget theory. The U.S. Congress is populated by professional politicians representing a range of constituencies, and it houses an independent analytical capacity. The federal budget process is dominated by entitlement programs rather than by the consideration of agency line-item budget requests, and the budget process is called upon to play a role in the development and implementation of fiscal and economic policy, including efforts to redistribute income. The economic and political perspectives are naturally salient in an expenditure-driven budget process that must consider the macroeconomic ramifications of alternative spending plans. The federal budget has historically been characterized as expenditure driven because there is no requirement that revenues and expenditures balance each fiscal year.

This characteristic and its many ramifications are the most important differences between national and state and local budgeting.

Local legislators are usually part-time legislators, if not full-time politicians, and the legislative body is in session only periodically. Local legislative bodies typically do not have access to technical bureaucracies and staffs of experts that compare to those assembled in the Congress. The public organization often drives the local budget process. The resource allocation processes of local governments center on substantive service delivery programs based in agencies under the authority of the chief executive, rather than on entitlement or other transfer payment programs. Most importantly, local budgets must balance, and local government policy makers cannot consider expenditures apart from revenues. Local government budgeting is thus revenue driven, in that the revenue constraint generally dominates decision-making. The various committees in the Congress can build the national budget from the ground up and then reconcile the total with available revenues—or not. The mandate to balance the local government budget requires a top-down view of the overall allocation scheme, and the public organization can provide such a perspective.

Although these differences can be arranged on a continuum, there would seem to be a qualitative gap between the federal and local budget processes that calls for different theoretical approaches on the part of researchers. The nature of the gap points to organization theory as a potential source of practical budget theory for local governments. A factor that may limit its applicability to county governments and some municipal governments, such as the commission form (an increasingly rare form in which elected legislators also serve as the executives of service agencies), is the number of elected executives in the political jurisdiction. In county governments, however, the elected officials tend to share the same constituency, which may constrain their capacity to function as completely independent political actors. They are also likely to share important administrative support systems that are usually under the control of the chief executive. The approach to budgeting outlined here may also be a fruitful way to study states with a single elected executive, particularly when the executive is endowed with administrative tools, such as the line-item veto, which expand his or her budgetary influence. However, multiple elected executives at the state level may respond to different constituencies, and fragmented organizational structures and authority systems may make the traditional research focus on agencies as independent political actors more appropriate.

Most local public organizations are also characterized by organizational fragmentation and weak central authority systems. Multiservice public organizations are highly differentiated; that is, they face a wide range of complex environments and they must mirror that complexity in their internal structures and available expertise in order to be able to respond effectively. These professionals tend to view the world from their own often narrow perspectives, and this can generate conflict within the organization. Private-sector firms house a variety of specialists, but these are all working toward a single goal that serves to integrate their efforts and to give substance and form to the umbrella organization. Even private-sector firms organized around a variety of product lines cannot match the degree of differentiation and the problems of integration found in the typical multiservice public organization. The centrifugal forces generated by differentiation in the face of weak integrative structures and processes can be so strong that the idea of a single organization falls apart. Individual agencies also respond to different segments of the public and different professional associations, and they function in separate intergovernmental networks. At the local level, however, the prospects for effective integration are enhanced by the fact that these centrifugal forces swirl around a single executive. One of the functions of the executive is to mitigate the deleterious effects of these forces on the capacity of the public organization to respond efficiently, effectively and economically to the range of demands for service emanating from its many political environments.

The service delivery systems of the federal government and most states can most accurately be characterized as ''holding companies'' rather than as single integrated organizations. That is why the traditional focus on political interaction may be more apropos at that level of government, and why this book is primarily targeted to local government budgeting. However, as demands to balance the federal budget grow stronger and the president is endowed with managerial powers such as the line-item veto, the organizational approach to the study of resource allocation systems in the public sector may become more relevant at that level.

One of the organizational purposes of the budget process is to enhance to capacity of the organization's managers to make optimal resource allocation decisions. One criterion for optimality is that the managers provide services that are responsive to the needs of the public, and that they do so efficiently, effectively and economically. The resource allocation process should function as a counterweight to the centrifugal forces generated by the highly differentiated nature of multiservice public organizations that serve to constrain the management capacity of the public organization. Alternative budget formats and processes should be examined for their relative utility in that regard, in light of the existing capacity of the management staff. In addition to the prescription that the resource allocation process should enhance the capacity of the management staff to make optimal resource allocation decisions in the short term, the second criterion for optimality is the preservation and development of the organization's economic base in the long term. The local government organization derives its resources from the economic base of its jurisdiction, and a basic function of professional public management is to maintain the organization's flow of resources.

The resource allocation process of the public organization serves a developmental function for both the internal structure of the organization and its relationship with its external environment. The need to maintain the economic base of the jurisdiction can function as a centripetal force in the public organization, in much the same way as the need to make a profit does in the private sector. This is not to say that the determination of the optimal course of action is not ultimately a function of societal values and political power. The maintenance of the organization's resource base also requires the provision of responsive services, the identification of which is obviously value laden. The approach outlined herein provides a framework for the development of theory to inform and to guide the actions of the participants, particularly the professional public administrators. Thus, the organization-based approach to budget theory also holds promise for the development of a normative theory of budgeting rooted in the public management professional.

The issues introduced in this section are explored in greater detail in the following chapters. In the following section, we describe some of the local government resource allocation factors that make an organization-based approach to budget theory a potentially fruitful one. We do not attempt to describe all of the relevant elements, and we only try to to indicate how our approach is more appropriate for local government than one centering on the legislative body and the political process. The following chapters in this book do not examine all of the elements of the local government resource allocation process, but rather examine salient issues in the context of our overall approach.

ORGANIZATION-BASED BUDGETING COMPONENTS

The organization-based approach to the development of budget theory is a potentially fruitful course if processes within the public organization that are not part of the formal budgetary process affect the resource allocation mix. These organizational processes should also be manipulable by public managers, and crucial elements of the formal budgetary process should also be controlled by management. Any theory of the resource allocation process at the local government level must then consider these elements, and the organizational context in which they occur would be the best approach. In a more applied vein, these elements would have great salience to program managers, because they would influence their budget allocations. Since these elements are manipulable, they could be used to overcome some of the centrifugal forces in the local government organization that constrain its capacity to provide responsive services efficiently, effectively and economically. This practical end would require guiding theory.

On the local government level, the executive organization determines much of what comprises the budget process, including budget format, which may directly affect budget processes, deliberations and outcomes. These issues are examined in Chapter 2. Although state statutes and local ordinances may specify baseline requirements, the executive organization also influences the timing of the process, the participants, the number and location of public meetings and their agendas, and hence the degree to which the budget process is open to the political environment. By limiting participation, the public organization can limit the extent to which individual agencies can appeal to distinct constituencies for support of their budget requests, and the structured analysis of budget alternatives might carry more weight in the decision-making process.

The executive organization can also influence the parameters of the budget process. The organization's zoning policies, comprehensive planning process and the capital improvement budget are products of the professional, executive organization. Although they are subject to legislative review, their developmental processes are usually less open than the formal budget process. These processes can establish parameters for the budget process that are legally binding, but these decision-making processes may not be as salient to the public and the governing body as is the operating budget process. These decisions affect the long-term financial viability of the jurisdiction, as well as the level of resources available to fund immediate service needs. The capital budget process and economic development issues are reviewed in Chapter 7.

The revenue forecasting process, which establishes the revenue constraint of the budget process, is also the responsibility of the organization and its analytical staff. Managers can exert pressures on forecasters in order to dampen demands for expenditures, to expand the fund balance, or to make more discretionary funds available during the fiscal year. Long-range forecasts monitor the financial condition of the jurisdiction and set policy agendas in that regard. Forecasting is examined in Chapter 2, and again in Chapter 5 with additional analytical techniques. The source of the values and assumptions that drive analytical studies are important to the extent that such studies influence policy outcomes, and professional management should seek to enhance that influence. The behavioral controls on budget professionals and the influences on their decision assumptions are also a significant area of interest, in light of evidence that state and local executives adopt an average of 95 percent of their budget recommendations (Thurmaier, 1995). The assumptions and values that drive structured analyses should be an area of interest for top management and researchers, as should the assumptions, values and perspectives that drive operational decision making.

The operational responsibilities of professional managers may also directly affect resource allocation outcomes. Productivity improvement efforts are usually conceptualized as technological improvements at the program level, and such efforts are the core of politically neutral, professional management. However, all technological fixes have allocative effects, because they make additional resources available to the organization. These resources result in increased service levels and thus alter the allocation mix, or they are re-allocated to other service areas outside of the formal budget process. Managers' efforts to increase the capacity of their agencies to meet their programmatic requirements through such means as training programs, investments in technology, and team-building or organizational development programs also inevitably affect resource allocation process outcomes. This is not to suggest that such efforts should not be undertaken by program managers, only that it is not possible to theorize about budgeting and resource allocation without considering the action of agency man-

agers and the organizational context in which they occur. Salient questions include: Are such efforts supported by the public organization? From what
perspective are they designed? How are productivity and efficiency measured?
Are there incentives for risk taking and experimentation in program delivery?

The implementation of performance or productivity measurement systems
usually entails the definition of agency missions, goals and objectives. The definition of these ends is clearly a political process, but this process and similar
productivity efforts are formally implemented as value-neutral administrative
management tools. However, the assumptions and decision-making perspectives
that underlie such efforts manifest different political values, and these should
again command the attention of top management. Program managers seek to
appeal to a wide variety of constituencies, and may adopt ambiguous or multidimensional missions in pursuit of political support. Such a scenario can con-
fuse allocation schemes and policy-making, but the formalization of missions
and goals can be threatening to program managers. Productivity issues in the
context of local government resource allocation are examined in Chapter 4.

A particular type of productivity improvement effort is the privatization of
public services or the contracting for services with private-sector organizations.
These options seek to replace part of the public organization's resource allocation system, which is based on organizational hierarchy and authority relations, with contract-based market systems. In theory, contracts negotiated by top
management would overcome the sub-optimal allocation of resources precipitated by weak authority systems. This would clearly affect the organization's
structure and the nature of the budget process. The negotiation of these contracts
also requires the establishment of missions, service levels and performance criteria. The contract development process takes place outside of the formal budget
process, although the contracts are ultimately ratified by the governing legislative body. The hidden costs of public organization oversight staff and programmatic support represent an allocation of resources that occurs totally outside of
the budget process. The internal costs of administering the contract are often
overlooked in the initial benefit-cost analysis used to justify the contract. Some
of the problems of costing public services are reviewed in Chapters 5.

The issue of hidden costs also applies to the provision of public services.
These costs can take the form of staff services that are funded through general
revenues, but which are consumed by a particular service delivery system. For
example, a purchasing department may devote 80 percent of its resources to
processing requisitions from the public works area, or a personnel department
may devote most of its staff hours to testing and processing police applicants.
These resources support the indicated services but they are not allocated to those
services' budgets, and the true costs of providing a given level of public safety
or public works service are hidden. These costs are even excluded from the
program budget format described in the following chapter. This issue is more a
function of organizational structure than of the budget process, and yet it has
tangible impacts on the outcomes of that process. The structures and processes

of the public organization are reviewed by the governing legislative body, but usually not during the formal budget process. Management policies regarding the design and operation of administrative systems affect the recorded costs of public programs, and hence affect the resource allocation scheme of the public organization.

Although legal limits may apply here, the level of budgetary control is also a management function, and it can have a significant impact on budget outcomes. The question is whether operating agencies are required to stay within budgeted amounts at the level of the individual object code, at the level of categories of objects codes (e.g., personnel, operating expenditures, and operating capital expenditures), or at the agency budget level. The minimal level of control is often established by the level at which the actual appropriations are made by the legislative body. More stringent controls imposed by the chief executive officer would limit the agencies' discretionary spending and centralize some programmatic decision-making. Program managers would be required to commit to program operations during the budget development phase, where top management can exercise greater oversight and then maintain that policy direction through budget controls. Top management may also authorize transfers between object codes and categories of codes. These aspects of the resource allocation system are to a large extent a function of management style and organizational preferences, and they can have a significant impact on budgetary outcomes. Management policies regarding year-end supplemental appropriations may also be important in this regard. Relevant issues include: Does the chief executive or the agency executive present requests for supplemental appropriations to the legislative body? What are justifiable grounds for supplemental appropriations? What controls exist to preclude the need for supplemental appropriations? These issues are examined in Chapter 3.

A concrete manifestation of the internal resource allocation system is the operation of internal service funds, or charge-back systems. These funds are designed to account for expenditures on services that are shared by operating agencies; examples are data processing, warehousing, and fleet maintenance. The resources necessary to cover the costs of providing the service are appropriated to the operating agencies, and are disbursed to the agency housing the service as the service is provided. Such systems are designed to bring market controls and incentives to the provision and consumption of the service. The operation of internal service funds raises a host of economic, managerial, and fiscal issues that have been largely unexplored. Among these is the fact that these funds are often allowed to carry forward a fund balance between fiscal years, rather than returning unexpended resources to the general fund for re-allocation. It thus becomes possible to stockpile funds outside of the formal budget process for significant capital purchases, although large purchases are usually subject to legislative review. Allocating costs to several agencies also allows managers to mask the magnitude of the costs of providing the service, and it becomes possible to justify service enhancements by tying them to politically irresistible recipients of the internal service, such as law enforcement. Conversely, by including an internal service agency's resources in the budgets of operating agencies, it becomes easier for the latter to cut expenditures by reducing the former's resource levels. We are reminded of a finance director who, when asked to trim his budget, eliminated the printing of monthly expenditure reports for the organization's program managers. These funds had been allocated to his budget to be disbursed to the data processing department as the reports were provided, because that agency was structured as an internal service fund and computerized databases were assigned to single departments for convenience in billing. However, the finance department was not the primary user of the reports, and the finance department could eliminate them without operational loss. Internal service funds are often characterized as self-regulating market mechanisms that relieve top management of their oversight responsibilities, but this abrogation can precipitate perverse effects on the organization's resource allocation system.

Enterprise fund agencies that provide specific goods and services to the general public are structured to operate much like private companies within the public organization. The fees that these agencies charge for their services are set at a level that will cover their operating expenses, debt service and capital expenditures. These fund balances are also carried forward between fiscal years, but these revenues are usually subject to strict budgetary controls. The more salient issue here is the degree to which the provision of the specific service is being subsidized by general fund revenues, or the extent to which general government services are being subsidized by the enterprise fees. The latter scenario is the more likely, because enterprise fees can be justified on a cost recovery basis, and they are usually more palatable politically than general tax increases, which may also be subject to statutory limits. For example, a city may decide to increase sanitation fees and transfer any surpluses to the general fund as charges for services, payment in lieu of taxes, or return on initial investment, rather than raising property taxes. Computational methods and formulas regarding charges for general governmental services and foregone taxes that a private enterprise would pay are often arbitrary and idiosyncratic. As noted above, the same holds true for internal service funds. We are familiar with the case of a purchasing director who shared an electronic database with his warehouse, which was structured as an internal service fund, and he was able to charge out the cost of the entire system as warehouse overhead.

The entire fund structure of the public organization affects budgetary outcomes. A variety of funds can be constructed to segregate general funds and give the appearance that they are earmarked for specific purposes. These funds are thus hidden from the formal budget process; examples include general funds that have been appropriated to general capital improvements but never fully expended, or state revenue-sharing funds received in a separate fund but available for general government expenditures. Routine maintenance projects may also be recast as capital projects, and the true cost of providing a given level of service in a specific area is hidden from the regular budget process. The recurring impact of capital projects on operating funds may also not be clearly determined or enunciated, and the capital program budget, which may be less salient to the general public, may commit the formal operating budget process to specific expenditures. Issues regarding fund structures and accounting policies appear throughout this book.

The structure of the revenue system is often viewed as a technical issue under the purview of the executive organization. However, revenues also influence the degree to which public services are responsive to immediate needs; that is, service delivery is not responsive if those who need the service cannot pay for it, or if the revenue system places too great a burden on the recipient. The proliferation of user fees, as local governments become increasingly dependent on own-source revenues, carries with it a host of equity issues and also threatens service-level adequacy. However, tax burdens and service mixes influence the locational decisions of individuals, and, thus, the locational decisions of firms that employ them. Tax systems that overburden businesses may have a direct influence on locational decisions by private firms that affect economic development, and hence on the long-term financial viability of the jurisdiction. The need to borrow to build the infrastructure in support of economic development must also be balanced with the need to maintain current service levels. Debt service should be ''leveled'' so that borrowing for future needs does not disrupt the flow of resources to current services. Revenue structures are examined in Chapter 6, and debt policies in Chapter 8.

The public organization influences resource allocation outcomes not just through its structure and administrative processes, but through the culture and values of the organization. The cultural values that are most salient for each employee may be those of their particular agency, and it is this parochialism that compromises the overall efficiency of the public organization. The most important organizational ritual around which top management can build core organizational values is the budget process. They can begin by requiring that their finance professionals carry out their own allocation responsibilities—for example, forecasting, cash management, and fund balance maintenance—in a way that reflects those core values. Top management cannot expect managers to put aside parochial interests and self-interested behaviors if their finance professionals do not manifest the values of risk-taking, experimentation and creativity, and adopt decision premises that reflect an organization-wide perspective. Both the finance director and the purchasing director cited in this section were clearly finance professionals, and when the centralized functions they administer augment the centrifugal forces endemic in the public organization, the center will not hold. In any case, a cursory review of the administrative processes, organizational structures and organizational values that affect resource allocation outcomes will demonstrate that any theory of local government resource allocation will be incomplete if it does not consider these elements.

THE INTERGOVERNMENTAL ENVIRONMENT

The local government public organization is a highly differentiated one, but unlike at most levels of government, the various agencies that comprise the organization tend to fall under a single executive. The prospects for achieving a level of integration that would enhance the efficiency, effectiveness, economy and responsiveness of the organization's mix of services rest on the single organizational dimension that runs through all of the agencies, and the only process in which each agency must acknowledge that it is a part of a single organization—namely, the annual formal budget process and the resource allocation process of the organization. The destructive effects of political conflict are also mitigated by the fact that all of the agencies in the local government organization serve more or less the same constituency. There is also usually a consensus regarding which services the organization should be providing, although particular constituencies may disagree on the level of resources allocated to individual programs.

The potential for conflict is also lessened because local governments are limited in their capacity to engage in income redistribution policies. Local governments must compete with other local governments for economic investment and tax-base maintenance. Highly progressive tax systems (in which high-income persons pay at a higher rate) on the local government level would encourage higher-income persons to exit the jurisdiction, and the costs of exit at this level are much lower than the costs, both financial and psychological, of exiting the national jurisdiction. However, recent efforts to push more responsibility for some income maintenance programs, such as welfare payments, to the local government level may disrupt this relatively placid political landscape. Local governments exist in an intergovernmental network in which they exercise the least amount of power.

All local governments are creatures of the states that create them. A 1911 ruling by an Iowa judge established that local governments possess only those powers specifically granted to them by the state. This means that each state must pass laws that are responsive to the needs of all of its municipalities, and this can be problematic in states with several large cities operating in different environments. Some states have established home-rule charter cities that are allowed to adopt their own ordinances and policies in any area, unless they are specifically prohibited from doing so by state law. This allows some cities do define their own organizational structures, expenditure patterns and revenue systems, rather than conforming to the single model defined by state statutes.

States are in a position to mandate that their cities provide specific services, to limit the range of revenue sources available to them, and to impose a variety of administrative, procedural, and reporting requirements. Some states have periodically lessened their own political burdens and fiscal problems by requiring local governments to provide services for which the state does not provide revenues or additional revenue sources. State-level politicians receive political mileage by providing services without assuming a financial obligation. However, the states often collect certain revenues for redistribution to the localities in which they were collected, operate formal revenue-sharing programs and grant programs, and function as financial overseers through financial reporting requirements. Thus, they lessen the administrative costs of collecting revenues, augment local revenues, and provide early-warning systems for financial problems. Some states have even passed legislation that limits their capacity to impose unfunded mandates on their local governments.

The federal government also imposes mandates on local governments, primarily through its grants programs. The federal government attaches to its grants conditions regarding affirmative action, wage rates, administrative tasks such as program evaluations, and other substantive policies deemed to be in the national interest. Local governments that become dependent on grant programs to fund the operation of core programs may find themselves facing a fiscal crisis if these funds are terminated, just as many local governments did when the general revenue sharing program of the federal government was terminated early in the Reagan administration. However, the most pernicious effects of grant programs, both federal and state, may lie in their ability to distort local spending priorities. For example, a recent federal law made funds available to local governments to hire additional police officers. The federal government offered to pay one-half of the salary of each officer for three years, after which the local government would assume the full costs of the officer. If the officer is not funded after three years, the local government must return the federal funds expended to that point. Local governments may take advantage of this opportunity whether they really need additional officers or not, and they may do so without considering whether they can afford the full cost after the initial three years. The federal government still makes a variety of grants available in specific areas, and even if the local government is required to provide 10, 20, or 25 percent of the total funds from its own sources, it may pursue the funds regardless of whether they really need the program or project. This distorts local spending priorities. One the other hand, local governments would not pursue certain projects, such as wastewater treatment facilities, without external assistance, because some of the benefits from these projects spill over to other jurisdictions that do not pay for any part of them. The funding of local projects with federal dollars also provides for greater redistribution of income, because the federal tax system is much more progressive than local government revenue systems.

Local governments also exist in local intergovernmental networks. School districts, municipalities, counties and special districts may share the same tax base and revenue sources. When local governments borrow, they must consider the issue of overlapping debt; that is, other local jurisdictions may be using the same tax base to service their debt. Local governments do not have exclusive use of their economic bases, thus complicating the need to maintain the long-term financial viability of the jurisdiction. This is particularly obvious in economic development efforts. Local governments compete fiercely to attract industrial and commercial investment, often offering tax abatements to attract a firm from a neighboring jurisdiction. But the benefits of regional economic development spill over to all the local governments in the region; for example, a commercial establishment in one area will attract workers who may build homes in another, or a manufacturing firm will attract ancillary industries to surrounding areas.

The intergovernmental arena has recently come to be characterized by greater fragmentation. Tax revolts, calls for smaller government, and the size of the national debt have generated greater competition for increasingly limited resources among levels of government and within the state and local levels. There exists no substantive national urban policy to guide policy makers or grant programs, and the scope of intergovernmental grant programs has been dwindling. The current era of intergovernmental relations has been referred to as "competitive" or "fend-for-yourself" federalism. There is no comprehensive program, substantive policy, or intergovernmental partner available to help local governments identify and meet their short-term needs or provide for their long-term economic viability. Local governments cannot afford to be passive in such an environment and simply react to fragmented, haphazard policies. In a case in which we were involved, a budget director sought analytical data to support her efforts to convince the local delegation to the state legislature to support a pending bill that would move the statutory exemption on the assessed valuation of real estate property from the first $25,000 to the second. Under the bill persons who paid no property taxes because their houses were worth less than $25,000 would pay on the full assessed valuation, and those whose homes were assessed at between $25,000 and $50,000 would pay more than they paid with the exemption on the first $25,000. A cursory analysis indicated that the local government in question would reap a $400,000 windfall, and the director was very pleased. When it was pointed out that support of the bill was tantamount to saying that the city needed $400,000 and planned to get it from its poorest residents, she disputed this interpretation; in her view, the bill was simply an opportunity to increase revenues, which was a good thing. Action was contemplated without consideration of short-term needs or long-term viability, much less the political firestorm that would result. Wiser heads prevailed in the state legislature, and the bill never came to a vote. Local governments must plan for their short-term needs and long-term goals before they can take rational action in a turbulent environment.

MANAGERIAL ISSUES

How do local government program managers view the annual budget process? Many program managers approach the formal budget process of their jurisdictions with a mixture of dread and defiance. The process is viewed as an intrusion by persons who know little about the program and probably care even less. The managers must take time away from their operations to complete endless paperwork that seems redundant and meaningless. They are often asked to supply data and measures of the effectiveness and efficiency of their programs that they view as simplistic, one-dimensional, and misleading. They find themselves writing justifications for expenditures that amount to little more than storytelling and game-playing. The formal budget process is reduced to a simple rule: Get as much money as you can in the expenditure areas that have the most support from policy makers, and try to secure the discretion to spend it as you really think it should be spent to provide for the efficient and effective delivery of services that are responsive to the needs of the public. However, the formal budget process becomes a wall between the professionalism of the program managers and the responsibilities of the organization's finance professionals, making the efficient, effective and economical production of responsive public services problematical.

The program professional may perceive that his or her interests conflict with those of top management and the organization's finance professionals. The latter may want to build up unallocated fund balances in order to provide for unanticipated emergencies or to fund pet projects of elected officials. Top management does not want to recommend tax increases, so these funds must come from existing programs. The organization's finance professionals know that reductions can be made in the budgets of programs without drastically affecting their ability to meet service needs, but they usually have little or no knowledge of the substance or the range of funded programs, and budget reductions are made in clumsy, damaging ways, such as across-the-board cuts or mandated reductions in certain spending areas. Program managers learn to protect themselves against such intrusions by padding their budgets, thus making the finance professionals' perceptions of the availability of slack funds a self-fulfilling prophecy.

The finance professionals in the local government organization probably enjoy their best relationships with the managers of enterprise fund agencies, such as potable water, wastewater treatment, and sanitation. First, these services are public health–related and highly technical, and any interference in the substance of their operations would be met with resistance from professional associations, bond-rating agencies, and the general public. Second, these agencies are funded through their own charges for services, and these charges cannot be used for any other purpose (aside from nominal charges for participation in general administrative services, such as the budget process, personnel office, and accounting systems, and payments in lieu of taxes that allow the agency to parallel the cost structures of private-sector firms). Hence, these agencies do not compete with other agencies for finite funds. General-fund agencies often seek to mimic enterprise-fund agencies. They seek to have funding sources earmarked for their exclusive use, such as gasoline taxes for public works road projects. They rely on state government or professional associations to set mandatory service or staffing levels, as in fire departments. Or they may employ professional accreditation processes to secure additional resources, as in police departments. The purpose here is to remove funding sources or expenditure cuts from the annual budget process. These are legitimate responses to the political environment faced by service professionals, but they also serve to constrain the capacity of the public organization to meet the service needs of the jurisdiction as a whole. The more pernicious "games" generated by this environment have caused some to question the ethical standards manifested in the typical local government budget process (Lewis, 1992).

As professionals, program managers seek the autonomy to design public service delivery systems, the authority to implement and operate those systems, and the resources to fund them. Each program manager is oriented to meeting the demands for his or her particular service. Top management and the finance professionals must see that the organization responds to the range of service demands emanating from the public. When these two responsibilities meet in a highly differentiated local government organization operating in a very political environment, the resource allocation process can become a war. Program managers perceive constraints on their authority to define their missions, attacks on their autonomy to implement the technologies that give them their professional identities, and raids on the funds that allow them to build the political support necessary for their agencies' continued survival. In response to this external threat, program managers seek to maximize their own budgets and hoard slack resources to guard against the deleterious effects of across-the-board cuts, they minimize the information forwarded to top management, they implement ambiguous goals in order to maximize political support, and they build rigid bureaucracies in order to maximize internal control and to manifest strong technologies.

If the role of the finance professional is to optimize the overall allocative scheme of the local government organization, he or she must take responsibility for the effects of the organization's structure, culture and administrative systems on the resource allocation process. The organizational scenario outlined above also militates against efficiency within each service agency. Program managers who feel they are in a state of siege are unlikely to take chances on potentially innovative technologies, or to pull the plug on outdated technologies for fear the resources devoted to them will be lost. Creativity and risk-taking require a supportive organizational structure. Top management and the finance professionals must give the program managers the discretion necessary for them to effectively employ their expertise, and they must provide administrative systems that reward experimentation. But they must also develop the capacity of program managers to make decisions that are optimal for the organization as a whole; that is, they must instill an organization-wide decision perspective in substantive program managers in place of limited, agency-level perspectives.

Program managers do not necessarily hide from top management because their programs are failing. This point is virtually moot in any case because funding is not usually tied to performance. What they fear are (1) possible miscommunications regarding program definition and relevant political constituencies; (2) policy or technological changes and the reallocation of program resources; (3)

measures of effectiveness and efficiency; (4) budget surpluses and mid-year requests for supplemental appropriations. Organization theory recognizes two responses to this kind of uncertainty that are relevant here: reduce reliance on information, or maintain slack resources; the latter manifests itself as padded budget requests and spending in areas other than those to which the funds were allocated, and the former in rigid hierarchies and self-interested budgetary "gaming" in place of organization-wide analysis. A theme that runs through this book is that the budget process can be used as a communication mechanism and to develop an organizational culture that supports the optimal allocation of the public's resources, and that the local government finance professional has a responsibility to utilize the budget process in this way.

The academic field of public administration has provided little guiding theory in this area. Research and pedagogy in the field has suffered from compartmentalization of its subject matter. The functions of the finance professional have been studied apart from the responsibilities of professionals in the substantive service areas. These come together in the practice of public management in the place we call the public organization. Efficiency, effectiveness, responsiveness and economy in the delivery of public services and the allocation of public resources are the hallmarks of professional public management, but the structural and behavioral constraints on the pursuit of these ends cannot be addressed by researchers who focus exclusively on budget formats and formal budgetary processes. These must be studied in the organizational context in which they exist, and a broader theoretical perspective must be employed to reconcile the responsibilities of professional management with the demands of democratic theory. The theoretical implications of the approach to budget theory described in this book are outlined in Chapter 9, in which avenues for further research are also indicated.

REFERENCES

Lewis, Carol W. (1992). "Public Budgeting: Unethical in Purpose, Product, and Promise." *Public Budgeting and Financial Management*, 4 (3): 667–680.

Rubin, Irene S. (1993). *The Politics of Public Budgeting* (2nd ed.). Chatham, N.J.: Chatham House.

Thurmaier, Kurt (1995). "Decisive Decision Making in the Executive Budget Process: Analyzing the Political and Economic Propensities of Central Budget Analysts." *Public Administration Review*, 55 (5): 448–467.

Wildavsky, Aaron (1961). "Political Implications of Budgetary Reform." *Public Administration Review*, 21 (Autumn): 183–190.

Chapter 2

Budget Formats

Budgetary decisions have to be based not only on relative needs as they are today but also on forecasts of what the needs will be tomorrow, next year, or in the next decade.

Verne B. Lewis (1952)

The annual budget process asks program managers for information in three broad areas. First, the manager must provide some indication of what the program will accomplish. This is a policy decision that is made by legislative bodies and elected officials when they authorize the program, but it is a truism in public administration that managers influence the missions of the programs they implement. This mission is often perceived as obvious or taken for granted, and this policy question is not a central one in budget deliberations. However, policy questions are at least implicitly considered, because alternative funding levels yield alternative levels of service.

Second, the manager must consider how the mission will be accomplished and what resources will be required. This is a technological or efficiency issue that is more clearly within the purview of professional public management. However, all technological efficiencies have allocative effects—that is, lower costs yield higher service levels if resource allocations are held constant. This is one of the reasons why professional managers cannot avoid influencing policy decisions regarding service levels. The first place that managers look for guidance regarding required resources is history, or what was required the previous year. Technological issues, just like policy decisions, tend to recede into the background during the formal budget process.

Budget deliberations thus tend to focus on the third issue: What will it cost?

These cost questions constitute the fiscal dimension of budgeting. Once again, the past is the most obvious source of information regarding costs. Each year more or fewer total resources are available to the jurisdiction, however, and allocation battles inevitably center on spending rather than on service-level alternatives or on technological efficiencies that can yield additional resources. Budget deliberations tend to focus on total spending or spending in specific expenditure categories, such as travel, printing or contracts. Important policy decisions may emerge as consequences of spending decisions, but budget deliberations are focused on fiscal policy rather than substantive policy. Technological changes are also considered in the context of fiscal policy rather than service delivery efficiencies. Thus, the capacity of this process to yield responsive policies delivered through efficient systems is questionable; economy rules here.

In his classic paper on budgeting, "The Road to PPB" (1966), Allen Schick makes the point that all budget formats serve three purposes. First, they function as control mechanisms; they hold public managers accountable for using public funds for approved ends. Second, they serve as guides to operations; they tell managers what is expected of them in terms of output, and they help managers plan their work. Third, they enunciate public policy, and, to varying degrees, they allow policy makers to plan how public funds will be used to achieve desired societal outcomes. Schick's contribution is to detail how each budget format optimizes one of these three functions of budgeting, although he emphasizes that all formats serve all three functions to some extent. He also suggests that the type of format employed in each jurisdiction is less a function of evolution and growth than one of choice regarding which function is to be optimized.

It is generally accepted wisdom that the adoption of a new budget format should be treated as a significant organizational change project. What is less well appreciated is the extent to which budget formats serve as vehicles for organizational change. A fourth function of budgeting should be added to Schick's list: budgeting influences the culture of the public organization through its effects on decision-making processes and incentive and reward systems, its centrality as an organizational symbol and annual ritual, and its reflection of the basic values of the organization and its assumptions concerning environmental relationships and the nature of human beings. This function of budgeting is becoming increasingly important as management control systems in modern organizations are less likely to be based on the firm footing provided by structure and procedures. Control systems rooted in culture and shared values are better able to provide for the creativity, commitment, flexibility and speed in decision-making required to compete in the twenty-first century. In order to preserve their legitimacy in the eyes of the public and to attract competent employees, in addition to enhancing their own efficiency and effectiveness, public organizations may have to adopt the organizational trappings of their private-sector counterparts.

The remainder of this chapter summarizes the elements of four budget formats in the context of local government budgeting. The implications that each format holds for organizational culture are also examined. The "results-oriented" or "outcome-oriented" budget format that has become a staple of the "reinventing government" movement is also examined in the context of organizational culture and the elemental paradox of public management: the public's simultaneous desire for effective public management and its need to control the discretion of public managers. After reviewing the importance of the revenue constraint as it relates to budget formats, we explore the organizational role of the budget office in the local government organization by employing the framework provided by the four functions of budgeting.

LINE-ITEM BUDGETS

Line-item, or object-of-expenditure, budgets are input-oriented budgets that optimize the control function. Managers are asked to indicate their planned expenditures in specific categories usually grouped into three broad areas: personnel, operating, and operating capital. Personnel categories, or line-items, include salaries, benefits, overtime and other funds paid directly to the employees of the organization. Operating expenditures are for items and materials that will be consumed during the fiscal year in the course of providing the services of the agency—for example, postage, uniforms, travel and subscriptions. Unlike personnel items, the operating items actually used by individual agencies may differ widely, but each agency selects from the same list.

Equipment and materials with useful lives longer than one year are requested under the area of operating capital. The line-items here are usually organized by cost—for example, items costing $500 to $1,000; $1,001 to $5,000; and $5,001 to $10,000. Less costly items might be requested under the category of "small tools" or "miscellaneous equipment" in the area of operating expenditures. Higher-cost capital items would be considered in a separate capital budgeting process, which is reviewed in Chapter 7. The determination of what goes into the operating-capital line-items and what goes into the capital budgeting process is a function of the size of the budget. Automobiles may be considered operating-capital items in a large city, and special-capital items in a smaller city. In any case, operating-capital items must usually be justified in great detail before they are funded.

In focusing on the funds expended in specific categories, the line-item format drives policy and efficiency considerations into the background. It centers budget deliberations on the cost questions, rather than on how the work is done or what ends are to be achieved. The first place that the manager looks to find the line-items that are relevant to his or her program and how much to request in each category is the previous year's budget. The fact that the manager is not encouraged to question mission or methods means that the budget will change only slightly, unless an obvious crisis needs to be addressed. An old rule of thumb in budgeting is to request the funds where one believes they will be approved and secure the discretion to use them as one sees fit; the safest harbor is the tried and tested one. Because it pushes the conscious consideration of policy into the background and encourages only small changes in budget schemes, the line-item format is the quintessential incremental budget. The theory of incrementalism began as a description of national budgeting in the United States during the 1950s, but it has achieved normative status in some circles. This theory holds that because public problems are so complicated and so little is known about their causes and interrelationships, policy should be made through incremental adjustments to existing programs rather than through the funding of grandiose, comprehensive plans to achieve specific goals.

Line-item budgets have significant strengths that account for the fact that they have persisted so long in the face of continuous efforts to reform the typical budget process. First, the line-item format can be used by all of the wide range of agencies that comprise the local government organization. Second, the format requires little or no analysis of the operating manager; calculations can be limited to adjustments to the previous year's requests due to inflation or increases in demand. Third, elected officials and legislative bodies feel more comfortable discussing "stuff" such as materials and travel funds and overall fiscal policy, rather than the arcane details of program technologies or policy analyses. Fourth, the fact that policy is pushed into the background minimizes the conflict associated with the allocation of finite resources. The general acceptance of the previous year's allocation scheme smoothes over potential conflicts, and the business of completing the budget proceeds more expeditiously. Policy conflicts have recently extended the budget processes of the federal government and the state of California beyond the start of the following fiscal year; non-essential services were curtailed in the former case, and public employees were paid with state "script" in the latter, which was graciously accepted by banking institutions.

Lastly, the line-item budget format optimizes the control function of budgeting, which was one of the ends of the local government reform movement of the early twentieth century. It provides a framework for accounting for the disposition of public funds. In some jurisdictions, operating managers are not allowed to transfer funds between line-items without administrative approval, and in some cases this requires legislative approval. However, managers usually have the discretion to determine how funds should be expended within the personnel and operating areas. For example, turnover may require more funds for overtime and less for salaries. Funds for operating capital are usually encumbered or reserved for the specific purpose for which the funds were requested. Elected officials prefer to pursue their control responsibilities through fiscal policy and policies regarding spending in specific categories, because, again, they are less comfortable dealing with the array of technologies represented by the broad range of policy areas they oversee. Control of policy and service levels is exercised through control of spending, and the policy decisions of past legislative bodies are thus implicitly ratified. Line-item budgets and their emphasis on control precipitate the behaviors and outcomes described in the incrementalist model.

Incrementalism is becoming less accurate as a description of, and less useful as a prescription for, local government budgeting, however, as local jurisdictions face increasing constraints on their capacities to increase revenues. Debt has spawned service devolution and fiscal withdrawal at the federal level. States are loading service and procedural mandates, both funded and unfunded, onto their local governments as they seek to deal with their own revenue problems and minimize any attendant political costs. It is a relatively simple process to apportion slices of a growing pie to hungry service managers and their political support groups, but "decrementalism" does not work so easily. Across-the-board cuts in times of decreasing revenues eventually impose serious hardships on salient services, and policy makers are eventually faced with decisions regarding which services should be terminated or severely reduced in order to fund the most basic services at viable levels. The potential for radical realignment replaces the practice of incremental adjustments to past decisions. The structured analysis of policy options may also assume center stage as policy makers seek information on which to base their policy decisions, or try to deflect any political costs associated with new resource allocation schemes.

The structured analysis of policy options does not usually play a significant role in line-item budget processes, for reasons that should now be obvious. Because line-item budgets force policy into the background, service managers focus on strategies to secure their share of incremental increases in revenues, or to protect themselves from decreases. Consideration of the relative merits of alternative policies gives way to the gaming, propagandizing and outright lying that has caused Carol Lewis (1992) to characterize the typical public budget process as inherently unethical. Competition among service agencies on the basis of narrow self-interest reduces the capacity of the organization to respond to the needs of its jurisdiction as a whole. Consideration of the long-term financial viability of the jurisdiction, like all policy considerations, becomes secondary. The line-item budget format engenders agency atomization, encourages self-interested behavior, and can create a climate of distrust in the organization. The typical local government organization is a highly differentiated one, and public managers should pursue administrative processes and organizational procedures that enhance integration, particularly in times of relative resource scarcity. Ironically, the line-item format's emphasis on control per se may create the type of organization it is designed to control.

PROGRAM BUDGETING

The quintessential program budget was the Program Planning and Budgeting System (PPBS) brought to the administration of President Lyndon Johnson by his secretary of defense Robert Macnamara from the Ford Corporation. However, a budgeting system that would serve to identify and communicate the ends of government was also a goal of the reform movement. Its focus on policy makes program budgeting the polar opposite of line-item budgeting. The pursuit of valued societal outcomes rather than the control of expenditures assumes center stage here. This dichotomy reflects the central dilemma of the reform movement: the simultaneous pursuit of effective government and controlled public administrators. Line-item budgets are input-oriented and built from the ground up in that they begin with the requests of the individual program managers. Program budgets require the enunciation of substantive policies in order to rationalize the allocation of resources to those ends. The federal government can fund antismoking programs and provide price supports for tobacco when policy is built from the bottom up, but the conscious selection of desired outcomes would require that this clear contradiction be reconciled. This requires the mobilization and centralization of political power, and the top-down promulgation of valued policy outcomes.

President Johnson achieved a landslide victory over his Republican opponent in 1964. The Democrats assembled large majorities in both houses of Congress, and Johnson himself was a veteran of Congress and knew how to work the system. He was able to assemble the political power necessary to dictate public policies from the top down. He identified goals in the areas of domestic, international, and defense policy. These goals became the missions of the agencies that comprised the federal government, and resources were allocated on the basis of their relative success in achieving desired outcomes. The policies, not the agencies, were the targets of the allocations. The format required the agencies to analyze the impacts of their programs in order to be able to demonstrate success. Thus, the role of structured analysis is also highlighted in this format, and PPBS put the field of program evaluation at center stage. President Johnson was able to extend his political reach into state and local government, and he partnered directly with community groups in regard to his domestic "War on Poverty" policies. He employed categorical and project grants that were narrowly focused on approved policy ends, and which also called for extensive evaluation of "what works."

President Johnson was unable to hold together the political coalition that enabled him to dictate policies from the top down without generating crippling conflict. Our Constitution was written to fragment political power, and major changes in substantive policies are more likely to be driven by ideas that capture receptive audiences at the grass roots. The use of structured analysis requires the enunciation of a single goal that must be optimized, but many government programs have multiple goals that represent the perspectives of multiple constituencies. PPBS also saddled agencies with extensive analytical responsibilities that threatened to overwhelm the annual budget process. Its emphasis on policy planning required a multiyear budget horizon, to which the electoral process is not well suited. Today, program budgeting at the federal level exists only in the functional classifications that cut across agency lines. The amount of funds expended in each broad functional area is calculated through "crosswalks" from the individual agency budgets to which the funds are actually allocated.

Centralizing the political power necessary to dictate policy from the top down may actually be more feasible at the local government level, where policy-making can come to be dominated by elites, especially in communities that feature more or less homogenous populations. However, the formal PPBS format never achieved widespread use at the local government level. Program budgeting encouraged the use of analytical techniques to identify the benefits of public programs, the development of performance measures to support these techniques and to communicate with the public, the conscious consideration of the long-term policy impacts of annual budgetary decisions, and the examination of the ends of collective action apart from the annual budget demands of existing agencies. Many local government jurisdictions organize their line-item allocations by program areas in their budgets, and they publish outcome measures that reflect the pursuit of enunciated missions and the accomplishment of established objectives. These programmatic areas usually follow organizational lines, however, and the fact that these data are published does not necessarily indicate that they guide budget deliberations.

Program budgeting spotlights some of the shortcomings of the typical budget process, but the nature of the political process militates against wholesale adoption of its elements. However, it has served to legitimize the use of structured analysis in resource allocation decision-making, and it has influenced the profession of public management. The prescriptions of program budgeting have been applied most effectively outside of the formal budget process. It may be too much to ask the formal, annual budget process to employ all of the elements of program budgeting, but it is not too much to ask of the professional public organization. The resource allocation process extends beyond the formal budget process, and the evaluation of the utility of alternative budget formats should include their effects on management capacity—that is, the capacity of local government managers to meet the actual needs of their jurisdiction in the context of enhancing the long-term financial viability of the jurisdiction.

PERFORMANCE BUDGETS

Performance budgets focus on the work being done in public agencies, and they seek to enhance efficiency—that is, to maximize production at a given level of resources. Resources are allocated to specific activities that produce immediate outputs, rather than to the line-items that indicate the materials consumed in the production process. Performance budgets may be viewed as input-oriented or output-oriented depending on whether the work activities are viewed as inputs to public policy outcomes or organizational outputs in their own right. In either case, performance budgeting is a bottom-up format in that it acknowledges the dependence of policy makers on the expertise of agency managers in their efforts to enhance overall efficiency. The focus here is on how much work is done, not explicitly on whether the work is worth doing given a particular policy goal. The maximization of efficiency, along with economy, effectiveness and control, was also a goal of the reform movement, and performance budgeting traces its history to those early efforts.

In performance budgeting, funds would be allocated to activities such as street sweeping or pothole repair. In line-item budgeting, the same funds would turn up in salary, small equipment, asphalt, and gasoline. The specific uses of these materials are not made manifest in the line-item format. In performance budgeting, the level of output that can be achieved with a given level of resources is usually indicated with performance measures; that is, X miles of street will be swept with the Y dollars allocated to the activity. However, once again, the policies that drive these production processes are not explicitly examined. Performance budgets serve best as guides to operations management. The managers know what is expected of their programs in terms of output, and they are better able to plan their production processes. The budget process is clearly dependent on the expertise and information provided by program managers.

Performance budgets encourage managers to make their production processes more efficient. Managers who produce more output at a given funding level will be able to maintain or increase their allocations. Managers who are less successful will be held accountable. Performance budgets can be coupled with a formal management-by-objectives (MBO) planning and evaluation system. The reporting of performance measures that can be tracked gives the budget process a multiyear dimension. However, elected officials may not be comfortable conducting budget deliberations on the basis of arcane technological issues. They may insist on maintaining parallel line-item budgets that will ultimately refocus resource allocation discussions on line-item expenditures.

The principal shortcoming of the performance budget format is that it is difficult to apply in many of the service areas encompassed by the local government organization. If demand for the program's output can be controlled, or the program is not required to meet all demands for its product or service, program managers are able to establish performance targets, and they can be held accountable for meeting them. In local government, public works and public utilities agencies, and programs whose production processes resemble those of private-sector firms, such as recreation agencies and libraries, are best suited to the demands of performance budgeting. For core local government functions such as police and fire, these criteria do not apply. For example, the police chief can only estimate the percent of crimes that can be cleared, because this is dependent on the types and number of crimes actually committed. These managers must respond to all demands for service, and they do not control demand; hence, they are unable to connect an identifiable level of service to a given level of resources. These agencies would be at a disadvantage in a performance budget process (or, alternatively, they could have an advantage over agencies that can provide more reliable data).

Performance budgets support incrementalist thinking to the extent that a focus on work activities can also be characterized as input oriented. However, they also provide a mechanism for the re-allocation of resources based on the rational analysis of production processes, and a forum for the discussion of substantive policy. In a line-item format, a program manager may endanger his total allocation if he or she tries to re-allocate among line-items in order to take advantage of a new technology in the field; decision makers may consider what is being given up separately from what is being requested. A focus on what can be produced at a given funding level unites these questions, and potential efficiencies make allocations more likely. Thus, performance budgets may reduce gaming in the allocation process.

Top management must determine whether their program managers are capable of employing the performance budget format. Possible issues are: Do managers currently use output measures to manage their operations? Is efficiency a core value in the organization? Are the operations managers competent and professional enough to be held accountable for output? Are elected officials amenable to this approach? How much of this organization can employ this approach, and what are the implications for those agencies that cannot? The performance budget format can also be used to develop these data, values, skills and communication channels. On the local government level today, performance budgets are rare, or they are developed in tandem with line-item budgets. Their greatest impact has been in the area of reporting output and workload measures in the traditional line-item format, and in encouraging managers to think in terms of efficiency. Both program and performance budgets are currently manifested as ''performance-based'' budgets. These are resource allocation decision-making processes that employ output and outcome data to allocate public resources, and these data are published in what are often traditional line-item budget documents. The concept of efficiency and the development of performance measures are examined more closely in Chapter 4.

THE ZERO-BASE BUDGET PROCESS

The elements of zero-base budgeting were described by Verne Lewis in a 1952 journal article in which he examined the applicability of marginal analysis to resource allocation decisions in the public sector. Jimmy Carter imported the format from the private sector to the state of Georgia when he was governor, and brought it to the federal government when he was elected president in 1976. The analytical demands of the system and the paperwork it entailed made it short-lived at the national level, but resource scarcity has renewed interest in it and its offspring, target-base budgeting. Zero-base formats seek to encourage non-incrementalist thinking and the re-allocation of resources while maintaining a bottom-up approach to budget development. Zero-base budgeting is differentiated from line-item and performance budgeting on this criterion, and from PPBS on the basis that program managers have a prominent role in the policy-making process. Like performance budgeting, the zero-base format relies on the expertise of program managers for the development of technological alternatives, but the policy-planning function of the budget process is more salient in the zero-base format, and the value of management expertise in the policy-making process is also made manifest.

Verne Lewis acknowledged that the allocation of public resources can never be merely a function of structured analysis, due to the absence of a single "bottom line" to be optimized. However, he believed that the political decision-making process could be informed by the comparison of alternative investments in public services at the margin. That is, given the level of resources invested to date in each area, where can the jurisdiction achieve the best returns on an additional increment of funds? Marginal analysis calls for successive comparisons of the effects of allocating an additional amount of funds to the various programs. All public programs share the overall goal of enhancing the general welfare, and each program targets an identifiable dimension of the general welfare. The return on an additional investment in each is expressed in terms of its specific policy area. The general welfare and its various dimensions constitute the common "bottom line" for budget deliberations.

In this format, each manager assumes he or she has no budget, and the previous year's funds will be allocated to the program in a number of discrete increments. Zero-base budgeting is an outcome-oriented format, because outcome-oriented measures are usually used to describe the impacts of these incremental allocations. For example, a police chief with a $1 million budget would be asked to indicate how the first $200,000 would be budgeted, and to describe the impact of these expenditures on public safety; he or she would do the same for the following four increments of $200,000. These increments are called decision packages. The format's policy focus is weakened when workload or output measures are used to give substance to each increment The program elements ranked highest in importance by the manager will be included in the first decision package, and the final rankings represent the manager's perceptions of the relative importance of the elements that comprise the program. The manager at the next level of the agency will assemble the packages of his subordinates to express his or her perceptions of their relative importance. The managers may also be asked to submit enhancement decision packages that represent their plans for any additional funds thay may be allocated. Oftentimes, an enhancement is ranked higher than an existing element, and the new element is funded by eliminating other elements of the program or packages in other programs. In this way the programs in the agency, and those in other agencies in the organization, are compared to one another at the margin.

This approach is potentially nonincremental in that it encourages managers to look within their previous allocations (which are usually passed forward without criticism in line-item formats) in order to find funds for new programs or technologies. Local governments are increasingly reliant on own-source revenues and subjected to increasing resistance to new taxes. Therefore, funds for new initiatives must come from existing allocations. Program managers face the same risks that they do when they open their past allocations to the possibilities of re-allocation, but at least innovative and creative managers can take comfort that all of the organization's allocations will undergo the same scrutiny.

The zero-base process can make agencies more aware of the goals of the other agencies that comprise the public organization, and can drive an organizational communication process leading to the general realization of a common mission—to provide for the general welfare of the jurisdiction. Top management can use the process to build the organizational trust necessary for a true discussion of the policy goals of the organization. This is not to say that the zero-base process ends the gaming that often characterizes the pursuit of public funds. Program managers may hide unpopular or marginally successful elements of their programs in highly ranked decision packages based on the assumption that higher-ups will not cut the politically popular and very visible elements that comprise low priority packages. An example of this gambit is the hypothetical "George Washington Monument" ploy, in which the National Park Service threatens to close the monument in an effort to avert, rather than deal more rationally with, anticipated funding cuts. More than one manager has been forced to reshuffle his or her packages when decision makers ratified the closing of their "monuments."

Target-base budgeting is a variant of zero-base budgeting in which managers are asked to assume that their budgets have been reduced to a base more than zero, usually 70 or 80 percent of current allocations. This form is more common, and it recognizes the fact that reductions beyond that point are not very likely, that the resulting programs and delivery systems would be radically different from the current context, and that the policy impacts of the initial increments from zero are negligible or difficult to describe. Agencies that collect user fees and charges must also describe the revenue effects of alternative funding levels in this format, in order to avoid eliminating more revenues than required to fund the decision package. The zero-base budgeting process is usually a superfluous one for enterprise fund agencies, but the periodic evaluation of the fee structures of such agencies in light of their service levels is advisable.

Among the shortcomings of the zero-base process are the time and paperwork associated with defining alternative service levels, and the analyses involved in establishing the connection between service levels and outcome measures. Elected officials may rebel against the time and effort involved in weighing the relative merits of even summary decision packages. Some managerial sophistication is also required, and suitable measures of policy outcomes may prove to be elusive (see Chapter 4). Like performance budgeting, the format is better suited to some service areas than others, but a less rigorous standard would likely be applied to outcome measures than measures of relative efficiency. The estimated effect of funding levels on outcome itself would often be a point of debate. The debate would, however, focus on policy outcomes, and all of the service areas have these in common. V. O. Key realized that the public organization may serve as a structure for "the canalizing of decisions through the governmental machinery so as to place alternatives in juxtaposition and compel consideration of relative values'' (1940: 1139). It is ironic that the rigid, hierarchical organizational form forced on public organizations in order to control the discretion of professional administrators may serve to deliver their summary judgments regarding the relative desirability of alternative resource allocation schemes and public policies.

RESULTS-ORIENTED BUDGETING

Results-oriented budgeting, or outcome budgeting, is a prominent plank in the platform of the ''reinventing government'' movement (Osborne and Gaebler, 1992). It seeks to reconcile the public's demand for greater efficiency and effectiveness in the delivery of public services through greater professionalism with the simultaneous demand for control of administrative discretion. These ends can be contradictory, because professionals need to exercise discretionary decision-making in order to realize their promise of enhanced efficiency and effectiveness. This issue has dogged the relationship between professional public administration in the United States and the politics of democracy and popular control of the policy-making process since the expansion of the administrative state in the late nineteenth century. The increasing complexity of modern society has resulted in greater reliance on scientific expertise, and the nature of the policy-making process means that groups can sidestep the formal policy process and seek to influence outcomes by dealing directly with the public administrators on whom we rely for professional program management. Thus, democracy seeks to control the management discretion on which it depends, and succeeds in constraining the capacity of professional management to meet society's needs.

Budget processes, personnel systems and purchasing procedures are the principal mechanisms through which control is exercised. James Q. Wilson (1989) has pointed out that the major difference between public-sector managers and private-sector managers is that the former do not control the factors of production to the extent that the latter do. The capacity of public-sector managers to hire, fire and reward employees, to purchase materials and enter into contracts, and to re-allocate available funds to adapt to changing situations or to adopt new technologies is severely limited. Hence, public-sector production processes, all else being equal, are inevitably less efficient. Private-sector managers are held accountable for the profitability of their enterprise, and they are granted the discretion to maximize this outcome by exercising their expertise in their use of inputs. In the absence of a tangible ''bottom line'' in the public sector, the accountability function focuses on management's use of inputs. The control function must be exercised in some fashion, or else it would compromise democracy's control of the public policy–making process.

Results-oriented budgeting seeks to increase the capacity of public managers to meet the needs of the public by moving the control function from the input side of the production process to the outcome side. Input controls are relaxed.

In the case of the budget and finance functions, this means fewer line-items, greater discretion in transferring funds between line-items, and purchasing processes unencumbered by excessive red tape. The professional administrators have more strength to "row" the ship of state, and the formal policy-making process can more effectively "steer" it (Osborne and Gaebler, 1992). Funding levels are based on policy impacts, as in the program budget format: what works gets funded and what doesn't gets fixed or eliminated. From a human resources management perspective, one expects to see gain-sharing programs and other incentives to encourage productivity improvements. Administrators have greater discretion in assigning personnel, and they themselves are subject to performance reviews that could result in termination.

Outcome measures play a large role in the zero-base budget format described above, and results-oriented budgeting is even more dependent on the development of valid policy outcome measures. If output or workload measures only are employed, the format is reduced to performance budgeting and MBO with fewer controls on inputs. Without outcome measures, policy controls would focus on outputs and the amount of work being done; this is the area of production processes and technologies, where administrators currently exercise and always require the most discretion. Only outcome measures would, theoretically, put the public's hand on the policy steering wheel, and allow professional discretion to be exercised where it is needed. Thus, the results-oriented format is constrained by the same measurement problems as the zero-base process and the evaluative component of program budgeting.

The identification of outcome measures is an integral part of the decision package development process in the zero-base format. As described above, the measures themselves often become the focus of the resource allocation decision-making process. The decision packages may have outcomes in a variety of areas. The politics of deciding which impacts are most important and which are most likely proceeds in tandem with the politics of allocating funds. This fluid quality may be lost when outcome measures become an element of a concrete administrative management system. In this scenario it becomes necessary for participants in the policy-making process to identify and agree on legitimate outcomes at the outset of the fiscal year and outside the resource allocation process. Results-oriented budgeting would seem to require the kind of consensus or centralization of political power demanded by program budgeting and top-down budgeting systems. Outcome measures may be imposed on administrators, and resisted. Managers realize that they serve a variety of constituencies, each of which may view their programs differently. This reality may lead to perceived contradictions in outcome measures in individual programs when these are viewed from outside the program.

Results-oriented budgeting may ossify the policy-making process in order to hold program managers accountable for a limited range of outcomes. Managers would have greater flexibility in the use of inputs, but this capacity to employ their professional expertise could only be applied in the pursuit of narrow goals.

The old adage of performance measurement applies: What gets measured is what gets done. In any case, the implementation of results-oriented budgeting would require an immense organizational development effort. Experimentation with a zero-base budgeting process would facilitate the development of the necessary consensus regarding outcome measures by allowing program managers to participate in the development process and by encouraging policy makers to consider a range of alternatives.

THE CENTRALITY OF THE REVENUE CONSTRAINT

Regardless of the format employed, budgetary decision making must usually be conducted within the constraints posed by available revenues. New policy initiatives and experimental programs were a feature of PPBS, but the centralization of political power necessary to drive policy-making from the top would also facilitate the consensus necessary to increase taxes and other revenue sources, if necessary. Zero-base budgeting encourages managers and policy makers to take a fresh look at service delivery, but they are also encouraged to look to other programs for the revenues to fund any changes. Performance budgets encourage managers to apply their professional expertise to service delivery in order to enhance efficiency and make additional revenues available under the existing constraint. Local government budgeting is revenue-driven, and all processes and formats operate under this constraint. Tax policy is inherently incremental, because large increases in tax rates are not well tolerated by those affected, regardless of the relative burdens they currently bear.

The centrality of the revenue constraint highlights the importance of the revenue forecast. The initial forecast of the revenue constraint for the next budget year normally occurs after the first quarter of the current year. Hence, budgeters must forecast twenty months into the future. The actual collections from the previous year are available to the forecasters at that time, but the current year's revenue have only begun to materialize. Good budgeters will continue to revise their forecasts as more data becomes available, but the initial estimate has great salience in the budget process. It sets the tone for the initial budget requests. Projected shortfalls require agencies to prepare contingency plans that could cause some consternation among employees. This can cause continuing morale problems, as employees are designated as nonessential or low priority. Forecasters may believe that frequent revisions might undermine their credibility, and the initial forecast can assume a life of its own.

Unfortunately, forecasters are under some pressure to under-forecast revenues. The initial estimate of the revenue constraint is a long-term forecast fraught with uncertainties, and the potential costs of under-forecasting are perceived to be considerably less than those of over-forecasting. Over-forecasting would precipitate disruptive midyear cuts as the organization's managers scramble to adjust to the dawning reality. Any under-forecasted revenues would simply be available at the end of the fiscal year and become part of a healthy fund balance. Better yet, resources would be available during the year for discretionary spending or to fund pet projects of elected officials. The costs of under-forecasting are limited to the loss of purchasing power due to inflation, which is partially recovered through interest earnings, and the less chaotic expenditure adjustments that can be made during the budget process. Deliberate under-forecasting also serves to dampen the political pressures for public spending.

The revenue constraint and its identification are discussed here because the reform budgeting formats are designed to move program managers away from the games associated with incremental adjustments to line-item budgets. They seek to encourage managers to use their professional expertise so that public resources are employed more efficiently, more effectively and more rationally. Finance professionals and top management want program managers to submit "real" budgets that represent honest efforts to meet the politically enunciated needs of the jurisdiction. Program managers seek to pad their budgets with slack resources in order to be able to deal with unanticipated events, and these resources could be used more productively elsewhere. However, finance professionals pad their own forecasts of the revenue constraint in order to protect themselves from the potential costs of over-forecasting, and the program managers bear the attendant cost.

As local government organizations become increasingly dependent on own-source revenues, the efficient management of these resources becomes increasingly important. Part of this management effort is to make these resources available to program managers on a timely basis. Budgeters should seek to forecast as close to the true revenue constraint as their skills and available technology will allow. They must also seek to enhance that knowledge and analytical capacity. Finance professionals cannot develop the organizational trust necessary for the operation of an efficient budget process without assuming the same risks they demand from program managers. A brief summary of forecasting techniques is presented in Chapter 5.

BUDGETING AS ORGANIZATIONAL DEVELOPMENT

Researchers have uncovered some evidence that budget format makes a difference in regard to the language employed in the budget process, the nature of budgetary communications, the criteria used to evaluate requests, and the substance of resource allocation deliberations. But it is less clear whether different formats yield different outcomes and better decisions. It seems reasonable to assume that substantially different processes would facilitate access and influence by substantially different interest groups, and hence yield different outcomes; or each process may hold an advantage for a particular type of service, and thus produce a better outcome for that service. But there is little evidence that format has a direct effect on outcomes.

The power of political elites coupled with the apparent apathy of the general public may limit the range of possible outcomes regardless of budget format.

The press of incrementalist thinking and the limits imposed by the revenue constraint may dampen any effects that format may have on budgetary outcomes. Alternatively, the effects of format on outcomes may evolve slowly, because format affects outcomes through other variables. One of these variables may be the capacity of the organization's managers to make better resource allocation decisions. This is the fourth function of budgeting introduced above to complement the three outlined by Allen Schick (1966). Formats can be used to influence the formal and informal communication processes that tie together the diverse service delivery systems that comprise the local government organization. They can serve to define the perspectives and premises that drive decision-making in each of the systems, as well as overall resource allocation schemes. The "better" decisions are those based on an understanding and appreciation of the needs of the jurisdiction as a whole, rather than on the perceived need to simply maximize the resources allocated to individual service areas. This is not to say that structured analysis can determine the one most effective resource allocation scheme in that regard, but rather that better decisions emerge from the necessarily political deliberations when decision makers adopt a perspective that is broader than the interests of their own agencies. This means that service managers must perceive that they are members of a single organization pursuing goals that integrate their individual service areas: to meet the needs of the jurisdiction for collective action as efficiently and economically as possible and to maintain the long-range financial viability of the jurisdiction. Each of these goals complements the other; responsive service delivery enhances the prospects for long-term financial condition, and no resource allocation schemes are feasible for long without attention being given to the underlying financial health of the jurisdiction.

The formal budget process is a promising vehicle for developing the desired management perspective because it is only during the formal budget process that individual service managers need even acknowledge that their agencies are parts of a single organization. Police managers can approach other centralized functions such as personnel, finance, and data processing as if they were simply extensions of the police department, or as agencies with which they have contractual relationships. In terms of an organizational concept popularized by Karl Weick (1979), the elements of the local government organization are "loosely coupled" on the dimensions represented by these relationships. However, municipal service agencies are more "tightly coupled" on the dimension represented by the resource allocation process; that is, a disturbance in one agency— whether it be a budgetary overrun, a surplus, or an emergency that calls for a re-allocation of resources—has immediate and direct implications for the other agencies that comprise the organization. The resource allocation process is also a symbol of the organization as a whole, and it is an annual ritual in which all of the service agencies participate.

Organizational culture and values are rooted in symbols and rituals. The organizational ends suggested here can only be pursued through the development of cultural values that transcend the professional and political values of the varied technologies that make up the local government organization. The highly differentiated nature of the organization and the corollary deference to technological expertise usually observed in regard to service delivery make it unlikely that the recommended organizational perspective can be "hardwired" into the structure of the organization or brought about by top management through administrative fiat. No formal decision-making process or structure can require the police chief to acknowledge that the recreation department also contributes to the goal of reducing crime and enhancing perceptions of security and, thus, his or her decisions in pursuit of resources to achieve these ends should be made from the perspective of this interdependence. The perception that the organization as a whole pursues shared goals must be a tenet of organizational culture and a central value of the organization. In summary, it is posited here that the relationship between budget formats and budgetary outcomes is mediated by the effects of format on organizational culture and values.

The budget format is also a suitable vehicle for developing these organization values and decision-making perspectives because the formal budget process provides the only occasion when the organization as a whole interacts with its political environment in an effort to identify the community's needs for collective action. The nature of that political environment will go a long way toward determining the level of integration required in the public organization, and it may serve as a constraint on the ability of management to develop those integrative perspectives. In more or less homogenous communities where the structure of the public organization reflects consensus values shared by service area managers, the use of outcome-oriented budget formats designed to achieve such consensus is facilitated, but not really required. Line-item budget formats can maintain the desired allocation scheme, and, if this does not compromise the long-term financial viability of the jurisdiction, the monitoring function can fall to the finance professionals. However, heterogenous populations and revenue scarcity can create political conflict in the environment and self-interested behavior in the organization that can compromise allocative efficiency and ultimately endanger long-term viability. Conscious efforts to develop the managerial perspectives necessary to pursue the former and provide for the latter should center on budget formats.

The relationship between budget format and organizational culture and its development is a potentially fruitful area for researchers. It can yield practical theories for managers that will enable them to employ formats not simply to produce a budget, but to build the capacity of their organizations to meet the needs of the public. Budget formats may also affect resource allocation outcomes through their effects on management capacity building. Zero-base, or target-base, budgeting may emerge as the format most suitable for pursuing capacity building as it is defined herein. It acknowledges the deference to functional expertise that necessarily characterizes local government management, and yet it provides a decision-making process that can serve as a vehicle for the development of an organizational culture and values that can mitigate the destructiveness of the centrifugal forces that can result from such deference. In Chapter 4 we suggest that the very process of developing the outcome-oriented measures required for effective zero-base processes can enhance the decision-making perspectives of service managers.

MANAGERIAL ISSUES

The optimal organizational location of the budgeting function depends on the nature of that function. The budget function can be reduced to little more than simply publishing the allocations. Requests may be submitted directly to the chief executive; top management may balance these requests with available revenues, and suggested expenditure decreases or revenue increases may then be submitted to the legislative body. The budget department simply assembles and promulgates the results. Even the oversight and execution of the budget could be reserved for the finance office and top management. At a minimum, however, the budget office is usually required to review requests for compliance with established fiscal policies, and it is sometimes commissioned to evaluate the policy implications of budgetary requests. As in program budgeting, the budgeting function can be used to pursue substantive policy outcomes from the top down, and, as outlined herein, the budget process can also function as a vehicle for the organizational development and management capacity–building efforts of top management.

If the development of substantive public policy is an explicit element of the budget process—as in program budgeting or zero-base formats—the budget office should be located as close to the chief executive officer as possible. In this scenario the budget department would be responsible not only for reconciling agency requests with overall fiscal policy, but for helping to rationalize substantive policies. This rationalization process must occur at a point where some level of organization-wide authority is centralized. The need for direct relationships with top management is particularly crucial if top management also seeks to assign organizational development responsibilities to the budget process. Due to the deference to substantive expertise that characterizes policy-making and operational decision-making in the highly differentiated local government organization, the centralization of policy-making would probably require an intensive organizational development effort.

A persuasive case can be made for placing the budget function in the finance office, particularly in light of the broad definition of resource allocation and financial management employed herein. This option would provide for a sharing of resources and information, and for the standardization of the latter. The lull in the budget process occurs during the first quarter of the fiscal year, at the same time that the finance office is racing to pull together the financial report for the previous fiscal year. Budget personnel would have direct access to financial expertise in the form of certified public accountants (CPAs) typically housed in the finance office. This would be a suitable placement if the budget function is only asked to publish the budget, just as the finance office assembles the year-end report. However, the finance office operationalizes what is very much a control function, and CPAs usually look to the professional accounting establishment for their operating norms and standards. This perspective often functions to constrain relationships with service agencies, which are more closely tied to local political context. Placing the budget function in the finance office may militate against efforts to build substantive policy bridges to service programs. Obviously, finance and budgets offices must share information in order to execute their immediate oversight and control functions, and to pursue their respective professional orientations: the finance office to attend to the long-term financial viability of the jurisdiction, and the budget office to maximize the capacity of the resource allocation scheme to meet the needs of the public. However, the latter must also be positioned to help instill these values in the decision premises and professional orientations of service managers.

Once again, the choice of optimal format depends on the goals of top management and the overall capacities of service managers. From the perspective described here, top management should move in the direction of focusing budget deliberations on issues of substantive policy, and should seek to enhance the decision-making perspectives of the organization's service managers in that regard. Both of these ends must be pursued jointly in order to optimize resource allocation schemes and to provide for the long-term financial viability of the jurisdiction. In light of these ends, it is hypothesized here that the zero-base, or target-base, format is the most effective format. Top managers can ameliorate some of the workload and capacity issues associated with the process by subjecting only one-quarter of the service areas to zero-base review each year—for example, public safety programs, public works agencies, parks and recreation functions, and the area of general administrative services. A stand-alone budget office located close to the chief executive would provide the necessary policy planning and continuity. The formal budget process could proceed with more traditional formats, and the decision-making process would be informed by the results of the zero-base reviews. Service agencies would have an opportunity to respond to problems identified in their zero-base review before nonincremental re-allocations become a possibility in the cycle's fourth year. Annual appropriations would take place in the context of policy planning, which is in turn freed from the capacity constraints inherent in the one-year timetable. This is the recommendation of Verne Lewis in the quotation that opened this chapter. In order to simultaneously pursue the ends of efficiency, economy and effectiveness, annual allocations must take place in the context of long-range policy planning. The local government organization functions as the repository for information regarding short-term needs, long-term trends, and internal management capacities.

REFERENCES

Key, V. O. (1940). "The Lack of Budgetary Theory." *American Political Science Review*, 34 (2): 1137–1140.

Lewis, Carol W. (1992). "Public Budgeting: Unethical in Purpose, Product, and Promise." *Public Budgeting and Financial Management*, 4 (3): 667–680.

Lewis, Verne B. (1952). "Toward A Theory of Budgeting." *Public Administration Review*, 12 (1): 43–54.

Osborne, David, and Gaebler, Ted (1992). *Reinventing Government*. Reading, Mass.: Addison-Wesley.

Schick, Allen (1966). "The Road to PPB: The Stages of Budget Reform." *Public Administration Review*, 26 (2): 243–258.

Weick, Karl (1979). *The Social Psychology of Organizing* (2nd ed.). Reading, Mass.: Addison-Wesley.

Wilson, James Q. (1989). *Bureaucracy*. New York: Basic Books.

Chapter 3

Budget Execution

Excessive attention to the development of formal calculational capabilities can (and this is particularly true in local government and in developing nations) divert scarce resources from the equally important tasks of building action capabilities.

Bertram M. Gross (1969)

In the above quotation, Gross refers to the analytical capacity of a public organization and the phenomenon of ''paralysis by analysis,'' but he follows up with ''one of the oldest verities of business and public administration: namely, that good staff services alone do not a good decision maker make'' (1969: 127). Budget execution entails a myriad of decisions regarding the implementation of public policy in a wide variety of service delivery areas. The flip side of execution consists of a range of control functions maintained by central staff agencies, such as finance, purchasing and budgeting. In the same way that most local government budgetary processes yield policy by default—that is, by not considering policies explicitly and simply ratifying the previous year's spending schemes—these control functions seek to maintain the policies manifested in the budget document by simply ensuring that spending follows budgeted authorizations. Good staff services alone do not a good organization make.

These control functions are exercised in an accounting framework structured specifically for control rather than to support the operational decision-making of service managers. This chapter begins with a review of this accounting edifice, and descriptions of the major control functions—budgeting, finance and purchasing—follow. The budget execution process is then viewed from the perspective of service delivery managers, and we explore ways to reconcile the need for control and accountability with managers' desire for autonomy and discretion to take responsive action. We close with an examination of the operation of internal service agencies, which manifests some of the basic issues of budget control and policy implementation.

THE FUND STRUCTURE OF LOCAL GOVERNMENTS

In the private sector, a single self-balancing set of accounts is used to account for all the activities and resources of a business. The business and the accounting entity are one and the same. In the public sector, governments are comprised of several accounting entities called funds. This is because government operations are diverse in nature, and a variety of fiscal entities are required to accurately record and summarize these operations. In addition, this segmentation facilitates compliance with legal restrictions placed on the use of some resources. Governmental fund structures also function as powerful controls on the use of public resources. There are three categories of funds—governmental, proprietary and fiduciary funds—housing a total of nine fund types.

Governmental funds are used to account for the financial resources expended in the course of providing—for want of a better word—a local government's "nonbusiness"-type activities. These are the activities, such as police, fire and recreation, funded from general taxes, fees, and some intergovernmental grant programs. There are four kinds of governmental funds.

General Fund

Each local government has one and only one general fund. It is the principle reporting entity for every local government. All of the financial resources of the government not required to be accounted for in another fund are accounted for in the general fund. The majority of the funds budgeted during the annual budget process come from the general fund, except in those governments that operate extensive enterprise fund services. The majority of the services typically associated with local governments, such as police, fire and recreation, are usually funded from general funds. Financial managers try to maintain a continuing fund balance of between 5 and 10 percent in order to respond to emergencies and to guard against overspending. Fund balances may also be formally reserved for specific purposes such as petty cash or encumbrances, and these funds are unavailable for appropriation. Unreserved funds may also be excluded from the annual budget process by designating them for tentative management plans, such as equipment replacement, or to respond to possible accounting changes. The term "designated" allows managers to accumulate funds in the general fund, the use of which, however, is not legally restricted.

Special Revenue Funds

These are used to account for funds that are legally restricted to specific purposes, with the exception of those held in trust or used for major capital projects. Noncapital intergovernmental grants would typically be accounted for in special revenue funds. Local governments may have more than one special revenue fund, and these funds often proliferate. Sometimes a special revenue fund is set up for revenues that can be accounted for as a special account within another fund, or they are used to collect general funds that are then transferred to other funds. In the latter case, general funds can be hidden in the fund balances of special revenue funds and excluded from the formal budget process.

Capital Projects Funds

General funds allocated for major capital projects are accounted for in these funds. Capital projects funded through enterprise revenues or trust funds are accounted for elsewhere. The legal segregation of these funds allows for the coordination of the financing and construction of projects that can extend over several years. Top management can also use these funds to divert revenues from the annual budget process and accumulate them for the acquisition of land for, or the construction of, politically popular capital projects, which often never seem to get built.

Debt Service Funds

These funds are used to account for funds accumulated to pay the principal and interest on the general long-term debts of the local government. Management practices in this area are tightly regulated by law and closely scrutinized by external auditors.

Proprietary funds are used to account for the operations of business-type agencies in the local government organization, such as potable water, waste water treatment or sanitation. There are two types of proprietary funds:

Enterprise Funds

These funds are used to account for the operations of agencies that "sell" services directly to customers, much like private-sector enterprises. A key difference is that these agencies usually operate as a monopoly within the jurisdiction, and the exchange of fees for some level of service is legally mandated. These agencies (for example, sanitation, wastewater treatment, and potable water) are each set up as individual enterprise funds. Each is totally funded from the fees it collects selling its service; even the debt the agency incurs to maintain its capital plant and equipment is funded through these fees. However, a local government may create an enterprise fund to account for the operations of a service only partially funded from its own fees, in order to determine the extent to which the service is being subsidized through general funds. Enterprise agencies may also be required to transfer funds to the general fund to cover the costs of their participation in administrative processes funded through general taxes, such as the budgeting process, the accounting system and the personnel function, as well as to make a payment in lieu of the taxes they would pay as a private-sector enterprise and to repay the general fund for its initial investment. Local governments are not required to structure these business-type agencies as enterprise funds, but these functions are often capital intensive, and governments can often obtain lower interest rates if an identifiable revenue stream is legally restricted to repay the debt necessary to fund capital facilities and equipment. The local government can also avoid straining legal limits on its capacity to issue general obligation debt. The operation of enterprise funds is thus closely scrutinized by external observers representing potential investors.

Internal Service Funds

These funds are used to account for the operations of agencies within the government organization that "sell" services to other agencies within the organization or to other governmental organizations. ISFs are mechanisms for allocating the costs of the goods and services provided by the ISF agencies to the agencies that employ them in their day-to-day operations, and they are designed to minimize these costs by bringing market controls to the use of the goods and services. ISFs are examined in greater detail in the last section of this chapter.

Fiduciary-Type Funds

Three types of funds are used to account for assets held by a government in a trustee or agency capacity. Agency funds account for assets held for others, such as taxes collected by a government for distribution to other governmental units. Pension funds hold assets accumulated to finance pension benefits. Trust funds hold resources designated for the purposes specified in a trust agreement—for example, funds donated for the purchase of library books. In an expendable trust fund, both the principle and accumulated interest can be used to buy the library books; in a nonexpendable trust, only the accrued interest can be expended for the designated purpose. Trust funds can create resource allocation problems for local governments. For example, what would happen to the general funds allocated for library book purchases if trust funds set up for that purpose proliferated? Assets seized or forfeited as a result of criminal activity are often liquidated and placed in trust funds designated for the acquisition of police equipment or the funding of capital improvements for police agencies. However, many police agencies continue to compete with other local government agencies for general fund resources for these purposes, despite healthy forfeiture-and-seizure trust fund balances.

We have consciously attached "political" issues to the descriptions of these fund types, because they are often simply presented as value-neutral accounting entities. Service agency managers tend to accept the restrictions and controls associated with their governmental fund structures as the nature of their legal environments, but these are as amenable to political manipulation as revenue structures (which service managers also usually accept as an environmental "given") and resource allocation schemes. As local governments become increasingly dependent on own-source revenues, managers must become more knowledgeable regarding accounting structures and policies. If current resources are the only ones available, managers must know where they are in order to function effectively.

ACCOUNTING AND FINANCIAL REPORTING

Funds differ on the basis of exactly what is accounted for in each fund, and the manner in which revenues and expenditures are assigned to particular accounting periods, usually a single fiscal year. The "what" of accounting is termed the measurement focus; the basis of accounting refers to the determination of the "when." Private-sector firms, proprietary fund agencies, pension funds, and nonexpendable trust funds employ the flow of economic resources as their measurement focus (or the capital maintenance focus), while governmental funds and expendable trust funds focus on the flow of current financial resources (or the spending focus). The term "measurement focus" is not applicable to agency funds. The accrual basis of accounting is associated with the economic resources focus, and the modified accrual basis is associated with the focus on current financial resources.

Accrual accounting recognizes revenues in the period in which they are earned regardless of when they are actually received, and recognizes expenses in the period in which they are incurred. Because general government functions do not necessarily earn money, modified accrual recognizes revenues when they are measurable and available to pay current liabilities in that period. The exact nature of these criteria may differ with the revenue source, as well as with the practices of particular governments. The modified accrual basis assigns expenditures to the period in which they will be liquidated with available financial resources. These criteria allow local governments considerable discretion in assigning revenues and expenditures to accounting periods, and this discretion is sometimes abused in order to balance current liabilities and available financial resources.

The accrual basis deals with "expenses" and the modified accrual speaks to "expenditures." The former represent reductions in economic resources, and the latter reductions in current financial resources. When a private-sector firm purchases an automobile, the purchase represents no net loss of economic resources. The $20,000 in cash becomes a $20,000 asset. The expense is incurred as the asset is used up in the course of doing business; if the life of the car is five years, the asset is expensed, or depreciated, at $5,000 per year. A general fund agency would record the total cost of the automobile as an expenditure in the period in which it was purchased, and the entire $20,000 would appear in a single accounting period. The $20,000 are expended when they are no longer available as current financial resources. The modified accrual basis does not provide information on the cost of doing business, because the automobile will also be used to provide service during the next four years. Private-sector firms and proprietary-type government agencies require data regarding the true cost of doing business in order to establish prices and set fees, pursue efficiency in their operations, pay taxes only on net revenues, report to stockholders and the financial establishment, and provide for the long-term economic viability. General government operations simply account for what happens to the money. This focus is based on elemental differences between business activities and general government operations, but it also reflects the emphasis on control rather than on efficiency and effectiveness that characterizes local government management.

All local governments must submit some sort of formal financial report to their respective state governments annually. They are also advised to make a complete set of audited financial statements by fund type available to the financial establishment. The Government Accounting Standards Board (GASB) encourages all local governments to prepare a formal document called the Consolidated Annual Financial Report (CAFR), which includes both summaries by fund type and the statements of individual funds. All of these reports, however, focus on the accounting entity, or funds that comprise the operations of the local government, rather than the local government as a whole. Nothing is said about what the reported transactions accomplished, or the "profit" of the local government operations, even its proprietary fund agencies. For private-sector entities, the calculation of this profit and its implications for long-term financial condition is fairly straightforward. In fact, two local governments could compile CAFRs that were identical in fund structures, financial transactions and fund balances, and these organizations could be in vastly different financial conditions. The poor condition of the infrastructure, low service-levels, and weak managerial capacity of the one would not show up in its financial report, and yet these would sharply limit its ability to absorb revenue reductions or provide for emergency expenditure increases. These eventualities would require service-level reductions that could precipitate emigrations, reduced property values, disinvestment, and the deterioration of the jurisdiction's economic base. For this reason, the GASB is considering requiring local governments to provide service effort and accomplishments measures in their financial reports.

The GASB is also considering moving the accounting focus from the measurement of current financial resources to financial resources, and adopting the accrual basis of accounting for governmental funds. A primary target here is reduction of managerial discretion in regard to revenue recognition. Revenues should be recognized in the period in which the underlying event generating the revenue occurs, and they are due and demanded; for property taxes, this is the period for which they are levied, if they are demanded, regardless of when they are collected. On the expenditure side, expenditures should be recognized in the period in which the liability is incurred. Additionally, any operating expenditures affecting long-term operating debt, such as accrued liabilities in the form of pensions, would be reported, since the focus would no longer be on current financial resources but the flow of financial resources in general. The GASB is becoming less concerned whether current-year revenues are sufficient to pay current services, and more concerned with the larger issue of whether the financial resources obtained in a given period are sufficient to cover the liabilities incurred during that period. Expenditures for capital outlays, however, will continue to be recognized when they are incurred, and the depreciation of these items will not be mandated. The overall thrust of governmental accounting remains to track the flow of dollars, although over a wider horizon, rather than establishing the costs of providing services and tying these to policy outcomes.

External auditors focus on the adequacy of internal financial controls, such as the structure of the accounting system, the segregation of financial responsibilities, and the functions of the internal auditor. This is done in order to be able to assess the fairness of the government's financial statements—that is, the degree to which the statements accurately represent the finances of the jurisdiction. However, an assessment of the actual financial condition of the government is not normally an element of the audit function. If such an assessment were expected of auditors, they could be held responsible for failing to identify potential problems. Internal auditors also devote most of their energies to testing the adequacy of the government's accounting system and financial controls, but they are more likely to be involved in performance audits, in which the managerial capacity and the operating efficiency of targeted agencies are addressed. By and large, however, neither internal nor external auditors target the long-term economic viability of the organization for analysis.

BUDGETARY CONTROLS

Controls on the budget execution process are exercised through the budget, the finance and the purchasing functions. In many local government organizations all of these function may be the responsibility of a single agency; in others these functions are assigned to individual departments. In this section, those controls that are budgetary in nature are reviewed, with the next section focusing on financial and purchasing controls.

The budget department deals with three budgets simultaneously. First, the analysts review the previous year's budgets, usually during the first quarter of the fiscal year, as the finance function prepares the annual report. These reviews focus on the amounts actually expended by each agency in light of what was budgeted, in an effort to identify areas that may have been overfunded or underfunded. Budget analysts should work closely with analysts or managers in the service delivery agencies in order to give programmatic substance to the analyses of budget variances. This information is used in deliberations for the development of the following year's budget, which is the second budget dealt with by the budget department. The budget development process occurs during the last three quarters of the fiscal year. Concurrently with both of these responsibilities, the budget department oversees the execution of the current year's budget.

This oversight responsibility centers on monitoring the rate at which each agency expends its budgeted funds in order to minimize the possibility of overruns. Agency budgets are often divided into equal quarterly allotments by line-item or line-item category, such as personnel, operating, and operating capital. If an agency expends its first-quarter allotment for office supplies in the first month of the fiscal year, the budget department may force the agency to wait for the start of the second quarter to purchase additional supplies, or may require overruns in the first quarter to be balanced by the end of the second. This practice helps to prevent large year-end shortfalls that could entail service cutbacks or require supplemental appropriations. The actual size of the allotments can be tailored to past spending practices; for example, the recreation department may expend the bulk of its budget during the summer months, in which case its allotments are adjusted to identify actual shortfalls and overruns, rather than those "false echoes" associated with uneven spending patterns. Allotments usually focus on operating expenditures. The personnel costs of fully staffed agencies are stable and routine, unless an error is made in preparing the budget, or an unforeseen emergency precipitates unusual overtime expenditures. However, the budget department exercises a position control function to ensure that all of the persons working in each agency hold positions that are authorized in the budget. Funds budgeted for operating capital are often encumbered at the beginning of the fiscal year, and cannot be used to purchase anything but the specific item that was budgeted.

Sophisticated computer programs have made formal allotment procedures largely obsolete. They provide monthly reports for budget analysts and agency managers that list the amount budgeted in the line-items of each agency, the amounts expended to date, and the amounts that will be expended by year's end if current rates continue; these are compared to budgeted amounts as in the quarterly allotment procedure, and potential problems are flagged early. These reports often include the funds budgeted for the previous year for each line-item and the amounts actually expended. More sophisticated programs display the funds requested for the coming year as the development of that year's budget proceeds, as well as the amounts approved to date. Thus, all three budgets are displayed in a single report.

In organizations using performance or program budget formats, the budget department may also be responsible for monitoring demand, workload, or activity levels, and for collecting and analyzing outcome measures. This arrangement can serve to build substantive bridges between the service agencies and the budget department, and the control function can be more effectively informed by service delivery issues. The allocative efficiency of future budgets can also be enhanced by this relationship. Good budget analysts generally resist the mindless application of fiscal criteria to budget control and development. The capacity of the budget department to build these bridges is often a function of the level of control exercised in the jurisdiction; that is, whether service agency managers are allowed to transfer funds among line-items within the same category or among categories, or if they must seek permission from the budget department, or even the city council, to alter line-item allocations. Tight controls tend to preclude substantive communication. Good budget analysts will focus their attention on the large line-items that are central to the functioning of their agencies, and they will balance overruns in some with shortfalls in others in order to maximize the flexibility of service managers. They will differentiate those variances that are due to legitimate changes in service delivery strategies or demands from those due to poor planning or price changes. In short, the analyst monitors spending in the context of service delivery as well as fiscal constraints. The danger here is that they could be co-opted by their service delivery agencies and function as advocates of the agency rather than guardians of the public fisc.

The expenditure monitoring function also occurs in conjunction with the revenue monitoring function. If revenues are not collected as projected, service program managers may be forced to cut expenditures regardless of their spending patterns. This is another reason for maintaining allotments. In jurisdictions with declining revenues or weak revenue forecasting capacities, service managers may learn to spend their budgets as soon as possible in order to avoid their share of reductions when revenue shortfalls become manifest. A strict allotment program precludes this possibility. This also demonstrates that, in addition to seeing that the service agencies execute their budgets as appropriated, the budget department has its own policy goals to pursue in the budget control process: that is, to protect the capacity of the organization to respond to potential revenue shortfalls.

In some jurisdictions that budget department may also exercise a pre-audit function. The relevant analyst will sign off on capital items or purchases exceeding a certain dollar limit. This review is required because the purchases will have a big impact on the balance of specific line-items; it ensures that funds are indeed available, and that the expenditures are still warranted by service delivery requirements. This responsibility spills into the controls associated with the finance and purchasing functions.

FINANCIAL CONTROLS

In pursuit of its responsibility to maintain the integrity of the accounting system and fund structure described above, the finance department records each expenditure in the organization's chart of accounts. Every purchase transaction is assigned a code number that indicates the fund, department, program, and specific line-item associated with the expenditure. The finance department will also encumber funds reserved for specific purchases, such as capital items, and render them unavailable for any other purpose. These records form the basis of the monthly expenditure reports received by service managers. Encumbrances usually appear as expenditures, and more than one manager has been shocked to find that the funds for his or her new vehicle had apparently been used for some other purpose, when in fact they had simply been encumbered until the vehicle was purchased.

The lack of communications regarding encumbrances illustrates the blind approach to the recording of transactions that often characterizes the finance function. This can be contrasted with the efforts of budgeters to build substantive bridges to service agencies. However, once again, the finance department must maintain the integrity of the accounting system, and it is understandably more sensitive to the possibility of co-optation than the budget department. Service program managers often view the finance department as a constraint on their flexibility in employing their budgeted funds, but they recognize that this function is rooted in professional standards and reporting requirements that are long-standing and unavoidable. For this reason, they may also view the finance department as less intrusive than the budget department.

However, the finance department also has its own policy pursuits attached to its control functions: namely, the maintenance of healthy fund balances. Finance professionals pursue this end in order, like the budget department, to be able to respond to short-term emergencies, but also to demonstrate that the jurisdiction is in good financial condition in their reporting functions. Healthy fund balances make investment attractive and please bond-rating agencies. The goal of maintaining these balances, however, sometimes conflicts with the needs of program managers for resources to meet demands for substantive services. The finance department may oppose requests for supplemental appropriations from unreserved fund balances because such appropriations compromise the finance department's own policy goals, rather than judging the requests on their own merits. While it is obvious that lower interests rates for legitimate borrowing mean more resources available for allocation to service delivery systems, managers should be aware that financial controls are not exercised in a value-neutral context.

The structure of the transaction processing system is also a responsibility of the finance department. It is a principle of accounting control that responsibility for making transactions should be separated from the maintenance of their recording in order to minimize the possibility for fraudulent transactions. However, the division of these responsibilities among several positions can create unnecessary red tape and constrain the capacity of program managers to provide timely delivery of services. Rather than accepting the structure of the transaction processing system as an unavoidable element in the environment of public management, the value of these controls should be weighed against the costs imposed on service delivery managers.

PURCHASING CONTROLS

The purchasing department defines exactly what can be purchased with some authorized expenditures and from whom. The department is most likely to be involved in expenditures for operating capital equipment or other expenditures that exceed a specified dollar limit. The local government's legislative body may also review expenditures for such costly items when they are made, even after authorizing the expenditures during the budget development process; this is to ensure the expenditures are still needed and still reflect the policy preferences of the council members. The purchasing department will work with the service agency to write specifications for the product or contract, and private-sector vendors will be invited to submit bids for its provision. Usually the lowest bid that meets the specifications is accepted.

The key role of the purchasing department is writing the specifications for the items. Purchasing managers seek to realize economies of scale and volume discounts by writing specifications that meet the needs of more than one service agency. For example, the parks manager may require a certain kind of four-wheel-drive vehicle to survey his or her domain, and the fire chief may need a slightly different type of four-wheel-drive vehicle to drive to the scene of a fire. The purchasing manager may try to reconcile these differences in order to solicit bids for both vehicles using a single set of specifications. This practice also reduces the costs of soliciting bids. The specification reconciliation process also signals the service agencies that they are members of the same organization—in much the same way as the budget process does—and should seek to make operational decisions from the perspective of what is best for the organization as a whole. The same perspective holds for stocking goods in a consolidated warehouse often operated by the purchasing department.

The purchasing function is perceived in much the same way as the finance function by service delivery managers; that is, purchasing managers are committed to professional standards and operational procedures that often limit the capacity of program managers to meet the needs of their constituencies, and this is unavoidable. We are aware of one purchasing director whose staff was very slow to confirm the receipt of items that had been purchased, and hence authorizations for the payment of invoices were not being forwarded to the finance department on a timely basis. The items were often delivered directly to the service agency that had requested them, and these were slow to verify that what had been received was what had been ordered and that the item was in good condition. But when the items were delivered to the purchasing department, that department was also slow to forward the items to the user for confirmation. The upshot of these internal problems was that the purchasing director was usually unable to take advantage of discounts offered by vendors for early payment of their invoices. Analysis indicated that this medium-sized city was losing about $80,000 by not using available discounts! One analyst suggested that the purchasing director request payment for the discounted invoice whether or not the required time criteria had been met, until the procedural issues could be addressed. The purchasing director replied that such an action would violate the ethical code promulgated by his professional association, although he acknowledged that most vendors would be grateful for any kind of payment and were unlikely to challenge the discount. Top management supported his position, because he was able to produce documents indicating that he was, indeed, a certified purchasing professional. If purchasing managers want service managers to adopt organization-wide decision-making premises in order to achieve economies of scale in purchasing goods and services, they should also.

SERVICE MANAGERS AND BUDGET EXECUTION

Budgets are generally built from the bottom up, and budget processes are heavily dependent on the expertise of service managers. Budget processes tend to focus on the funds allocated to line-items, and the implications that these allocations hold for substantive policy are clear only to service managers. Hence, these managers are very influential in the policy-making process. But once the legislative body makes its appropriations, these policies—and, once again, what they are is not always clear—become ours as well. The expenditure of public funds in the pursuit of these policies must therefore be strictly controlled, so that service managers cannot alter or subvert them. As in the budget development process, these controls focus on the flow of funds rather than on the substantive policies, and these controls serve to constrain the capacity of service managers to realize those policy goals. For service program managers, budget execution means policy implementation. For budgeters, accountants and the purchasing department, budget execution means controlling expenditures.

In response to the constraints posed by spending controls, program managers are apt to bring the same kind of "gaming" that characterizes the typical budget development process to the execution phase. In the development phase, gaming strategies center on getting as much money as possible in whatever area is feasible. In the execution phase, these strategies focus on getting the flexibility to spend those funds where they are needed the most in terms of achieving policy objectives. The initial battlefront is the level of control exercised on line-item appropriations. At a minimum, program managers prefer that the level of control be set at the line-item category level rather than at the individual line-item, so that they are able to use funds within those categories as they see fit. A control function that concerned itself only with the bottom lines of their budgets would maximize their decision-making flexibility.

An examination of the strategies used in expending funds for capital outlays illustrates the dilemmas faced by service managers as they execute their budgets. Consider the manager who was fortunate enough to justify the purchase of an additional vehicle during the budget development process. The case for the vehicle was made on the basis of enhancing efficiency in pursuit of the policy defined in the mission of the agency. As discussed above, these funds are usually encumbered immediately by the finance department, but the manager must still decide whether to purchase the vehicle as soon as possible, or to delay purchase in case the funds are needed elsewhere—to respond to an emergency or to compensate for an unforeseen shortfall in some line-item. Seeking approval for the transfer of funds would take less work than trying to get a supplemental appropriation, despite the encumbrance. However, delay might mean that the funds could be transferred to another budget due to the same kind of emergency, or fall victim to shortfalls in overall revenue collections. The actual impact of either decision on service delivery may be slight, but the important point here is that the decision is made without explicit consideration of service quality. The need to deal with the internal control function limits the capacity of the manager to maximize effectiveness, and the length of the purchasing process and its cumbersome bidding phase are not even addressed.

The wages and benefits appropriated for approved but vacant positions constitute another pool of funds available to the service program manager. The decision here is whether to accelerate the hiring process in order to fill the positions or to use the funds to pay overtime to existing personnel in order to maintain service delivery levels. The latter option allows the manager to maintain a degree of flexibility in the use of the funds, as well as to grant existing personnel wage increases that might not otherwise be available. Ideally, the decision should rest on criteria that reflect service quality, but the very existence of the positions may not be based on those criteria. Police managers may find it easier to secure funds for additional sworn personnel in the face of rising crime rates than to get funding for training, travel to conferences, professional memberships or wage increases that might be demanded by other employees of the jurisdiction. Funds allocated to vacant positions can be used for overtime, or reprogrammed to other purposes during the fiscal year. Indeed, filling the vacant positions might prove counterproductive because that option might stretch available resources in related areas, such as training, overtime and uniform allowances.

On the other hand, vacant positions may be lost if they are not filled on a timely basis (though this is unlikely in the case of police positions). The old saw of "spend it or lose it" applies to personnel line-items as well as operating expenditures. However, it is in the latter that service managers should probably be allowed the greatest amount of discretion. Unlike capital outlays, operating expenditures do not usually represent expenditures for a single costly item that must be justified in great detail; nor do they have the permanence and ancillary costs associated with employment positions. Operating expenditures also represent the "how" of public policy, or the technologies to be used in the pursuit of policy goals, and the identification of optimal service delivery technologies is the reason why professional managers are employed. But the budget development process forces managers to get the money where they can, and does not encourage them to speak in terms of optimal technologies. Thus, service managers must seek the discretion to move funds among operating line-items in order to implement and adapt service delivery technologies. We are familiar with a case in which a city's internal auditor was reviewing his budget submissions with a new budget analyst, and the analyst questioned him about a $15,000 request under contractual services. This amount represented less than 5 percent of the auditor's budget, but a substantial part of his operating expenditures. He relied that he did not know what that line-item was used for, but that amount had always been in that line-item. The analyst disallowed the request, and the budget director reassigned the analyst.

Public managers sometimes find that they must return to the legislative body for a supplemental appropriation. An important piece of equipment may need to be replaced, an overtime budget may have been overexpended due to some emergency, or a new program may have been suggested or a new technology made available. In any case, funds have not been allocated for that purpose, and waiting for the following budget process may result in denigration of service delivery. Less often, a manager might feel he or she has a better chance of getting a project or item funded through the less visible supplemental process than in the more competitive budget process. Revenue collections may have exceeded expectations, or a particular council person may champion the project. In a jurisdiction we observed, the city manager assembled all requests for supplemental appropriations and took them to city council for consideration. Some were funded and some not, but the number of requests grew steadily. It was suggested that he change his policy and let each manager present his or own request in person, and the requests for such an opportunity dwindled rapidly.

Over time, budget execution for service program managers becomes less and less about implementing public policy and more and more about simply spending line-item allocations. The pursuit of substantive policy goals must be undertaken within the constraints posed by controls on budget execution, and the controls themselves come to define the operational environment. Managers are exhorted just as often and as loudly to make sure that their personnel take their vacations on schedule (so that vacation time does not accrue) as they are exhorted to meet operational demands. The accounting framework that drives these controls is not even designed to provide the managerial information that could enhance service delivery efforts. The results-oriented budget format reviewed in Chapter 2 moves the accountability and control function to the monitoring and evaluation of policy outcomes, and allows service managers more discretion in how they employ available resources. However, we suggested that the outcome measures that would support the implementation of such a system have not been fully developed. The move to results-oriented budgeting would have to be a gradual one for most jurisdictions in any case, because organizational culture and values of the typical local government organization do not support it. The place to start to instill the values necessary to support the rational pursuit of policy goals is the budget development process. The values that drive the budget execution process—that is, what should be the policy implementation process— are developed as a product of the resource allocation process of the public organization.

We have also pointed out that private-sector managers have a readily available measure of their policy effectiveness: namely, profits. However, in the not-too-distant past, the blind pursuit of short-term profits for quarterly reports weakened the global competitiveness of some segments of this country's economic infra-structure. It was learned that market controls on the decision-making perspectives of private-sector managers must also encompass the long-term economic viability of the enterprise. Local government managers are also accountable for the long-term economic viability of their jurisdictions, and this criterion helps to define rationality in the allocation of public resources. Unfortunately, there is no real political constituency for this end, but neither did there appear to be a constituency for it in the private sector.

MANAGERIAL ISSUES

Important issues in local government resource management are manifested in the operation of and allocation of resources to internal service fund agencies (ISFs). The ISF is the only fund type geared to the internal operations of local governments, and one of the few accounting mechanisms that is management oriented rather than oriented to meeting the needs of external users of financial reports or optimizing the financial control function (Chang, 1987). This section examines the operation of local government ISFs.

As above, ISFs are agencies that provide goods or services to other agencies in the government organization or to other governments on a cost-reimbursement basis; that is, the price charged to the user agency is designed to cover the costs of providing the good or service incurred by the ISF. Services that have been structured as ISFs include warehousing, fleet maintenance, data processing, bill collecting, office space allocation and engineering services. These charge-back mechanisms help local governments account for the total cost of individual programs by allocating the costs of these support services to the programs that use them. The centralization and sharing of these functions may make them more economical to provide, and they are able to take advantage of economies of scale. ISFs also bring market controls to the use of the service or product; the ISF is more sensitive to user needs because the agencies are now "customers," and the user agencies are more efficient in their use of the service or product because these agencies are being charged for its use. ISFs make all managers more aware of costs and the need to control them, and they spotlight the value of managing resources more productively.

In order to maximize the efficiency of the ISF as a market mechanism, the organization's user agencies should be afforded the option of purchasing comparable services or products from private vendors. This is often the case with in-house suppliers in private-sector firms. More often than not, however, local government agencies are required to deal exclusively with the in-house ISF. It is unlikely that an ISF with a limited customer base could compete effectively with private-sector firms, and the local private sector would object to allowing the local government ISF to compete in the open market. The goals of public sector ISFs are convenience, certainty, and responsiveness to a limited customer base; economy may be a secondary goal. We are reminded of the case of a private-sector warehouse manager who was hired to improve the operations of a local government consolidated warehouse structured as an ISF. In an attempt to reduce overhead charges he sought to institute a "just in time" inventory policy. Using modern warehousing techniques, he determined that the public utilities agency used an average of two large, custom bolts every month, and he decided that two months' supply on hand would be adequate. These bolts were used to refurbish potable water pumping stations. One station was refurbished every year, and all twenty-four bolts were required at the same time. Some private-sector warehouses might have declined to service this customer, because the specialized product stayed on the shelf too long; the ISF manager had no choice in the matter.

Private-sector managers are evaluated on their ability to reduce costs, enhance productivity and maximize profits. Public-sector managers are evaluated on their ability to stay within their budgets. In many cases, the private-sector vendors will appear to be a more economical choice for public agency managers. This is because the charges for using the ISF service appear right in their budgets, and in overhead charges when they purchase a good. However, the costs of shopping among vendors, negotiating volume discounts, achieving economies of scale, and centralizing access that appear in overhead charges can be hidden in the user agency's budget when the agency by-passes the ISF. The costs of road crews stopping at multiple vendors for supplies before going to the job site, the costs of the administrative assistant calling for prices when a large printing or copying project is needed, and the costs of maintaining a large volume of supplies which could become obsolete or damaged, for example, are hidden in the agency's line-items and in reduced service levels. The centrifugal forces at work in multiservice local government organizations that serve to lower decision-making perspectives to levels that are sub-optimal for the organization as a whole will always make ISFs look like an uneconomical alternative.

In their text on governmental accounting, Robert Freeman and Craig Shoulders contend that flexible budgets should be employed by ISFs, so that the "level of activity of an IS Fund will be determined by the demand of the user department for its services" (1996: 444). Fixed appropriations to the ISF would constrain its ability to respond to user agency needs, and separate appropriations to the various user agencies would also limit ISF activity. However, in our experience the latter scenario is usually the case, because flexible budgets may compromise the capacity of the jurisdiction to balance its budget. The user agencies would still have some discretion in the use of the funds, because the

ISF could draw down its fund balances to cover any projected shortfalls in its own revenue stream. However, the absence of a true flexible, or open, budget compromises the capacity of the ISF to function as a market mechanism for allocating resources within the local government organization during the budget execution process. The flexible budget option would also facilitate an abuse of the ISF mechanism identified by Chang and Freeman (1991), namely the practice of reclassifying general-fund programs as ISF activities in order to circumvent the constraints of the formal budget process. For example, rather than justifying a fixed appropriation for the data processing department, the department is structured as an ISF, and user agencies are granted open-ended authority to purchase services from the department as long as their needs are being met.

The fixed-budget option at least signals agency managers that they are sharing the costs of some central services, and that they are all part of a single organization. However, the ISF will not function as a market mechanism for allocating those costs. The allocation of central service costs is ultimately a management decision, and it is best if this decision is made by the users as a group. In Chapter 1 we outlined a case in which the finance director was able to cut his data processing budget without hurting his own operations because the cost allocation scheme had been poorly designed. In another case, fleet-maintenance user charges reflected the hourly rate of the mechanic who actually serviced each vehicle. If vehicles had been randomly assigned, the effects of wage differentials would have also been randomized. However, management decided that emergency vehicles should have first priority, and other vehicles were serviced by supervisors when the mechanics were busy with police and fire vehicles. This meant higher bills for recreation and public works vehicles, and the costs of the management policy were being borne by those most inconvenienced by it.

If management policies override market mechanisms, these policies should be the product of a joint effort and an organization-wide decision-making perspective. In one case, a task force of data processing personnel, data processing users, and fiscal analysts was assembled to develop an equitable cost allocation system for the data processing department, which was structured as an ISF. They designed a system in which the user was billed on the basis of the value of the service to the user rather than on the basis of costs incurred by the data processing department. The users would have closer control of their data processing line-items, and they would be better able to plan for their future needs. The data processing department would not bill for cost overruns in system development projects, and they would be allowed to balance their ISF accounts over a three-year period rather than annually. The department would also make available a range of system support and maintenance plans from which the users could choose. The internal auditor of the jurisdiction, however, contended that the potential need for short-term transfers from the general fund to the data processing ISF, and the implementation of a pricing-structure that did not reflect actual costs did not constitute good accounting practices. Despite the potential for enhanced departmental productivity and user responsiveness, the plan was rejected. Management ceded its responsibilities to the myth that the ISF mechanism manifests market controls, and, as in the case of the purchasing director above, certification triumphed over rationality.

Good staff services do not necessarily yield good substantive policy decisions. Public managers implement public policy as they execute that annual budget. The crucial issue for the effectiveness and responsiveness of those service delivery systems, as well as their efficiency and economy, is the decision-making perspective adopted by those who manage them. In a case we witnessed involving the operation of a consolidated warehouse structured as an ISF, a "board of directors" comprised of the warehouse manager, user agency managers, and central staff analytical personnel was able to cut the warehouse overhead charge by 25 percent and improve service to the user agencies by adopting decision-making premises that reflected an organization-wide perspective. We believe that the professional expertise of local government managers must be applied in an organization-wide context in order to yield rational resource allocation outcomes. The centrifugal forces that characterize highly differentiated local government organizations precipitate sub-optimal decision-making perspectives. Administrative systems alone cannot generate sufficient centripetal force to overcome sub-optimization, and the imposition of self-regulating market mechanisms is not a viable alternative to the development of the necessary managerial perspective.

REFERENCES

Chang, S. Y. (1987). *A Study of the Basic Criteria and Standards for Internal Service Funds*. Lubbock: Texas Tech University Press.

Chang, S. Y., and Freeman, Robert J. (1991). "Internal Service Funds: The Neglected Stepchild's Neglected Stepchild." *Government Accountant's Journal*, 40 (3): 22–30.

Freeman, Robert J., and Shoulders, Craig D. (1996). *Governmental and Nonprofit Accounting: Theory and Practice* (5th ed.). Upper Saddle River, N.J.: Prentice-Hall.

Gross, Bertram M. (1969). "The New Systems Budgeting." *Public Administration Review*, 29 (2): 113–137.

Chapter 4

Budgeting for Productivity

Real efficiency . . . must be built into the structure of a government just as
it is built into a piece of machinery.
            President's Committee on Administrative Management (1937)

Private-sector firms develop annual budgets, too. Like public-sector budgets,
these are estimates of expenditures by the functional areas that comprise the
organization. The most obvious differences between private- and public-sector
budgets is that the former are not legal documents, and the general public does
not participate in the budget development processes of private firms. The resulting documents are more flexible than the typical public-sector budget. Private-sector managers have the discretion to alter their annual resource allocation
plans in response to changes in the internal or external environments of their
organizations. Internal changes include the adoption of new technologies, the
development of new procedures, and the design of new products that make
changes to the plan of operations embodied by the original budget desirable.
Examples of changes in the external environment of the firm include the birth
of new competitors, new government regulations and new markets.

   Private-sector managers receive information regarding the profitability of their
firms on a daily basis, so they are able to re-allocate resources to those activities
that are most profitable or most crucial to profitability in light of changing
circumstances. Profitability, variously expressed as income, return on equity,
market share, and rate of growth, serves as a common "bottom line" for all of
the firm's activities. This unifying goal is absent in multiservice local governments. Production technologies and relevant cause-and-effect relationships are
also better understood in the typical private enterprise. This knowledge makes

responsive, effective re-allocations feasible. If something is not working, the cause is usually identifiable and alternative courses of action are available. Consensus on goals and general agreement on the relative efficacy of alternative activities allow private-sector firms to allocate resources on the basis of rational planning, structured analysis of readily available data, and a relatively straight-forward calculus.

The reform movements that sought to "reinvent" government in the United States at the beginning of the twentieth century pursued two basic goals. One of these goals was to bring business practices such as rational planning and structured analysis to the administration of public service delivery systems. These reformers conceptually separated the administration of public policy from the development of policy. They sought to enhance the efficiency of the former by isolating it from what they viewed as the ravages of partisan politics. Others desired a humane, responsive government that could take positive steps to address quality-of-life issues and provide for the general welfare. At the same time, some of these reformers wanted to strengthen the accountability of government administrators through the implementation of control mechanisms such as accounting, budgeting, and personnel classification systems. The environment of public management has come to be characterized by the often conflicting demands for efficient and effective administration of the government's business, and popular control of the required professional discretion. This conflict is rooted in the different political agendas of the various reform groups; some desired a better and a more active government, others wanted smaller and less expensive government, and some may have simply sought to limit the growing political power of ethnic minorities. From the beginning it was clear that enhancing productivity in the public-sector would entail more than simple calculation.

It is not our intention to oversimplify the resource allocation processes of private-sector firms, but rather to reduce them to their basic elements in order to demonstrate that these elements are not often present in public-sector organizations. The absence of these elements has enormous implications for public-sector budgeting, for efforts to enhance productivity in the provision of public services, and for local government management in general. The relative productivity of an organization depends on the capacity of its managers to apply their collective expertise to changing circumstances, and to gather data regarding the nature of those circumstances and the range of alternative courses of action available to them. In this chapter, we explore the nature of local government productivity, the types of performance data available to public managers, the issues associated with developing program performance measures, and the prospects for integrating performance measurement with the formal resource allocation process. In addition to the issue of bringing productivity data to resource allocation decision-making, we also examine the potential for utilizing the formal budget process itself as a tool for developing the capacity of the local government organization to provide efficient and responsive services.

DEFINITIONS OF PRODUCTIVITY

A production system is comprised of three broad stages: input, throughput, and output. The input stage refers to the resources used in the production process. These inputs may be personnel, equipment, raw materials or a combination of resources expressed as money. The throughput stage encompasses the work being done. It is here that the inputs are employed, changed or consumed. The output is the thing produced, the service provided or the changes made in the environment of the production system.

The efficiency of the system can be defined as the cost of producing a unit of output, and its productivity is the amount of output produced per unit of input. In each case, the specific type of output unit and the most crucial input unit is a function of the nature of the specific production system under consideration. These definitions are market-oriented definitions of efficiency and productivity. They focus on the productive capacity of the system and the cost of each unit of output for the purposes of establishing a unit price. The production system must produce enough units of output at a cost per unit that will allow it to sustain itself; that is, it must produce a profit. This is not to say that this approach has no utility for the production systems of governments, only that it may not capture elements of productivity that are particularly salient in the public sector.

In the public sector, efficiency generally relates outputs to inputs, and this includes the dollar costs of producing a unit of output. Productivity must be more broadly based, however, because the production system does not sustain itself through dollar profits but rather by meeting a politically enunciated need of the community. Productivity must capture the effectiveness of the production system in meeting that need. The effectiveness dimension includes the quality, responsiveness and adequacy of the service delivery system. An efficient production system is one in which the units of output are valued more than the inputs required to produce them. This calculation is complicated by that fact that the evaluation of the elements of effectiveness is often subjective and not amenable to quantification. Productivity simply refers to the overall capacity of a system to produce goods and services efficiently and effectively over time.

The pursuit of productivity is something closely associated with professional, competent management. Professional managers will make production decisions on the basis of scientific criteria, use modern decision-making methods and organizational processes, employ state-of-the-art technologies, and actively seek to maximize the efficiency of the entire production system. Professionalism also means that managers will not appropriate inputs or outputs for their own use, or seek to produce outputs that are not highly valued by allocating resources to sub-optimal production systems. As we have indicated previously, controls placed on managers to guard against self-appropriation and sub-optimal allocations can constrain the flexibility they require to pursue productivity. These controls are more likely to be found when there is disagreement regarding the value of the outputs or uncertainty regarding the effects of technological changes, or where the value of the outputs are difficult to measure, as is often the case in the public sector.

Allocative efficiency refers to the degree to which the allocation of resources to the various functions or divisions of the organization is optimal for the organization as a whole. We have indicated that the pursuit of this end is an element of professional management, and the maximization of allocative efficiency is often a matter of simple calculation in private-sector firms. However, these calculations may break down in the face of multiple product lines, particularly when these products are geared to market segments that require different production strategies. This scenario of multiple products supported by different constituencies clearly characterizes the local government organization. It should be clear that the business of the public sector is characterized by many of the factors that militate against a purely technical approach to the concept of productivity. In the following sections, we will examine the ramifications of the conflict between technological efficiency and the potential for managerial misfeasance, variable valuations of outputs by the public, uncertainty regarding cause-and-effect relationships in the pursuit of solutions to societal problems, and the lack of unambiguous information feedback systems in the context of local government productivity. However, one of the most crucial issues in public productivity is the lack of output measures necessary to calculate efficiency ratios and to monitor the effects of technological changes.

MEASURING LOCAL GOVERNMENT SERVICES

The public sector provides many services by default, in that private markets are not able to produce them at an optimal level, or sometimes at all. Markets fail in some areas because the potential providers or purchasers of the good or service are not able to reserve all the benefits of the purchase for themselves, as in the case of national defense or mosquito control, or prices cannot provide for the optimal use of a shared resource, as with an aquifer or fishing grounds. It is also often not possible to divide such goods and services into discrete, measurable units to which prices can be assigned. Thus, the problem of measuring the outputs of public service delivery systems is based on the fact that these goods and services are provided by the public sector *because* they are difficult to measure.

Political systems are less precise in determining "customer" preferences for goods and services than are market mechanisms. Whenever a person buys a pair of shoes, he or she is, in effect, voting for that particular style, material, size and color of shoe. The dollars that are spent on that pair of shoes constitute information to the production process, and this detailed, precise information is collected continuously. If the firms in the business of making shoes want to be successful, they adjust their production processes in response to this information (they also seek to influence "votes" through advertising).

Our elected representatives are responsible for production decisions in the public sector. However, during their election campaigns they represent various positions on a range of issues, and the fact that they were elected does not reveal the preferences of the voters on any specific issue. Additionally, each elected official usually represents a different political constituency. Polling is sporadic and expensive, does not reveal strength of convictions, and does not indicate how familiar the respondents are with the specific issue under consideration. Thus, in order to maximize productivity, public-sector service providers must actively seek answers to the questions for which private-sector managers are provided information on a daily basis: what do our customers want and how well are we meeting those needs?

There are five general categories of performance measures: input, workload, output, outcome and impact measures. We should be familiar with input measures. These detail the things used in the production process. It is usually not a problem to express all inputs in terms of the dollars required to acquire them. Thus, all of the inputs can be grouped to form the input side of an efficiency ratio, or efficiency ratios can be expressed in terms of specific inputs, such as personnel. A police department would count the number of detectives and the number of vehicles available to them as inputs to the investigative process. A recreation department or public works agency would detail its personnel and salient equipment as input measures. Again, these could be coupled with workload, output, or outcome measures to form efficiency ratios. Inputs are the primary elements of object-of-expenditure, or line-item, budgets.

Workload measures focus on the components of the throughput process. These summarize the activities undertaken within the organization to assemble and change the raw materials into products or to service the clients in the environment. A police detective division would be interested in monitoring the number of cases assigned to each detective, or the number ultimately investigated. A recreation department would count the number of softball games it sponsored or swimming lessons it administered. Workload measures are usually expressed as the amount of an activity conducted by each employee, or some other input measure. As seen in Chapter 2, workload measures are an integral part of performance budgets, where the inputs are expressed as budgetary dollars, and decision makers can focus on the amount of work that can be accomplished at a given level of inputs. A public works division would calculate the miles of streets that could be repaved with available resources, with a view toward increasing the productivity of the division over time.

Workload measures sometimes overlap with output measures in the public sector, but output measures properly focus on the immediate products of the production process and the activities that comprise it, rather than on the activities themselves. For example, a recreation department would be hard pressed to distinguish between the number of softball games as a workload measure and the number of people participating as an output measure, but the difference often comes down to such hairsplitting. For the police investigation division, an appropriate output measure would be the number of cases cleared (by identification or arrest) and this can be expressed as a percentage of the number assigned for investigation—that is, as a percentage of the workload measure. Like workload measures, outputs can also be combined directly with inputs to form market-like productivity measures, such as the number of cases cleared per investigator or the number cleared per $10,000 budgeted. These can be used to calculate efficiency measures or the total cost per unit of output. Such calculations can be problematic in the public sector, however, due to the nature of the budget process and the accounting system's focus on the flow of resources over time rather than on the actual costs of production.

Outcomes refer to the immediate changes in the environment of the organization that are produced by the outputs. For the private-sector organization, outcomes may include the overall profitability of the firm, as well as its market share, rate of growth, and return on equity. These measures are obvious elements of the goal of the firm, and they are valid indicators of the effectiveness of the firm's operational strategies and resource allocation plans.

The overall mission of the public sector enterprise is to enhance the quality of life in a community and to protect the general welfare of its people. Understandably, it is often difficult to identify unambiguous outcomes for such a broad mission. In addition, the specific element of the environment targeted by an individual public agency is usually subject to influences that are outside the scope of its strategic approach or resource allocation plan. For example, a positive outcome for the investigative function might be a decrease in the crime rate in the community; however, crime rates are clearly influenced by factors that are unrelated to the police mission. Positive outcomes may also depend on other organizations. The police agency would like to see a high percentage of its arrests result in successful prosecutions, but it must rely at least in part on the competence and capacity of the prosecutor's office. A recreation department may identify a 50 percent participation rate as an appropriate outcome and measure its actual outcomes on the basis of what could be an arbitrary standard.

The difference between outcomes and impacts is often simply one of time horizon, and these measures also tend to bleed into one another. In the private sector, impact measures may plumb the long term profitability of the industry of which a particular firm is a part. In the public sector, impacts refer to the ultimate effect of the organization or program on the societal problem that it was designed to address. The police agency might be concerned about the feelings of security among the residents. Once again, perceptions of a secure environment are influenced by a host of factors; indeed, a high level of police visibility may engender feelings of security in some residents and insecurity in others. Similarly, can the managers of the recreation department legitimately claim that they are in the business of enhancing the health of the residents of the community when their efforts can have only a marginal impact?

The mission of a public organization should, nevertheless, indicate the societal issue or problem it is charged with addressing and how the environment will be different if it is successful in its efforts. The mission of the agency operationalizes the policy that society has chosen to pursue in a particular area. The ambiguity of public-sector outcome and impact measures is rooted in the necessary connection between public policy and organizational mission. Public policies are usually multidimensional, and the areas targeted are subject to a host of influences. Responsibility for a public policy is often shared by more than one agency, and policies sometimes manifest conflicting elements. Additionally, public policies are rarely settled, and the political conflicts that drive the policy-making process inevitably spill into the public agencies charged with implementing them. These factors lead to problems in regard to the reliability and validity of public-sector measures as indicators of the effectiveness of the public agency in carrying out its mission.

The validity of a measure refers to the degree to which it is actually measuring what we assume it is measuring. Reliability refers to the consistency or precision of that measure over time and among users. A measure can be very reliable and still not be a valid measure of the targeted phenomenon. The reliability and validity of measures are of particular concern in the social sciences, which deal with abstract concepts and phenomena that are not directly observable, are only hypothesized to exist or are difficult to define. If the integrity of the accounting system is maintained, the validity and reliability of the measures typically used by a private-sector firm are usually not in question. The data reflect some aspect of the firm's "bottom line," and the ratios employed are commonly accepted as valid measures of the various elements of profitability. These ratios can even be used to compare the relative performance of firms in the same production sector. However, efforts to measure public-sector production systems must deal with a range of issues related to validity and reliability.

The ambiguity of public missions is a product of the complexity, multidimensionality, interrelatedness and apparent intractability of the societal problems public organizations address, as well as of the nature of the policy-making process and each agency's need to maintain a broad base of political support for its mission. In order to plumb the efficiency and productivity of production processes in this environment, multiple measures are often required, and these may not capture the full range of the mission. These multiple measures may even yield contradictory data. This clearly compromises both the validity and reliability of the measures. The actual goal of the production process becomes questionable, and hence accuracy in measurement becomes meaningless.

Factors that are beyond the control of public-sector organizations also influence the phenomena that are used to measure the outcomes and impacts of their production systems. For example, crime rates are influenced by poverty rates, economic cycles and social mores, in addition to the operational efforts of the police agency. Indeed, the police may have only a marginal impact on crime rates, and police managers may shy away from this measure as an indicator of the effectiveness of their efforts. The validity of such "uncontrollable" measures as indicators of the outcomes of the production process, as well as their reliability over time, is questionable. Comparisons between similar production systems in different public organizations are also problematical when the measures are influenced by additional factors that may vary widely among jurisdictions.

Most importantly, the meaning of the measure is a function of the political values of the interpreter. An increase in the feelings of security in a community does not indicate successful performance by the policy agency to someone who does not value that outcome. Is an increase in the efficiency and effectiveness in processing welfare claims a positive outcome if one believes that psychological and economic costs should be attached to applying for welfare in order to reduce the number of claims? The ambiguous missions that emerge from the policy-making process allow people to interpret agency performance on the basis of their own particular values. Conflicting interpretations of ambiguous missions can also exist within the same public organization. Such a scenario can constrain management's ability to optimize the allocation of its resources. Indeed, efforts to develop a single, shared mission for the managers of the organization may be one of the important factors in building the productive capacity of the organization.

On the other hand, ambiguity allows public agencies to maximize political support. The elemental conflict between production efficiency and popular control in the public sector is apparent here, and public managers must address both. Public agencies are active participants in enunciating the substance of policy. When the recreation department establishes a 50 percent participation rate as a desirable outcome, it is making policy, reducing ambiguity in its mission and providing for the coordinated pursuit of production efficiency. It is also risking the loss of political support from those who might oppose such a mission. This indicates that, in some cases, one might expect public agencies to resist the development of efficiency and effectiveness measures.

The salient point in the present discussion is that it is difficult to separate the evaluation of the performance of public agencies from the assessment of the desirability of the substantive policies which they are charged with implementing. Efficiency ratios inevitably contain elements of effectiveness—quality, responsiveness and adequacy—which raise issues of political appropriateness. Thus, the reliability and validity of productivity measures are constrained by the fact that the interpretations of the measures differs with the measurer. Additionally, what is being measured is usually the formal mission of the organization rather than the overall performance of the organization, which may be trying to respond to conflicting demands from multiple constituencies. Public-sector measures do not speak for themselves, and it should cause no surprise that public-sector managers tend to fall back on relatively "harmless" and less controversial workload indicators as measures of their efficiency and effectiveness.

THE CONTEXT OF LOCAL GOVERNMENT PRODUCTIVITY

This section examines some of the key issues that affect the efforts of local government managers to enhance the productivity of their service delivery systems. These include factors related to the role of local governments in the federal system, the internal structure of the typical local government, the nature of public-sector productivity, and incentives for pursuing productivity. Although we highlight factors that constrain productivity efforts, we nevertheless recognize that such efforts are the hallmark of professional management. In the following section on the possibilities for integrating budgeting and productivity, we will outline potential remedial measures and identify how the local government management environment can be made more supportive of productivity enhancement efforts.

The fragmented structure of local government militates against the efficient production of essential public services. Small, overlapping jurisdictions can preclude the attainment of economies of scale. Intergovernmental structures and fiscal transfers in the form of grants and revenue sharing can facilitate the necessary cooperation, but our federalist system also allows the national and state governments to mandate the provision of certain services by local governments. These mandates, usually not funded by the mandating level of government, can result in a local government resource allocation plan that is sub-optimal from the local perspective.

Even when grant funds are made available for the provision of certain services or projects, these funds can distort local priorities. A program or project for which there is relatively little demand in a community may become a top priority simply because another level of government has made funds available to support it. Earmarked funds, such as gasoline taxes limited to expenditures for road maintenance and improvements, can result in the overproduction of those outputs. If these service areas have an exclusive source of funds, the local government is faced with using these funds, or reducing or refusing them. Like mandates, intergovernmental constraints on the use of resources can limit the ability of management to optimize allocative efficiency and maximize overall productivity.

Internally, local governments are comprised of a variety of service delivery systems. Each production process requires unique technologies and particular knowledge, and the management of the umbrella organization is characterized by deference to the substantive expertise demanded by each of its components. This structure—often more of a holding company than an integrated organization—can generate enormous centrifugal forces in the organization. Fierce competition for scarce resources in the absence of a central, unifying goal will inevitably result in the sub-optimal allocation of organizational resources. In private-sector organizations, each component recognizes that the others are necessary for the successful pursuit of the firm's goals. This is not necessarily so in the local government organization, where each component attempts to secure resources in order to pursue its own particular goals. Indeed, it is only during the annual budget process that each substantive service area need acknowledge that it is a part of a larger organization. The agencies that comprise the local government organization focus on securing resources rather than on using them productively. This political conflict yields winners and losers within the organization, and inevitably results in the sub-optimal allocation of the resources of the organization as a whole. A more rational approach to resource allocation within the organization would allow it to engage its political environment more productively.

A second internal factor that militates against the effective pursuit of productivity is the nature of local government accounting systems, which often precludes the tracking of the actual costs of providing a given service. The measurement focus of accounting for general fund expenditures is on the fund's current financial resources. The general fund deals with current operations, and the accounting emphasis is on appropriated funds that are allocated and expendable. If a recreation department purchases a vehicle in year one, the entire cost of the vehicle is accounted for in that year even though the vehicle may be used to provide recreation services for many years into the future. Thus, the cost of recreation services is overreported for year one and underreported for the additional years in which the vehicle was used. This measurement focus and the modified accrual basis employed to account for general-fund resources do not provide a basis for managerial accounting. Managerial accounting provides the information necessary to support decisions about program costs based on the analysis of past performance and projections of future costs. These are the data required for effective productivity analysis and the construction of meaningful efficiency ratios. Thus, the most salient information system in the organization does not support productivity efforts. As another example, the depreciation of capital investments is not accounted for in the general fund. Depreciation data are not recorded because there are no tax benefits to be realized, and the accounting focus is not on the assets of the government or the actual costs of providing the service under consideration. However, such data would constitute a useful measure of the productive capacity of the equipment and the financial condition of the jurisdiction.

We have described how the public-sector environment is characterized by a lack of agreement on goals and a paucity of knowledge regarding the relative effectiveness of alternative means. Thus, the emphasis is on controlling what organizations do, rather than on maximizing their effectiveness, and this control orientation constitutes an enormous obstacle to providing incentives for increasing productivity. This control function is exercised through formal rules and regulations, budgetary policies and personnel classification systems. Public-sector managers do not effectively control the resources available to them, and it is difficult to pursue productivity in the absence of discretion in the deployment of resources. Operating managers may not be able to respond to changing circumstances when their resources are deployed on the basis of budgetary decisions made months in the past. Sometimes a manager finds it easier to go to the budget process to get an additional employee to do the work of a nonfunctioning one, rather than going through the laborious process of terminating the latter. Managers have little incentive to take responsibility for productivity if they are not given the necessary decision-making authority. Professional managers who have served in both sectors consistently cite the lack of flexibility and discretion in dealing with budgetary and personnel decisions in the public sector as a salient difference between the two sectors (Allison, 1980). The results-oriented budgeting system described in Chapter 2 represents an acknowledgment of these constraints and an attempt to mitigate their effects.

Two developments in the environment of local government management have spurred efforts to increase productivity. The first is the privatization movement and the second is growing resource scarcity. The privatization movement seeks to eliminate some public services and contract with private-sector firms for the provision of others, as well as for the provision of some administrative support functions. This movement has put enormous pressure on some public service systems to remain competitive with private-sector providers. Privatization and resource scarcity have also forced local governments to turn to user fees to support some services. User fees make the service providers more aware of the costs of providing the service, since prices must be set to recover that cost. These prices in turn affect the demand for the service, and the providers are encouraged to keep costs at a minimum. Fiscal stress also forces local governments to look to productivity enhancements as a way of stretching available resources (Stipak and O'Toole, 1993).

The connection between the pursuit of productivity and incentives is well supported in the public management literature, and the crucial role of the human resource management function in this regard is receiving increasing attention. However, pay-for-performance schemes face serious obstacles in the public sector. The aforementioned classification systems are among the most formidable. Merit pay increases usually make up only a small part of an employee's annual pay increases, which are invariably tied to seniority. If an employee is at the top of his or her classification, the merit increases do not apply. Management positions may be exempt from formal classification systems, but these have salary ranges attached to them, and informal "equity" standards inevitably influence pay increases.

Legislative bodies are also reluctant to appropriate funds for bonuses or gain-sharing programs (that is, programs in which productivity gains are shared with the responsible department and/or its personnel and the umbrella organization). Indeed, many productivity efforts entail an investment in development of human resources that decision makers may view as excessive, even if the return in increased productivity appears to justify the expense. These include training programs, team-building workshops and management development courses. Indeed, the payoffs from these investments often come in the form of increased commitment and motivation on the part of the participating employees. Rather than searching for incentives for productivity, perhaps managers should be seeking ways of motivating employees who are often disillusioned by mindless rules and regulations, endless red tape, a lack of resources and an apparently uncaring bureaucracy.

Pay-for-performance plans are also hindered by the state of the art of performance appraisal. The assessment process is viewed as a burdensome one even in the private sector, and it can often be disruptive. Supervisors are reluctant to take responsibility for giving subordinates negative feedback regarding their performance. These problems are compounded in the public sector, where outputs of productive processes are often difficult to quantify and measure; the appraisal process comes to be viewed as a purely subjective one in which favorite employees are rewarded. In other cases, pay-for-performance and management-by-objectives systems may be biased in favor of those programmatic areas where objectives are easier to quantify, or they may force managers to focus solely on quantifiable ends.

Public managers are also encouraged to spend their entire budget. Unexpended funds may indicate that the manager's agency is overbudgeted. Thus, managers may be reluctant to engage in productivity efforts that may cut costs if they do not have the authority to reprogram the available funds. Indeed, in many cases the funds saved by a productive manager are used to increase the budget of a less efficient one in order to alleviate recurring "crises" and eliminate bothersome midyear supplemental appropriations. In the same way that the external controls built into traditional personnel classification systems make it difficult to reward productive performance, the typical budget process includes strict fiscal controls that precipitate disincentives to the implementation of productivity programs.

The quotation that opened this chapter indicated that "[r]eal efficiency . . . must be built into the structure of a government"; if this is so, then it is clear that the current structure, with its emphasis on deploying controls rather than facilitating effectiveness, is inadequate. The multiple objectives emanating from the political environment in which public managers operate and the nature of public services militate against the effective pursuit of productivity. But can the productivity of local government organizations be significantly enhanced through the adoption of new organizational charts and administrative systems? A rigid structural approach may compromise the discretion of individual substantive service managers necessary for productive service delivery. It would seem that the only incentive for public managers to maximize efficiency lies in their personal sense of professionalism, in that the pursuit of efficiency in production systems is the mark of professional management. However, public-sector organizations do not provide fertile ground for the development of responsible professionalism. The administrative systems and decision-making processes of public organizations are structured to constrain professionalism so that it remains responsible, rather than encouraging the development of that responsibility. This points to the need to develop an organizational culture that supports the professional orientation to productivity, and one that seeks to raise the decision-making orientations of substantive service delivery managers to the perspective of the public organization as a whole.

The study of the productivity of public-sector organizations has begun to move from a narrow, fragmented focus on technological "fixes" in specific program areas to an examination of the broader organizational structures and administrative systems that may inhibit productivity. Some researchers have speculated that the productivity movement that was so vibrant in the 1970s may have waned partly because academia had produced little applied theory to guide practitioners (Balk, Bouckaert and Bronner, 1989). The development of useful applied theory will necessitate placing productivity within a general theory of public management. Such a theory must address the essential conflict between democracy and expertise that manifests itself for the public manager as the dilemma of control *versus* effectiveness.

ALLOCATIVE AND TECHNOLOGICAL EFFICIENCY

As described previously, the public-sector resource allocation process is characterized by the separation of the paying of the services from the process of deciding what services will be produced (Rubin, 1993). This is the antithesis of private-sector market transactions, and the unavoidable result is the over-production of some services and the underproduction of others, as interest groups and public agencies compete for resources on the basis of political power rather than demonstrated need and established efficiency. Taxes are extracted from all of the participants to fund programs favored by the winners in the policy-making process. In such a scenario, people are inevitably forced to pay for things that they do not want. Thus, many people complain about the productivity of government agencies simply because they do not value the outputs, and not necessarily because the production process is inefficient or wasteful.

In fact, there is no political constituency for the optimal allocation of public resources at any level of government. Once again, following V. O. Key (1940), the optimal allocation of public resources is an issue in political philosophy rather than a problem for structured analysis. Individuals and political groups define optimality from their own unique perspectives. Thus, there would appear to be little room for professional public administrators to pursue allocative efficiency in the employment of public resources through the structured analysis of alternative resource allocation plans. It would seem that professionals must satisfy themselves with the pursuit of technological efficiencies within the constraints posed by the political system.

However, technological efficiencies have allocative effects. When a program or department is made more productive due to changes to procedures, the addition of new equipment, the restructuring of the organizational chart, the redesign of jobs or some other means, the initial result is an increase in the level of service or number of products provided by that program or department. For example, based an on analysis of its patrol deployment scheme, a police department redesigns its patrol zones and its allocation of patrol officers to shifts. The project results in a better response time and, one would hope, a decrease in the crime rate and an increase in the citizens' feelings of security. It does not immediately yield a decrease in costs; this can only be realized if the previous response time were deemed to represent an acceptable level of service, and the police budget were cut back to return response time to that level. Under this option, the funds realized through productivity enhancement are now available for re-allocation. If policy makers were satisfied with the previous level of service and savings accrue to the general fund in the form of a smaller police budget, any incentive to adopt technological efficiencies is considerably weakened.

This scenario does not necessarily rest on the assumption that decision makers are aware of the policy implications of their budget decisions, and that jurisdictions budget for service levels rather than funding levels. As we saw in Chapter 2, this is rarely the case. However, policy preferences certainly influence budgetary choices, even if service levels are not explicitly connected to funding increments during the decision-making process, and satisfaction with service levels would influence policy preferences. Hence, technological efficiencies invariably affect allocative mixes by increasing service levels while holding resources constant, or by yielding additional resources for re-allocation. The relationship between allocative and technological efficiency means that the latter also has political implications.

The allocative effects of technological efficiencies become particularly salient when the productivity enhancement under consideration requires an investment of additional funds. The enhancement may entail the purchase of new equipment, the training of current personnel or the creation of new positions. This investment may be recouped in the form of increased productivity in a short period of time, but the immediate result is an increase in service levels rather than a decrease in expenditures. Even if expenditures are reduced so that the previous service level is funded at a lower cost, decision makers may resist making short-term investments in order to realize long-term economies.

Just as significant as the connection between allocative efficiency and technological changes is the general lack of knowledge regarding how to enhance technological efficiency (Downs and Larkey, 1986). Many of the problems addressed by public programs are "wicked problems" (Harmon and Mayer, 1986; Rittel and Webber, 1973). These are societal issues that are amenable to a variety of definitions, that are complex and interconnected, and that are not amenable to structured analysis because they are difficult to measure. Problems in service areas like garbage collection, road resurfacing, and fire suppression are relatively "tame," because, like the private-sector problem of maximizing profits, they are governed by tested technologies and known cause-and-effect relationships. However, solutions to problems such as crime, unemployment, racial strife, poverty and social welfare are a function of the political definition of the problem, and cause-and-effect relationships are usually ambiguous in any case. To strive for productivity when we can't agree on what the salient issues are, have little idea what to do about them, and generally have no indication whether what little we are doing is working can be futile. Lack of knowledge regarding "what works" also precipitates the phenomenon of the efficient bureaucracy in the failed organization; that is, professional administrators can be very efficient in delivering a technology that simply does not work.

As a result of this lack of direct measurements and tested technologies, David Ammons (1985) points out that "performance myths" sometimes constrain efforts to improve productivity. For example, regular and highly visible patrol by marked vehicles is generally accepted as a viable, effective police tactic. A police department that did not engage in such tactics would be viewed as unprofessional. However, a series of studies has clearly demonstrated that regular patrol does not result in greater feelings of security among the citizenry or increases in arrest rates. Myths can also manifest themselves at the organizational level. John Meyer and Brian Rowan (1983) describe the "institutionalized organization," which is structured to reflect myths regarding how organizations should be structured rather than in response to the demands of its operational environment. Such a scenario is more likely in the public sector, where organizations must secure resources from the political arena rather than from direct exchanges with their environments. Public-sector organizations may value perceived legitimacy over actual effectiveness in order to maintain their viability. Once again, the nature of the public organization emerges as an important variable in enhancing productivity and providing for technological and allocative efficiencies.

INTEGRATING PRODUCTIVITY AND BUDGETING

The local government organization operates in a very political environment, and the simple measurement of policy outcomes required for structured analysis inevitably entails political considerations. We identified the pursuit of technological efficiencies as the essence of professional public management, and, although formal incentives for substantive service managers to seek technological efficiencies may be lacking, all technological efficiencies have allocative effects. Hence, professional management cannot escape its ownership of public policy outcomes, and public-sector professionals cannot pursue productivity and effective public management unless they function as politicians. They are not simply professionals who inform the political process and facilitate the bargaining and negotiating process, but rather active policy advocates. Analysis meets politics in the public organization, and productive and effective public management depends on the nature of the political values that guide analysis and define productivity. In the absence of integrative values to be pursued and unifying goals to be optimized, professional management is reduced to the maximization of individual budget allocations. Hence, productive public management is actually destructive of optimal resource allocations in local government.

In Chapter 2, we described how the use of results-oriented measures in the budget process allows for the shifting of the control function from inputs to outcomes. Program managers can focus their energies on the efficient pursuit of substantive policies, and they are able to make discretionary judgments regarding the most effective use of available resources. They are then held accountable for the attainment of policy goals, rather than for simply following the spending plan outlined in the budget document. However, the loosening of input controls and the creation of broader discretionary decision-making authority may augment the centrifugal forces generated in highly differentiated local government organizations. The traditional control function was largely exercised through the budget and finance functions, and the movement to outcome monitoring will likely require these offices to exercise more analytical functions in regard to policy outcomes. As we suggested in Chapter 2, a results-oriented budgeting format should probably not be implemented in an organizational environment such as the one described in the preceding paragraph, particularly if the political environment of the organization is characterized by conflict regarding fundamental values. In short, the nature of the budget process as an administrative system is not the answer to the productivity dilemma in the public sector.

The idea of holding public managers responsible for policy outcomes and the prospects of a policy-monitoring function tied to the budget process spotlight the issue of the policy role of the finance professional in local government. In private-sector firms, the finance professional monitors both the short-term profitability and the long-term viability of the enterprise. It is in these policy areas that the finance professional speaks, and that voice is recognized as a legitimate one within the firm. Although the firm's top managers may disagree on the most effective way of pursuing those goals, there is usually consensus that an optimal resource allocation strategy in that regard exists, that it should be discovered and implemented, and that the finance professional can speak to that issue. In the public sector, however, it is probably not possible to identify a political constituency that supports any objective definition of the optimal allocation of public resources. Political groups tend to define optimality in terms of their own short-term needs. Long-term viability is not considered or is similarly defined.

What is the policy goal of local government finance professionals? They seek to achieve a policy outcome for which there is no other political constituency: the optimal allocation of the public's resources. But from what perspective do they define optimality? They define optimality in terms of their professional responsibility to the organization: an optimal allocation is one that supports the long-term financial viability of the jurisdiction that funds the organization. This perspective is politically neutral in that it is rooted in the fundamental responsibilities of the finance professional, and the legitimacy of this role is augmented by the fact that there is no political constituency for the long-term financial viability of the jurisdiction. But people define long-term financial viability in terms of their own particular circumstances, so isn't this determination simply a reflection of "political philosophy"? We do not mean to imply that the determination of financial viability is a function of structured analysis, although the issue is more amenable to the application of expertise and analysis than many short-term political issues. This is an area in which finance professionals can exercise an educative function, and it is one they can take ownership of because long-term financial viability is rarely explicitly considered in the resource allocation process.

In short, we propose that the finance professional take ownership of the "profitability" issue—that is, provide a voice for the allocation of resources that optimizes the long-term viability of the local government jurisdiction. The responsibilities of the finance professional in this policy area should be formalized and made explicit, so that substantive policy issues and economic development decisions can be made in the context of the overall viability of the jurisdiction. These include planning, land use, infrastructure and service areas, as well the traditional finance focus on fiscal policies and revenue sources. This charge is based on the absence of a political constituency for this perspective, and this responsibility entails stimulating political debate rather than precluding it through executive fiat. The promise of professional public management will not be realized until the policy role of public managers is acknowledged and made manifest, and the same caveat applies to professional financial management.

We have contended that the pursuit of productivity is an essential element of professional management, and we have suggested that what we have broadly defined as the finance function is an essential element of public management. In order to pursue productivity, public-sector managers must engage their political environments as politicians, but it is important that the local government professionals engage their political environment as elements of an integrated organization rather than as individual political actors. The policy goals of the finance function can serve as the necessary integrative force. We have contended that the pursuit of optimality in the annual resource allocation scheme of the jurisdiction, in order to provide for the long-term viability of the public organization, should be an end of all public management professionals because without organizational viability, no resource allocation scheme is long viable. Hence, all public managers must assume this professional finance responsibility in order to pursue productivity in their individual service areas. Finance professionals must educate the organization as well, through organizational development efforts that encourage managers to adopt this perspective in their decision-making. Productivity applies not just to the structure of public organizations, but to their cultures and values as well. The budget process, which is administered by the organization's finance professionals, is the most suitable organizational process for developing the organization-wide decision-making perspectives necessary to support productivity goals. It is not the role of the budget as an administrative system that connects it to productivity, but its role as a cultural symbol and an organization-wide communication system.

Researchers are beginning to recognize that the productivity issue cannot be effectively approached as a series of technological "fixes." They are beginning to connect productivity with broader administrative systems and organizational structures, but the necessary organizational integration cannot be achieved through the installation of such "hardware" alone. The local government public organization cannot engage a multifaceted, contentious political environment with a multifaceted organization exhibiting that same contentiousness. It must develop unifying values and goals within the organization that are grounded in a common professional orientation. An emphasis on hardware yields a professional organization that houses politicians; what is required is the development of a cultural software that supports a political organization staffed by professionals.

MANAGERIAL ISSUES

This section outlines a process for designing and implementing a performance measurement system in a local government organization. Performance measurement data can be used to communicate the accomplishments of a government to citizens, to monitor the effects of specific productivity improvement programs, to evaluate the overall effectiveness of public programs, to assess managerial effectiveness, and to clarify the trade-offs involved in allocating resources and help rationalize that decision-making process. Performance data are also useful to long-range service planning efforts, the determination of user charges, the analysis of revenue needs, and the identification of potential revenue gaps. The system outlined here is geared to meeting the needs of the annual budget process.

Performance measurement systems designed to meet the needs of the budget process should focus on the results of public programs. As indicated previously, the wide variety of government programs can only be meaningfully compared on the basis of their ultimate effects on the welfare of the community. It is difficult to make a rational decision on whether to hire more police officers or more traffic sign painters, or whether to fund more arrests or more traffic signs. But the relative attractiveness of each choice becomes clearer when one considers increased number of arrests and the decrease in traffic accidents, and clearest when one can compare the effects of both alternatives on overall feelings of security within the community. However, as we discussed above, results-oriented or outcome measures are the most difficult to identify for public programs.

The development of measures of program outcomes is facilitated when the local government employs a program structure in its budgetary process. If the budget is not built around a formal program structure, such a framework should still be employed in the measurement development process—indeed, the process should begin with its design. The need for a program structure becomes more evident as the size of the local government increases and the number of service departments proliferate. While it is possible to develop input and workload measures at the departmental or agency level, outcome or results-oriented measures require a different type of supporting framework.

Outcome measures plumb the extent to which the ultimate purpose of each program has been achieved, and it is necessary to enunciate this purpose so that appropriate measures can be derived from it. The mission statement of a program describes the purpose of the program or how the environment will be different if the program achieves a tangible degree of success. Once again, the mission development process is imbued with political overtones; it is the process through which professional managers decide what the public and the legislative body had in mind when they created the agency. The mission statement should be developed without reference to how it might be measured. After the mission statement is constructed, a series of three or four goals are developed that flesh out the details of the mission or describe different aspects of it. Actual measures should not be considered during this process either, because a plausible and significant goal might be ignored if it is perceived as impossible to measure.

Mission statements and goals describe the thrusts of government programs, and their ultimate purposes may never actually be achieved. For example, a police program such as the investigative process may be designed to eliminate criminal activity, and one of the goals may be to investigate crimes in order to identify and prosecute the offenders. Although the goal describes an aspect of the mission, it is unlikely that all offenders will be ultimately identified and criminal activity totally eliminated. Objectives, on the other hand, should reflect achievable and measurable ends; at least one or two objectives should be identified for each goal, and at least one measure for each objective. Thus, each program should have from three to eight measures that reflect the purpose of the program. This developmental process becomes cumbersome when agency missions are not separated into programs. The program framework also makes it possible to connect the workload and output measures that will inevitably and unavoidably be a part of the system to the results desired from the program as expressed in its mission.

An example of an objective for the police investigation program might be to reduce the number of burglaries by a given percentage within a specific time period. Another might be to increase conviction rates through more investigations. The focus here should be on increased effectiveness, efficiency and responsiveness in terms of the results achieved. Workload-oriented objectives should be avoided as much as possible. For example, the percent of cases assigned for investigation or the percent of cases ultimately cleared represent more intermediate outcomes than crime rates or conviction rates. Participants in the developmental process may be more familiar with these workload-type measures, and they may insist on reporting them. Measures should focus on the dimensions of quality/effectiveness, cost/efficiency or time/responsiveness; but the quantity dimensions, in terms of both input and output, are difficult to ignore. The need to maintain the "purity" of the measurement system needs to be balanced against the need to promote its acceptability, and the identification of real results-oriented measures will probably be the product of an extended developmental and educational process.

One of the authors participated in two program measurement–system development projects. One was in a small beach community, where it was necessary to identify programs, as well as to formulate a mission statement, goals, objectives and measures. A three-member development team met with the city's managers over an eight-week period. The second project, in a much larger city, proceeded in a similar fashion, but the program structure was already in place (the city had 104 identifiable programs in its budget). However, the developmental process in this case extended for eighteen months. The six-person team was comprised of in-house management and analytical staff members from various departments. A minimum of three members of the development team met with the management staffs associated with each program on at least two, and usually three, occasions.

The development of the mission statement was often more difficult than the identification of suitable measures, particularly when the focus on results-oriented measures was relaxed. Sometimes this was the result of a poor program structure; that is, the program was actually comprised of more than one program, and the management staff experienced some conflict in arriving at a single mission statement. This conflict occurred even in an area as ostensibly straightforward as the public library. Is the library an educational institution, a reference service, a recreational agency, a storehouse of culture, or a research institution? Different constituencies may see the public agency in different lights, and the agency must respond to them all. Such environmental factors may compromise the rationality of the measurement system, in that some measures may conflict with others. At the outset of the development process, it may be necessary to accommodate these factions, but the development of a single mission that encompasses these various perspectives should be a long-range goal of the measurement system. Another area of conflict, this time directly with the development team, was the identification of goals, objectives and measures that reflected the fiscal responsibilities of the management teams in programs that employed user charges, such as those of the recreation departments. The management teams saw their responsibilities in terms of substantive programmatic functions, and they generally felt that the primary responsibility for fiscal policy lay elsewhere. The fact that general-fund agencies cannot lay claim to such funds for their own use causes them to overlook their responsibilities to the organization as a whole.

In short, conflict in the development of mission statements is unavoidable, because the developmental process is essentially a political one. Mission statements and goals formalize the ends to which resources will be allocated, objectives highlight responsibilities and expectations, and measures make accountability more feasible and success or failure more manifest. Once again, productivity improvement does not simply lie in the application of technical expertise. It entails making choices in the allocation of public resources. If the pursuit of efficiency is the essence of professional management, professional public administration is an inherently political enterprise and its efficacy is enhanced when this fundamental fact is acknowledged.

The outcome data should be reported on a monthly basis in order to build commitment and continuity, and to provide for analysis of trends in the data stream. In short, if departments report their data on a quarterly or yearly basis, the managers may tend to forget as the performance measurement system retreats to the background. In addition, several years' worth of annual data would be necessary for meaningful analysis, and the system would be viewed as window dressing in the interim. At the outset, operating managers should be allowed to report their program results data through any means with which they feel comfortable. Some departments may be automated and wired for electronic transmission to a central location; others may have existing forms based on mechanical reporting systems; others may have in place operating systems that produce the data as a by-product; and others may be starting from scratch. The point here is to minimize the costs of compliance to the operating departments in order to encourage participation and enhance development.

If the program is supported by the top management staff, funds may be made available to provide for computerization of the system and standardization of the reporting process. Once again, productivity programs usually require some up-front investment. An additional area for investment may be the training of managerial staff in the development, reporting and use of outcome measures. The development of meaningful outcome measures for many programs may point to the need for regular surveys of clients, participants, and the citizenry in general. Thus, a third area for investment may be the development of a capacity for regularly scheduled surveys targeting specific programs or groups of programs. This effort would include internal surveys of the users of staff functions, such as budgeting, purchasing, data processing and employment. Program managers tend to be amenable to citizen surveys, because these allow various constituencies to respond to the program as they perceive it; structured analytical studies tend to adopt a single view of the program that must be optimized.

Minimize costs and focus on available data. Do not try to measure everything, but select measures that indicate problems soon enough for corrective action to be considered and taken. Implementation and further development are facilitated when the operating staffs can participate in the design stage. Program measurement systems that feature measures developed through a bottom-up process, as lengthy and haphazard as such a process may be, are more likely to be accepted by the operating departments. Any management studies or actions that emerge from the analysis of the measures are also more likely to be implemented if the measures have meaning for the targeted agency.

As we indicated previously, results-oriented measures can be used for a variety of purposes, and the primary use will indicate the most suitable agency to collect and analyze the data. The managerial issues surrounding the location of a centralized analytical capacity in the local government organization are ex-

amined in the Chapter 5. However, it should be clear that the data do not speak
for themselves, and analysis is required to turn data into information that can
form the basis for action. Managerial action is the ultimate test of whether the
measures are used. The development of an analytical capacity and management
response team may call for additional investment. However, if an initial trend
analysis indicates that a program problem may exist, top management can assemble an analytical study team from existing managerial and staff personnel
who have the skills, knowledge and experience necessary to examine the problem. These would include substantive programmatic knowledge, relevant analytical skills, and experience with the processes and interrelationships within the
organization. Indeed, the program measurement–system team that drives the
measurement development process could be the first of these "focus groups,"
which are described in greater detail in Chapter 5.

In this way, the individual departments that comprise the local government
organization are afforded access to the managerial and analytical skills existent
in the organization as a whole. These teams serve to broaden the perspectives
of the participating analysts and managers, who come to appreciate the roles of
their specific agencies in terms of a larger mission to enhance the welfare of
the community. The development and diffusion of an organization-wide managerial perspective may help to counter the enormous centrifugal forces that characterize the typical multiservice local government. The management staff can
eventually minimize the sub-optimal resource allocations that emerge from the
interservice conflict during the formal budget process. These managerial development efforts can facilitate the building of an organizational consensus regarding the elements of an optimal resource allocation plan. Such a plan would be
based on managerial expertise applied in a political environment, rather than
simply reflecting political power. The performance measurement system can
help top managers develop a conducive organizational environment. It demonstrates that the various agencies are part of a common enterprise that employs
integrative evaluation criteria and manifests a shared culture and definitive service delivery values.

REFERENCES

Allison, Graham T., Jr. (1980). "Public and Private Management: Are They Fundamen-
    tally Alike in All Unimportant Respects?" In OPM Document 127–53–1, *Setting
    Public Management Research Agendas: Integrating the Sponsor, Producer, and
    User.* Washington, D.C.: Office of Personnel Management.
Ammons, David N. (1985). "Common Barriers to Productivity Improvement in Local
    Government." *Public Productivity Review*, 7 (2): 293–310.
Balk, Walter L., Bouckaert, Geert, and Bronner, Kevin M. (1989). "Notes on the Theory
    and Practice of Government Productivity Improvement." *Public Productivity and
    Management Review*, 13 (2): 117–131.
Downs, George W., and Larkey, Patrick D. (1986). *The Search for Government Produc-
    tivity: From Hubris to Helplessness.* Philadelphia: Temple University Press.

Harmon, Michael M., and Mayer, Richard T. (1986). *Organization Theory for Public Administration.* Boston: Little, Brown.

Key, V. O. (1940). "The Lack of a Budgetary Theory." *American Political Science Review,* 34 (2): 1137–1140.

Meyer, John W., and Rowan, Brian (1983). "Institutionalized Organizations: Formal Structure as Myth and Ceremony." In John W. Meyer and Richard Scott, eds., *Organizational Environments: Ritual and Rationality.* Beverly Hills, Calif.: Sage, 21–44.

President's Committee on Administrative Management (1937). *Administrative Management in the Government of the United States.*

Rittel, Horst W. J., and Webber, Melvin (1973). "Dilemmas in a General Theory of Planning." *Policy Sciences,* 4 (2): 155–169.

Rubin, Irene S. (1993). *The Politics of Public Budgeting* (2nd ed.). Chatham, N.J.: Chatham House.

Stipak, Brian, and O'Toole, Daniel E. (1993). "Fiscal Stress and Productivity Improvement: Local Government Managers' Perspective." *Public Productivity and Management Review,* 17 (2): 101–112.

Chapter 5

Analytical Techniques

How does one convince administrators to collect information that might help others, but can only harm them?

Aaron Wildavsky (1979)

Very few, if any, local government elected officials will allow the structured analysis of policy alternatives or administrative issues by technical professionals to make their decisions for them. However, the application of analytical techniques to the enterprise of delivering public services allows professional administrators to influence and inform the development of substantive policy and the structure of service delivery systems. Wildavsky's quote (1979: 212) above reflects the view that professional administrators have little incentive to assess the effectiveness and efficiency of their programs when such studies could result in budget reductions and the termination of programs rather than new initiatives and re-allocations. Wildavsky focused on the national level, where the political bargaining, fragmented decision-making structures, weak administrative systems, and incremental politics that characterized the resource allocation process seemed to preclude a strong voice for structured analysis. The local government public organization, as differentiated and internally conflicted as it is, may provide a more hospitable environment for the effective application of analytical techniques to the operation of public service delivery systems. Indeed, one could make a case that this responsibility is professional public administration's reason for being.

In this chapter, selected analytical techniques are introduced, and their respective utilities are examined. Elected officials do not let analysis drive the policy process partly because they are often ignorant of, and hence distrust, what goes on within the "black box" that is the technique. Data goes in one end of the box and an answer comes out the other, but what went on in the box? There is intelligence in this skepticism. Most analytical techniques call for a range of assumptions on the part of the analyst, whose responses often reflect a host of value judgments. The sources and bases of the values that guide analytical judgments are not always clear. Data do not speak for themselves. Analysis turns data into information, but does not necessarily discover any objective truth. The extent to which top management can establish a shared, organization-wide perspective for the assumptions and value judgments demanded by analytical studies will go a long way toward determining the utility of these techniques in local government decision-making. Once again, this goal would seem to be more feasible in the local government organization than at the national level, where agencies function as more or less independent political actors with individual constituencies, support groups and administrative systems.

FORECASTING

The importance of the revenue constraint in the budget process was established in Chapter 2. The strong pressures to under-forecast this constraint were also reviewed. Within-year forecasts and longer-range forecasts are also employed. Within-year forecasts of revenues are used to update the forecast of the revenue constraint for the following year, and to provide for the productive management and timely investment of cash on hand. Simple spreadsheets can be employed to track the percent of the budgeted amount of each revenue source that is collected each month, and this is can be compared to a five-year average of the percent of actual year-end amounts previously collected each month for each source. This will indicate whether the budgeted amount for the current year will be collected—that is, what are the prospects for the budgeted amount becoming the actual year-end total given collections to date in light of historical averages? Projected shortfalls can be addressed on a more timely basis, and projected surpluses can be used to fund within-year supplemental requests, or investment schedules can be accelerated. Additionally, the forecast of the year-end collections in the current year is the best data for estimating the budget constraint for the following year.

These data also guide the timing of investment decisions. The keys to a successful cash management strategy are to mobilize the funds as soon as possible and to control disbursements. These goals maximize the amount of funds available for investment and the length of time that they can be invested. The cash management function in local government is facilitated by the fact that 60–80 percent of expenditures are in the form of regular payroll checks, which are relatively easy to calculate and project. The maturities of investment instruments can be scheduled to make the necessary liquid funds available on schedule. The monthly expenditures of individual agencies can also be tracked within the current year, as in the allotment schedules described in Chapter 3.

The forecasting methods described in this section are more applicable to the long-range forecast of the revenue constraint during the budget process, and to the longer-range forecasts of revenue and expenditure trends and the overall financial condition of the jurisdiction. Three categories of forecasting techniques are introduced: judgmental methods, extrapolation, and the more sophisticated causal and econometric modeling. The Financial Trend Monitoring System developed under the auspices of the International City/County Management Association or ICMA (Groves and Valente, 1994) is also reviewed as a tool for monitoring the financial condition of local governments. Expenditure forecasting should be followed with an analysis of the desirability of the forecasted levels, as well as an assessment of whether these levels will meet the needs indicated in forecasts of underlying demographic trends. For example, in order to complete his or her forecast, the analyst should determine whether recreation expenditures are increasing at a rate adequate to meet the projected needs of the number of children and teens in the jurisdiction. However, the wise analyst will apply the same scrutiny to individual revenue sources, because trends in the revenue mix can be as significant as overall revenue levels (as detailed in Chapter 6). Lastly, forecasts can identify future revenue gaps that must be filled with increases in revenue (in light of projected trends in the revenue mix) and/or reductions in expenditures (in light of identified demographic trends).

Budget managers or analysts who have been with a particular jurisdiction for a long time can seemingly pull revenue forecasts out of their pockets. They know who to call at public utility agencies for information regarding growth trends, in order to project revenues from utility taxes and franchise fees. They have a contact at the state revenue office for information regarding intergovernmental aid (which is particularly important when the state uses a different fiscal year than the local jurisdiction). They seem to have a feel for the appropriateness of budgeted revenues, and for the adequacy of collections to date in light of budgeted amounts. This scenario exemplifies judgmental forecasting, or forecasting based on substantive knowledge and experience. A potential problem here is that the organization becomes dependent on the expert. When the in-house expert inevitably departs, the resulting feelings of inadequacy and vulnerability may engender even more pressures to under-forecast.

There are techniques that formalize the application of expertise and experience to the forecasting problem. In the Delphi technique, experts exchange opinions regarding a forecast with one another anonymously through a moderator, who provides limited feedback to the participants. The experts may be asked to provide explanations for their opinions, and these explanations are shared, but criticisms from the other participants may not be forwarded. The moderator keeps asking the same questions, and, it is hoped, a consensus forecast emerges from this iterative process. The Delphi technique is designed to shield the experts from group pressures to conform to majority opinions or to abandon unpopular views. Less formal processes can resemble juries, in which the majority forecast carries the day. Budgeters left in the lurch with the departure of their in-house expert may turn to these group approaches.

Extrapolation techniques simply summarize past trends and extend them into the future. They are differentiated principally by the quantitative method employed to summarize and project. These range from the moving average and regression analysis to the Box-Jenkins technique and general adaptive filtering. These methods demand some expertise and they have extensive data requirements. However, in his book on the subject of local government budgetary forecasting, Howard Frank (1993) contends that many local governments collect the necessary data as a matter of course, and the knowledge for initial experimentation with these methods can be acquired in a short period. "User-friendly" microcomputer programs have made these methods more accessible.

Regression analysis seeks to describe the straight line that summarizes past data, and it is sensitive to random variations in the data stream. The moving average can be used to smooth out the randomness in data exhibiting little trend. Only a pocket calculator is required to employ these two methods. Single exponential smoothing weights recent data points more heavily in calculating the trend line, and double exponential smoothing adds a second coefficient to smooth any trend in the time series. General adaptive filtering (GAF) seeks to identify a set of weights that will optimize the forecast of a data stream; it is useful in forecasting time series exhibiting seasonal trends. The Box-Jenkins technique involves the analyst in an iterative process in order to identify the nature of the series, evaluate and diagnose this initial estimation, and then employ the resulting model to forecast the series. GAF and Box-Jenkins require some sophistication on the part of the user, and neophyte analysts should limit their initial efforts to the single and double exponential smoothing models, and similar techniques such as the Holt and the Winter models. Time series models require monthly data that must be "cleaned" to eliminate the effects of changes in enabling legislation, recording methods, and any other unusual events. These techniques have established a strong track record in the private sector, and they hold considerable promise in forecasting local government revenues (Frank, 1993).

Rather than simply extrapolating from the past, analysts may seek to understand the dynamics of the processes that generate the jurisdiction's revenues. In causal modeling, analysts try to explain the relationships among the factors that drive revenues and expenditures, and they employ that knowledge to forecast future trends. Multiple regression is one method employed to establish these explanations. Simple regression focuses on the relationship between time and revenue collections, but multiple regression employs a variety of variables. The relationship between each variable and revenue collections is assessed, and the power of the resulting model rests in its capacity to account for variations in collections. Econometric models mathematically structure the relationships that drive the economic activity from which revenues are ultimately derived. These feature simultaneous equations that can be used to simulate the workings of the economic base, and the models can be used to determine the revenue effects of such variables as tax rates, unemployment rates or military base closings. Oftentimes, researchers are called upon to employ more traditional methods to forecast levels of some of the variables used in these models. Causal models of any sort, and econometric models in particular, are difficult and expensive to construct. They are data-intensive and call for extensive research. This does not preclude their use by local governments, but the fact that these models have to be recalibrated every time a significant change occurs in the structure of the local economy may curtail their use. Several state governments have developed and used such models very effectively to address fiscal and substantive policy issues, but at that level the exit of a single large firm or several smaller firms would not significantly affect the structure of the model.

This does not mean that local governments cannot develop the capacity to monitor the structure of their economic bases and the bases of their various revenue sources, as well as important demographic and financial trends. Analysts can track and forecast trends in variables considered to be important in a particular jurisdiction without constructing a model of how the economic base functions. The ICMA's Financial Trend Monitoring System (Groves and Valente, 1994) focuses on thirty-six variables that may affect local government financial condition. The required data are usually readily available, and each indicator is monitored individually. The analyst should be armed with a theoretical model of local government financial condition in general in order to interpret and give meaning to the data. The analyst must also have a sound knowledge of the local context, because, as will be demonstrated in the next chapter, the factors that determine the relative financial health of a jurisdiction can be highly idiosyncratic. Ultimately, it is the knowledge and values of the analyst that comprise the "black box" through which data are filtered and become information.

In light of the immense pressures to under-forecast the budgetary revenue constraint in the typical local government organization, why would budgeters invest the time, effort and funds necessary to establish a sophisticated forecasting capacity? The organization's culture must support investment in efficiency, encourage risk taking, and reward experimentation in order to make the forecasters' personal efforts worthwhile. Forecasters must also perceive that the budgetary process requires more of the individual agencies than efforts to maximize their own budgets. If agency budgets are padded as a matter of course, budgeters will pad their forecasts. Why should they (or the program managers featured in the next section on program evaluation) take the risks indicated by Wildavsky at the outset of this chapter, if no one else does? The pursuit of efficiency, economy and effectiveness, which are the hallmarks of professional public management, entails more than the simple application of technology. It requires an enabling organizational culture, supportive reward systems and other administrative processes, and a sense of shared enterprise that yields a common decision-making perspective.

PROGRAM EVALUATION

Program evaluation is an umbrella term for the application of a range of economic and social science research techniques to the task of determining the relative success of a public program. Carol Weiss (1972) makes the point that programs designed to improve the general welfare of the public in a particular area, such as public safety, essentially reflect a theory of how that can be accomplished. The typical police patrol program manifests the theory that if professionally trained police officers patrol their jurisdiction in highly visible police vehicles, citizens will feel more secure; communication and electronic data processing technology will also allow patrol officers to respond to criminal incidents more quickly and effectively, and people will become more secure in fact, as crime rates are reduced through increases in apprehension rates. Actual police patrol programs may not achieve these outcomes for two general reasons: either the underlying theory of random patrol is wrong, or the theory is not being correctly operationalized by the police agency in question. A public agency may be very efficient, economical and even effective in carrying out its programs, but if a program is dutifully reflecting an incorrect theory, the program will fail to achieve desired outcomes. In fact, knowledge regarding cause-and-effect relationships in social issues such as crime, race, poverty and even economic development is little more than primitive. Still, analysts study relationships between program variables in order to assess the correctness of the theory the program manifests, and to determine whether the theory has been correctly implemented.

Evaluation studies that focus on whether the program's design reflects its underlying theory and whether the actual elements of the program conform to the design are called formative, implementation or process evaluations. Evaluations of administrative systems, operational procedures and selection criteria fall into this category. Studies which assess the extent to which desired outcomes have been achieved are called impact, outcome or summative evaluations. Evaluation research is plagued with the same problems as social research in general: conceptual confusion, measurement limitations and lack of experimental controls. Paradigmatic debates from the social sciences also spill over into program evaluation. Some would reject the cause-and-effect model borrowed from the physical sciences described above, and they focus on the importance of understanding the particular contexts of social programs. The goals, technologies and structural elements of a public program are the product of the interaction among legal mandates, the perceptions of the various participants, and local context; the capacity to transport successful programs to other contexts may be limited, so programs should not necessarily be assessed using external criteria. The "scientific" model is also limited by the fact that public programs manifest multiple goals and respond to multiple constituencies and "stakeholder" groups, such as clients, professionals in the field, funding groups, interest groups and oversight agencies. The assessment of the relative success of a program may be contingent on the perspective adopted by the evaluator in regard to these issues.

Weiss (1972) contended that sound evaluation studies require a coherent definition of the program. Michael Patton (1986) suggests that the process of clarifying the causal links of a program can serve to develop a shared understanding among the internal and external participants in the program. Rather than testing the program's theory of action, the theory of action becomes the focus of the evaluation. This approach puts the evaluation study somewhere between the process and outcome evaluations described above, and it recognizes the fact that a program is not simply a machine to be tested but rather a product of an organic process rooted in a local context that must be understood. This organizational-development role for evaluation reflects the role for program measurement described in Chapter 4. A precipitate of this view is that comparisons between programs in different contexts may not be very meaningful.

But comparison is the essence of evaluation. Outcomes can be compared to established standards, but such standards are rare in the public sector. Programs can be compared to other similar programs, but, as above, local contexts can be very idiosyncratic and very influential. The outcomes for clients served can be compared to the situation for those not served, but it is difficult to construct such experimental or quasi-experimental studies outside of the laboratory; it may not be feasible to exclude participants, or to match participants with nonparticipants on salient variables. Evaluation efforts may be limited to studying the same group before and after the program was established, and, as a corollary, monitoring the same program over time. The latter provides for continuous process evaluations based on outcome indicators, and gives managers data to support experimentation with program procedures and technologies and with adjustments in goals and objectives. Such experimentation is necessary to maximize responsiveness to local needs for services. This is essentially an extension of the program measurement system described in the previous chapter.

Formal, summative evaluations demand time and analytical capacity. The time constraints associated with the annual budget process preclude a formal role for program evaluation. In Chapter 2 we suggested that a zero-base decision-making process that extended over a four-year period might be more amenable to the structured analyses of funding schemes and alternative service levels. The annual budget process militates against both structured analysis and the explixit consideration of substantive policies. Either the budget cycle must be extended as we described, or the public organization must provide the necessary continuity and institutional memory to weave a rational whole out of the threads of the annual budgets. At the end of this chapter, we explore a way to enhance the analytical capacity of the organization as a whole, as well as to provide the common decision-making perspective also necessary to optimize the rationality of resource allocation schemes.

As we suggested in the introduction to this chapter, however, analysis can only inform the policy-making process, which is essentially a political process.

For example, the only scientifically rigorous evaluation ever undertaken of the random patrol theory described previously was the Kansas City preventive patrol experiment (Kelling et al., 1974). Fifteen police patrol zones were matched in groups of three on the basis of demand for police services and socioeconomic variables. Three different levels of patrol service were implemented in the zones in each group: the normal level (the control group); a proactive level that featured three times the normal level of patrol; and the reactive group, in which no random patrol vehicles were assigned. The evaluation study included citizen surveys, the assignment of trained observers to patrol vehicles, and the examination of official records. The results indicated that police officers patrolling in marked vehicles had no real effect on the public's perception of security, and did not yield increased apprehension rates; neither did crime rates increase in sections of the city that were deprived of a visible police presence entirely. The results have been widely ignored by the police establishment. Existing institutional arrangements and service delivery technologies represent power in place and provide for the flow of some level of resources. Studies that purport to show that alternative arrangements and technologies would yield more efficient and effective services more economically must ultimately confront that power and must be connected to the origin of those resources.

Wildavsky's point about the lack of incentives for managers to collect, analyze and report information regarding the relative effectiveness and efficiency of their programs is particularly relevant to program evaluation. First, the culture of the organization must encourage and support such efforts. Second, such support must include assurances that through such efforts managers can, indeed, "help themselves." Third, the effort must be attached to administrative systems shared by all of the various services that comprise the local government organization. The best vehicle is the annual budget process, which offers potential "carrots" to encourage participation and feasible "sticks" to discourage avoidance. Organizational support should also include the capacity to fix potential problems; in the last section of this chapter, we outline one possible course of action.

BENEFIT-COST ANALYSIS

In benefit-cost analysis, all of the benefits associated with a public program or project are compared with all of the costs associated with it in an effort to determine the internal efficiency of the program, and hence enhance the allocative efficiency of public spending. This technique was an important element of President Johnson's PPBS format in the mid 1960s. The benefits derived from the program each year for a fixed period are identified and quantified in monetary terms, and these are reduced to their present value using algorithms derived from the formula for compound interest. The determination of the present value of future benefits requires the selection of an appropriate discount rate that represents the opportunity costs of leaving the necessary funds in the private sector. The same analysis is conducted on the program's stream of costs. If the value of the discounted benefits exceeds the value of the discounted costs, the program is worth doing. Four issues immediately emerge: the capacity to identify and quantify the outcomes of public programs; the rationale for the discount rate; the ability to identify the costs associated with a public program; and the rationale for the selection criterion.

As indicated in Chapter 4, the public sector provides many services simply because markets cannot. These services are difficult to measure and to divide into salable units. In many cases, all of the benefits of the service cannot be appropriated by the purchaser. Program benefits spill over to nonpayers, and "free riders" are inevitable. The spillover problems can be particularly vexing at the local government level, but benefit-cost analysts can avoid the problem by not recognizing benefits that accrue to non-payers or citizens in other jurisdictions, or by weighting these less than those accruing to the jurisdiction that funds the program. We recall a benefit-cost analysis of a program to provide police patrol officers with take-home vehicles—the analysis went from positive to negative when the analysts decided not to recognize the crime prevention benefits associated with parking marked police vehicles in residential areas outside of the sponsoring jurisdiction, because two-thirds of the patrol officers did not live in the city that employed them. Economists have also identified a variety of ways to assign monetary values to the outcomes of public programs, including determining the value of a human life, but the measurement problem persists and has limited the application of the technique to areas where the outcomes of public programs are more tangible, such as infrastructure projects and capital improvement programs. In the analysis of the police take-home vehicle program cited above, the analysts made a variety of assumptions in order to identify, quantify and assign a monetary value to the crime prevention dimension of the program.

In cost-effectiveness analysis, a truncated version of the benefit-cost model, the analyst examines alternative methods of achieving a common goal, and if they each manifest similar benefit streams, the analyst can simply focus on determining which option is the least costly. The cost-effectiveness model provides for technological efficiency, but the promise of allocative efficiency is compromised because no effort is made to determine whether the cost supports the pursuit of the goal. Secretary of Defense Robert Macnamara, who brought PPBS to Washington, encouraged the use of cost-effectiveness analysis to judge the relative worth of alternative weapons systems. The goal of national defense is well supported, and cost-effectiveness is better suited to the analysis of alternative methods to pursue such goals, or to technical projects such as administrative systems or the acquisition of electronic data processing systems. However, the costs of public programs can be almost as elusive as their benefits, and this issue is examined in greater detail in a following section of this chapter.

Because it reduces all relevant factors to their dollar values, benefit-cost analysis manifests an objectivity that can be quite seductive. We have suggested that the analyst must make assumptions regarding the boundaries of the problems and the identification and quantification of the program's benefits, but the criteria for judging the worth of the program are also rooted in value judgments. Edward Gramlich (1990) details the evolution of these criteria from the initial Pareto optimality criterion, which held that a public program was worthwhile if at least one person was better off as a result of the program and no one was worse off. That stringent standard was replaced with the criterion that the number of gainers should exceed the number of losers, and the gainers should theoretically be able to compensate the losers. However, compensation required that the gainers value their gains higher than the losers valued their losses, and differences in the marginal value of a dollar meant that the selection criteria must consider the distribution of income in the jurisdiction. The equity of the distribution of income is ultimately a function of political values. Analysts may assign weights to the losses and gains that fall to various income groups as a result of a program, but the determination of the size of these weights is a value judgment.

E. J. Mishan (1969) makes the point that benefit-cost analysis is based on the debatable idea that the welfare of a community is equal to the sum of the welfares of the individuals that comprise it. We have indicated that local government finance professionals must attend to the long-term financial condition of their jurisdiction because there is no political constituency with a vested interest to do so. Finance professionals must bring this perspective to benefit-cost studies. The selection of a discount rate should also reflect the idea that societies tend to underinvest in collective actions. People can appropriate all of the benefits of their resources through immediate consumption, but resources devoted to investment, although they may ultimately raise the investors' income levels, also yield benefits to future generations. This view would hold that the discount rate applied to the analysis of public programs should be set lower than the cost of borrowing in private markets to compensate for this myopia, but there is no objective way of determining the "correct" public rate. A public program may be drawing on resources that are not being utilized in the private sector, such as unemployed persons. Additionally, the sources of public funds have particular effects: taxes tend to cut into consumption patterns, while borrowed funds compete more directly with private investment. Because most of the costs associated with a program occur early and the benefits accrue later, lower discount rates make it easier to justify public investments.

The net benefits criterion tends to favor large investments over smaller projects. Large projects might yield a higher level of net benefits, but the ratio of benefits to costs might be greater in a smaller project yielding less net benefits. Thus the benefit-cost ratio is also used as a selection criterion. In local government, benefit-cost analysis is primarily employed in the capital budgeting process. Kelso (1984) has outlined a decision-making procedure for capital projects using benefit-cost data: the projects with positive benefit-cost outcomes should be ranked from highest to lowest on the basis of their benefit-cost ratios, and analysts should move down the list until the budget constraint is reached; this method will maximize the net benefits that can be derived from that list of projects in light of the budget constraint. However, once again, analysis can only inform the policy-making process, and if net benefits are maximized with projects submitted by a single agency, or projects located in only one council district, the list will be revised to reflect organizational and political rationality.

Given the fact that political and organizational criteria will impact the final funding scheme, why should managers undertake benefit-cost studies? As described in Chapter 7, the capital budgeting process on the local government level tends to be less accessible to the general public than the operational budget process. The large sums involved, the complicated financing mechanisms required, and the irrevocable nature of the decisions make policy makers more dependent on the expertise of planning, engineering and finance professionals. Within the professional public organization, the capital budget process asks program managers to supply information, or at least participate in an analytical process, that can only help him or her. Managers may pad their operating budgets in order to protect their programs from environmental shocks, and they may even seek to maximize their operating budgets for personal aggrandizement. But none would like to be saddled with the long-term political costs of operating a capital facility that was not cost efficient in order to maximize their short-term budgets. In the broader perspective, benefit-cost analysis can help to rationalize investment in capital projects within the short term constraints posed by political and organizational structures.

Lastly, the social problems that are targeted by public agencies are complex, cause-and-effect relationships can be disjointed and temporally unstable, and potential solutions may cut across agency lines. Marciariello (1975) contends that traditional benefit-cost analysis does not consider the time-varying dimensions of the social systems in which social problems are imbedded, but rather assumes that the existing system is stable at the time of the analysis. He suggests that the local government environment in particular is characterized by pervasive dynamic effects, and he employs a complex, dynamic benefit-cost model to establish the relative benefits of urban projects. An exploration of the details of his approach, as well as an in-depth treatment of "static" benefit-cost analysis, is beyond the scope of this brief section. However, for the purposes of this chapter, it is important to note that the successful application of structured analytical techniques such as benefit-cost analysis requires more than a passing knowledge of the political, social, economic and organizational dynamics of the local government jurisdiction. The character of the local government environment can be highly idiosyncratic, and cause-and-effect relationships can vary geographically as well as temporally. Professional managers must understand the contexts in which they apply analytical techniques, and one of the goals of the finance professional should be to amass contextual knowledge so that it informs the analytical process, just as analysis seeks to inform the political process.

DATA ENVELOPMENT ANALYSIS

The documentation and measurement of performance is becoming increasingly important in government. Results-oriented budgeting systems call for the removal of budgetary controls on the manager's use of the factors of production and for greater managerial accountability for production outputs and policy outcomes. Government, in short, should be "run like a business." Once again, however, the "bottom line" that would facilitate this running is often hard to find. Data envelopment analysis (DEA), a technique based on linear programming, helps analysts measure and improve the performance of an agency, program, service or any "decision unit" by allowing them to determine its relative efficiency. The decision units must be comparable—for example, they could be police departments or multiple sites of a single program. Efficiency is usually expressed as the ratio of outputs to inputs. In the private sector, the output can be valued in dollar terms. Public-sector organizations generate a variety of outputs that often cannot be reduced to a single measure. Individual ratios will yield different pictures of efficiency, and the resulting ambiguity does not serve decision makers well. Likewise, a multiple-regression model of the relationship of inputs and outputs would require that all outputs be combined into a single measure of production (Sexton, 1986). DEA does not require that multiple outputs be expressed as a single indicator or aggregated into a single index, and it also allows for multiple inputs. A shortcoming of DEA identified by Thomas Sexton is that the technique "assumes that each unit of a given input or output is identical to all other units of the same type" (1986: 28). For example, all hours of police investigation are considered equivalent regardless of the skill levels of particular investigators, and all cases solved are considered equivalent regardless of the quality of the investigation.

DEA permits each decision unit to assign weights to each input and output, provided that each decision unit in the population can use the same set of weights to construct its own weighted output to weighted input ratio. This allows for differences in the way in which similar units employ staff, equipment, supplies and technology, and decision units are able to manipulate the weights in order to maximize their efficiency ratio. A description of the linear programming methodology employed is beyond the scope of this brief introduction to DEA, but the process uses the ratio of total weighted outputs to total weighted inputs to construct an efficiency frontier from those units rated at 100 percent efficiency. The relative efficiencies of other units can be expressed as a function of the frontier; units employing twice the input to achieve the same level of output, for example, are rated at .5. DEA can be used to perform multijurisdictional efficiency comparisons, to summarize and visualize salient performance information, to allocate resources more efficiently, to obtain information for strategic planning efforts, and to identify over- and underachievers. It is important that all inputs and outputs be identified and included in the model, but these need not be reduced to common units of measurement. The DEA technique identifies the potential for improvement, but the DEA results do not directly identify reasons for efficiency shortfalls or point the way to improvement. The technique does let managers know what inputs they are overutilizing and what outputs they are underproducing, and it will also identify those employing a very idiosyncratic mix of inputs. Additionally, the operating practices of the frontier units can be examined in order to identify "best practices" for others to emulate. Ronald Nyhan and Lawrence Martin (1998) suggest that the DEA model can also account for contextual variables that are not controllable but are often influential in determining outputs. The argument is often made (it is made in this book) that multijurisdictional comparisons of local government services are not practical because of the importance of contextual factors that are often idiosyncratic.

Nevertheless, DEA appears to be better suited to the comparison of multiple sites of the same service, or to programs that are similarly situated (such as schools), than it is to the comparison of the relative efficiency of services among local government jurisdictions. First, the structure and functional responsibilities of the same service area may differ among local governments, and they may not be able to share the same weights. Second, accurate cost data may be lacking, and the costs of support services or internal service-fund functions may be allocated in different ways. The application of DEA to local government services may be limited to clearly defined subprogram activities and operations. Although software packages are readily available, the technique requires some expertise and the communication of the results to policy makers so that they can inform action that may be problematic.

The central problem with using efficiency studies to inform the policy-making process, however, is the unavoidable political dimensions attached to running government like a business. James Q. Wilson's comments on the work of the Grace Commission (the President's Private-sector Survey on Cost Control) are appropriate here. In 1984 the Grace Commission claimed that it had identified over $400 billion that could be saved if government were managed more efficiently. Shortly after the report, an analysis by the General Accounting Office reduced this claim to $100 billion by eliminating recommendations for which no savings could be estimated and others that had been counted twice. About $60 billion of this "would require not management improvements but policy changes: for example, taxing welfare benefits, ending certain direct loan programs, adopting new rules to restrict Medicare benefits, restricting eligibility for retirement among federal civilian workers and military personnel and selling the power produced by government-owned hydroelectric plants at full market price" (Wilson, 1989: 319). Most of the remaining savings would require the hiring of additional personnel, were based on phantom productivity increases for which no procedures were specified, or called for greater reliance on private-sector suppliers and contractors. This case illustrates our previous point that efficiency in the delivery of services that one is politically opposed to has no meaning— indeed, it is something to be avoided if it results in increased service levels.

The studies of relative efficiency that DEA makes possible would probably be most useful to program managers evaluating their own operations, but such managers are likely to be less interested in interjurisdictional comparisons because they are more sensitive to the uniqueness of context.

COSTING LOCAL GOVERNMENT SERVICES

A major caveat underlying the various analytical techniques discussed in this chapter is that they require accurate service cost data, and these are often not readily available. As previously described, this is partly due to the fact that local government accounting systems focus on financial control rather than managerial accounting. Managerial accounting provides financial information that assists in planning, control and evaluation of the costs associated with the provision of public services (Steiss, 1989). Cost accounting assembles and records all the elements of cost incurred to achieve a given end, to carry on an operation, or to complete a specific unit of work (Kelley, 1984). From an analytical perspective, the costs of a service or program should be weighed against the benefits anticipated from its provision prior to the commitment of public funds. Once a commitment have been made, costs should be monitored and controlled to ensure that they are appropriate and reasonable for the service or program provided; that is, analysts should determine whether additional costs that were not part of the initial plan have been incurred. The overall performance of the service or program should also be evaluated to improve future decisions regarding resource allocations; that is, analysts must identify whether the anticipated benefits have been realized and the program or service is working as designed. These are the benefit-cost and program evaluation efforts described above. Cost information can also be used in making purchasing decisions, evaluating the option of contracting for the provision of selected services or activities, designing fee structures, reimbursing indirect costs associated with federal grants, and assigning the costs of central staff services to enterprise fund agencies (Kelley, 1984).

The total costs of a program include both direct costs—those that can be assigned specifically to a particular service or program—and indirect costs—those from ancillary services or central staff functions that cannot be directly assigned to one service or program. Variable costs are those that increase with increases in the level of service provided, as with salaries or operating supplies; fixed costs, such as rent or capital equipment, do not change with marginal increases in service levels, but all costs are variable in the long run. Unit costs are average costs, or the costs of producing a recognizable unit of a given service or program. Marginal costs are the total costs associated with a specific increase in service level, while sunk costs are those that were incurred before a change in service level; there are no marginal costs in sunk costs. Kelley (1984) defines avoidable costs as those that are not incurred when a particular course of action is taken, and opportunity costs as the value of the benefits that would have materialized if an alternative course of action had been taken. Opportunity costs are a cost incurred by the course that was actually taken, and avoidable costs are the benefits from that course of action. If a police officer is laid off, the avoidable costs are his or her salary and benefits less any payments for unemployment insurance; these are the marginal costs associated with a decrease in service, and they include only variable costs until service is decreased to such a level that patrol cars are sold and substations are closed. Knowledge of these types of costs is required for analytical studies to support managerial decision-making, but the typical local government accounting system traces only expenditures, or decreases in current financial assets.

Activity-based costing seeks to assign costs to outputs through the activities undertaken to produce them. Activity-level costs give managers information about where costs can be cut, efficiencies realized and productivity enhanced. For local governments, these efforts should focus on individual services and the activities necessary to delivery them; services become cost centers. The identification of all activity costs incurred to produce a service are not always self-evident. In Chapter 3 we described a fleet-maintenance internal service agency that followed a policy of servicing emergency vehicles, such as police vehicles, first, and the higher-cost supervisory personnel often had to work on the non-emergency vehicles, such as recreation department vehicles. The budget allocated the higher costs to the agencies with the nonemergency vehicles, while activity based costing would have assigned them to the police emergency-vehicle maintenance activity—even if they were actually paid by the recreation department. The first step in activity-based costing is defining the service, so that one knows what one is costing. Agencies and even programs usually house more than one service, and budgets usually describe lines of responsibility for funds rather than management responsibility for the services these funds fuel (Kelley, 1984). If possible, units of service delivery should also be identified. Ultimately, managers will be able to answer questions like: What does it cost to fill a pothole? What activities are contributing to the rising costs of the bookmobile service? What can be done to lower the costs associated with police officers waiting to testify at the court house?

The allocation of most of the direct costs of each service is a straightforward process; these can usually be found in budget documents or derived from budgeted figures. Problems can arise when a single person works on more than one service, or more than one service is operated from a single set of offices, but time and rent can be allocated through simple calculations. Difficulties arise in the allocation of indirect costs, such as administrative overhead and the costs of central staff services. Central administrative costs can be allocated to departments based on their percentages of the total budget, and these can be added to departmental administrative overhead and allocated to services on the same basis. However, the city manager and city council may spend more of their time on police matters or public works issues than they do on fire suppression issues or matters regarding recreation; if these patterns can be documented, they can form the basis of a more substantively meaningful allocation scheme.

The accurate allocation of the costs of central staff services presents even greater challenges. Like administrative overhead, these can be assigned as a percentage of the budget, but operational differences will probably emerge and these are difficult to ignore. In the case of a centralized personnel department, for example, the police department may have more turnover than other agencies, and public safety positions usually require more stringent selection procedures. It may be possible to identify the core functions of the personnel department— recruitment, selection, testing, grievance processing, etc.—and weight them for cost. The average number of times each agency is served in each area can be calculated, and the core functions can be weighted differently for different agencies to account for factors like the more stringent selection procedures for public safety candidates. The internal service-fund mechanism is designed to facilitate these allocations but, as we demonstrated in Chapter 3, these are often lacking. The "step-down" method of allocating staff services is designed to account for the services rendered by central staff agencies to other central staff agencies; this procedure yields greater accuracy, but it can be quite complex and requires the services of fiscal analysts or professional accountants.

The accurate allocation of administrative and service overhead is particularly important in regard to enterprise fund charges. If the overhead is underestimated, the general fund will be subsidizing the enterprise fund with discounted staff services and managerial oversight. If it is overestimated, the integrity of the enterprise fund is threatened. The same care should be taken in designing fee structures; if the enunciated policy holds that the full cost of the service should be covered by the fee, then it is necessary to identify all costs. However, most fees consider only the variable costs associated with the service. For example, the recreation center and the recreation director would still be there if a particular recreation program were not funded, so only the direct, variable costs incurred by the department to operate that particular program would be recovered through the fee. Accurate fee estimation is also necessary when a jurisdiction is considering "contracting out" a service. In order to justify the contract, it is necessary to determine exactly what it costs the jurisdiction to provide the service. In this case, the total avoidable costs should be considered; for example, a city manager may have devoted considerable time to a program, but his or her salary and benefits will still be paid by the jurisdiction when the service is contracted.

Local government finance professionals should seek to provide service managers the cost data they require to manage their programs more efficiently. Calls for productivity improvements, the pursuit of technological efficiency, and the rational analysis of alternatives necessary to optimize the resource allocation scheme do not resonate when the accounting function seeks only to optimize its control function. The provision of the data itself encourages the pursuit of the ends by creating expectations, serving as an example and contributing to the development of a supporting organizational culture.

MANAGERIAL ISSUES

A crucial issue in the application of structured analysis to the delivery of public services is the question of where that capacity should be located in the public organization. Should it be added to the budget office, placed in the finance office; should it constitute a separate centralized agency, or should each agency house its own analysts? Things to consider here are access to information, existing analytical skills, knowledge of the substantive service areas that will be the targets of analysis, capacity to implement the results of the analytical studies, the decision-making perspective that will guide analytical assumptions and value judgments, and the level of investment required. Various options optimize one or more of these criteria.

The creation of a stand-alone analytical agency attached to top management will require substantial investment or the reassignment of existing analysts. This investment may not be feasible in times of relative resource scarcity, and such "luxuries" are the first to go when resource limitations dictate cuts in service levels. Depending on the amount of resources available, this option could maximize skill level, as well as create the organization-wide decision-making perspective necessary to optimize resource allocation schemes. Alternatively, if analysts are assigned to the individual service agencies, their decision-making criteria would be more narrowly focused. However, the decentralization option would make data more readily available, and the analysts would be more likely to develop knowledge regarding the operation of their substantive service areas. In light of the deference to substantive expertise that characterizes the local government organization, a centralized office dedicated solely to analysis would be less likely to successfully implement the findings of analytical studies, despite the closeness of top management.

The finance agency typically houses professionals trained in the application of analytical techniques, and these would have ready access to financial data. Once again, however, the finance department is oriented to fiscal control, and the substantive service agencies are likely to view analyses completed there as threatening, and hence to resist implementation. Fiscal analysts and auditors may also avoid performance audits, organizational analyses and management studies of services that may require a review of substantive policy. They typically focus on the analysis of control systems, such as purchasing, the revenue collection process and the maintenance of inventories. The decision-making focus here is organization-wide, but limited to fiscal dimensions.

Some analytical functions, such as forecasting, will be placed in the finance or budget office, despite the vested interest of both in maintaining a healthy fund balance. Locating the overall analytical function in the budget office entails some of the same problems and opportunities associated with the finance office placement. However, these analysts will probably be more comfortable discussing substantive policy issues with their service agencies, because they inevitably do so as a normal part of the budget process. In addition to its control function, the budget office also operationalizes an enabling function in making resources available to agencies. The budget office builds bridges to the service agencies, and its organizational perspective is broader that that of the finance office, but the analyses conducted there will also have budgetary "teeth." Many of the operational and organizational issues that will be the subject of analytical scrutiny will emerge from the budget process—zero-base, performance, program or otherwise.

We recommend a combination of a decentralized analytical capacity in the service agencies and a centralized function in the budget office. Each agency must have some in-house analysts to support daily operations and long-range planning, and the budget office will already house a variety of analysts. We make this recommendation not just to take advantage of the strengths of each option and to minimize their weaknesses, but to create a synergistic relationship that will enhance the role of structured analysis in the resource allocation process and optimize the decision-making perspectives that underlie analytical studies. Whenever a problem is uncovered in an agency—through the resource allocation process, performance measurement system, or in another way—a group comprised of analysts from the budget office and analysts from the targeted (and any affected) agencies, as well as managers and personnel with relevant knowledge, skills or experience, should be convened to address it. These ad hoc "focus group" members would work on the analytical project on a part-time basis, sharing assignments and meeting periodically until a recommended course of action is identified.

This option promotes economy and technological efficiency because all of the agencies that comprise the local government organization would have access to the managerial and analytical skills extant in the organization as a whole, and these skills would be further developed. The "focus group" concept may also serve to enhance allocative efficiency, as service on the teams broadens the decision-making perspectives of the participating managers and analysts. They may come to conceptualize the roles of their individual agencies in terms of the larger mission to enhance the overall welfare of the community members. The development and diffusion of an organization-wide managerial perspective may help to counter the enormous centrifugal forces that characterize the typical multiservice local government organization. These managerial development dynamics can facilitate the building of an organizational consensus regarding the elements of an optimal resource allocation plan.

REFERENCES

Frank, Howard A. (1993). *Budgetary Forecasting in Local Government: New Tools and Techniques.* Westport, Conn.: Quorum.

Gramlich, Edward M. (1990). *A Guide to Benefit-Cost Analysis* (2nd ed.). Englewood Cliffs, N.J.: Prentice-Hall.

Groves, Sanford M., and Valente, Maureen Godsey (1994). *Evaluating Financial Condition: A Handbook for Local Government* (2nd ed.). Washington, D.C.: ICMA.

Kelley, Joseph T. (1984). *Costing Government Services: A Guide for Decision Making.* Chicago: Government Finance Officers Association.

Kelling, George et al. (1974). *The Kansas City Preventive Patrol Experiment: A Technical Report.* Washington, D.C.: Police Foundation.

Kelso, William A. (1984). "Benefit-Cost Analysis and Program Evaluation." In Lloyd G. Nigro, ed., *Decision Making in the Public Sector.* New York: Marcel Dekker, 9–42.

Marciariello, Joseph A. (1975). *Dynamic Benefit-Cost Analysis.* Lexington, Mass.: D. C. Heath.

Mishan, E. J. (1969). *Wefare Economics: Ten Introductory Essays.* New York: Random House.

Nyhan, Ronald C., and Martin, Lawrence L. (1998). "Assessing the Performance of Municipal Police Services Using Data Envelopment Analysis: An Exploratory Study." *State and Local Government Review.* Forthcoming.

Patton, Michael Q. (1986). *Utilization-Focused Evaluation* (2nd ed.). Beverly Hills, Calif.: Sage.

Sexton, Thomas R. (1986). "The Methodology of Data Envelopment Analysis." In Richard H. Silkman, ed., *Measuring Efficiency: An Assessment of Data Envelopment Analysis.* San Francisco: Jossey-Bass, 7–29.

Steiss, Alan W. (1989). *Financial Management in Public Organizations.* Pacific Grove, Calif.: Brooks/Cole Publishing Co.

Weiss, Carol (1972). *Evaluation Research: Methods of Assessing Program Effectiveness.* Englewoods Cliffs, N.J.: Prentice-Hall.

Wildavsky, Aaron (1979). *Speaking Truth to Power.* Boston: Little, Brown.

Wilson, James Q. (1989). *Bureaucracy.* New York: Basic Books.

Chapter 6

Local Government Revenues

The art of taxation is the art of plucking the goose so as to get the largest possible amount of feathers with the least possible squealing.

                                                                J. B. Colbert (1684)

Local governments are becoming increasingly dependent on their own-source revenues, and, in many cases, the era of popular tax revolts has resulted in severe restrictions on their capacity to increase local taxes. Local governments can no longer simply "pluck the goose" to support their current service delivery systems. In today's competitive economic environment, it is incumbent on finance professionals to explore new approaches to taxing and spending policies. Evaluating current tax structures and exploring alternative revenue options in a productive manner require an integrated, comprehensive approach to resource allocation issues. The mix of public services offered by local governments and the manner in which they are funded can be important factors for persons deciding where to reside, and the health of the economic base that provides the revenues that fuel those services is obviously influenced by these location decisions. Finance professionals must look beyond the annual budget cycle and take a strategic view of the revenue structure so as to provide resources to fund public policies over the long-term.

REVENUE MANAGEMENT

The term "revenue management" is not simply a new fad, but rather represents a fundamental shift in how local governments sustain and promote a financially sound economic base over the long-term. Revenue management involves several essential considerations that can be categorized under three general headings: revenue development, revenue analysis and support systems. The developmental aspect of revenue management is concerned with establishing a tax structure that considers both short- and long-term resource needs. Conventional revenue management stresses a time horizon that reflects election cycles and short-term political needs. The objective of the analytical process is to systematically examine the salient characteristics of each revenue source available to local governments, including yields, equity issues and cost of administration, with a view to clarifying alternatives and their implications. The support systems deal with the day-to-day management of the revenue sources, and these produce the data required by the revenue development and analytical processes.

Revenue management is defined as the assessment and maintenance of a local government's capacity to generate sufficient funds from all available sources to support policy decisions regarding service levels. These decisions may entail the maintenance or extension of existing programs or services, the production of new services, or the sale of bonds to fund supporting infrastructure and facilities. This is not to say that revenues must be available to fund all demands; the annual budget process always manifests a degree of fiscal stress, in that trade-offs must be made among competing demands for expenditures. Revenue management efforts must address these short-term issues, but they are also concerned with ensuring that funds are available for expenditures crucial to maintaining the economic base of the jurisdiction. These efforts may clearly conflict, and we have suggested throughout this book that professional management must constitute a constituency and serve as an advocate for the long-term perspective, thus informing short-term policy decisions with their long-term implications. Public managers are able to avoid this responsibility by approaching the revenue structure as an environmental "given" or constraint over which they have little control. This option, however, may no longer be tenable.

One of the authors was involved in a case (previously described in Chapter 1) in which the budget director of a medium-sized city was asked to assess the impact on the city of a proposed change in a state statute that exempted the first $25,000 of assessed evaluation from the local property tax (see below for a short description of the mechanics of the property tax). The change would move the exemption to the second $25,000, so that all property owners would pay something, and those whose homes were currently evaluated at less than $50,000 would pay more taxes. Analysis indicated that the amendment would yield the city an additional $400,000 annually in a general-fund budget of $120 million, and the director recommended to the city manager that the local legislative delegation should be asked to support the amendment. The equity issues associated with increasing the taxes of the poorest members of the community were easily brushed aside with comments that everyone should pay something, despite the fact that the burden would fall largely on retirees with fixed incomes and racial minorities. But the crucial point here is that the decision was taken without regard for its effect on the economic base and long-term financial health of the city, and without reference to the city's particular demographics. Indeed, the director was surprised that the yield was so substantial. Revenues were required to fund current services, and the environment had simply made available a source.

Revenue management is a proactive approach to revenue structures. An integrated revenue management system is concerned with establishing revenue performance standards, documenting revenue performance, comparing actual with expected performance, initiating corrective action, and creating a support structure that facilitates the approach. Ultimately, however, the articulation of an integrated revenue system requires an organizational culture that promotes a strategic approach to revenue management. This entails developing a common vision regarding the most productive methods available for funding services in the short- and long-term, identifying where the local government currently stands in relations to its revenue capacity, exploring alternative means of achieving the stated vision, and instituting a program for measuring progress. Although the model is depicted as linear in character, successful revenue management demands continued learning and adjustments. We contend that the definition of optimality in regard to a jurisdiction's revenue structure, as well as its expenditures mix, can be highly idiosyncratic. The application of professional management in this regard requires knowledge of the social, political and economic dynamics of the community, and the development of such knowledge and its application in resource allocation decision making are core responsibilities of professional local government management.

This chapter examines local government revenues in the context of the revenue management process. The first section reviews the environment of local government revenue structures and focuses on how local governments can evaluate specific revenue sources by employing public finance concepts, such as tax equity and efficiency. Second, the characteristics of major revenue sources are reviewed. Next, we examine the concept of revenue capacity, or the ability of a jurisdiction to fund current and future service demands, and we review some measures that governments can take to enhance their capacities. The third section identifies the support structures necessary to implement a successful revenue management system. The chapter closes with an examination of the issues of fiscal stress and financial condition.

LOCAL GOVERNMENT REVENUE STRUCTURES

The capacity to fund a policy decision is constrained by a variety of factors. The "separation of payer and decider" that characterizes the allocation of public resources through authority systems described by Irene Rubin (1993) means that, unlike market exchanges, the act of paying for government services does not tell the producers of the service what to provide. We have previously described the imprecision of the political process in this regard. It also means that government will inevitably use a citizen's taxes to provide a service he or she does not want. Private-sector firms also produce things that some people do not want, but they do not use those persons' funds to do so because those persons do not purchase the good or service. Thus, there is an inherent reluctance to pay taxes, even when someone wants 99 percent of what government produces. The paying of taxes is the only occasion when most citizens feel the coercive power of the state, and this anti-tax phenomenon tends to hold down public spending regardless of the efficiency of the production process or the desirability of the product.

As we have previously described, local governments are creatures of their respective states with no constitutional autonomy (except for home-rule municipalities), and the revenue-raising capacities of local governments are defined by state constitutions, statutes and regulations. The federal and state governments have at their disposal all the tax and revenue bases within their respective boundaries. Local governments have only those resources that have been expressly granted to them by their states. Sources of own-source revenues that have been generally made available to local governments are the property tax, user fees and enterprise charges, and sales and excise taxes; the income tax is also available to cities in ten states. In addition to limiting access to sources of funds, states place limits on rates that can be levied. The property tax remains the tax most closely associated with local government, and the major sources of local revenue will be examined in greater detail below.

Determining which revenue sources are to be utilized and what tax burden local taxpayers will bear is as much a political issue as what government will do with the funds. Dominant political attitudes regarding the appropriate level of government intervention in the local economy, the nature and level of services to be provided, leadership styles and management practices impact the revenue structure of local governments. Political winds are difficult to measure and anticipate, and political cultures can be highly idiosyncratic. Some local governments may have the need and the capacity to generate additional revenues, but the prevailing political philosophy may mean that any proposed tax increase is destined for failure. Raising revenues is even more problematic during election years. Increasingly, local government leaders are relying on strategies that close the "payer and decider" gap; that is, tax increases are tied to or earmarked for specific programs or projects. Earmarking tends to reduce flexibility, and some needs may be overfunded while others go unmet. User fees also attempt to close the described gap, and these have proliferated in the wake of tax revolts that have capped taxing powers. In other jurisdictions, the political support necessary to raise taxes may be there, and the jurisdictions may have room under their legal caps to raise taxes, but the citizens may simply not have the capacity to pay.

Special districts developed to provide specific services through independent taxing authority, in an effort to circumvent tax caps, have fragmented some local jurisdictions and rendered policy planning and coordination, as well as the maintenance of the common economic base, somewhat problematic. The evaluation of the economic framework in which a community must generate resources to sustain policy calls for a regional perspective. The revenue streams of most jurisdictions are integrally tied to the economic health of adjacent communities. The expansion or recruitment of a business in one area of the region will impact the revenue capacity in the others because population dynamics, economic health and economic development are not constrained by legal boundaries. Each jurisdiction must consider its own housing stock, the education and skills of its workforce, the age mix of its citizens, and the nature of its commercial, retail and manufacturing sectors. But the economic health and vitality of the entire region must be viewed in the revenue management process, despite the constraints that may exist on efforts to pursue cooperative policy planning and economic development activities.

Internally, revenue managers should examine the equity of their revenue structures in light of the distribution of goods and services provided, and the efficiency of their revenue sources in terms of the costs of compliance, the costs of administrations, and their effects on private economic activity. The precise impact of the revenue structure on the incomes of individuals in a given community cannot easily be determined, although estimates of impacts may be derived by a careful study of the components of the tax base and tax rates. However, the tax burdens may not fall on the initial tax base, due to tax shifting. The capacity of local governments to engage in redistributional policies is extremely limited, because high-income people are able to leave a city or even a state with less emotional and fiscal costs that they can leave a nation, at which level redistributional tax policies are more feasible. However, a local government can, from general taxes, provide some services that are more likely to be used by lower-income people without jeopardizing its competitive position.

The efficiency of a revenue source refers to the costs of collecting it, including the compliance costs borne by the payer. Payer cost may be operationalized as monetary costs, such as the price of a postage stamp to mail a property tax payment, or it may be operationalized as a convenience cost (for example, the amount of time required to complete forms), and these can be more difficult to quantify in dollar terms. These two dimensions contribute to the tax burden of the payer. Even the administrative costs borne by the government, such as record keeping, auditing and enforcement, are, of course, ultimately borne by the taxpayer. The efficiency of a tax also refers to its effects on private economic decisions, such as the decision to consume or save and the choice between work and leisure. An efficient tax would impact these choices only minimally.

Tax equity does not necessarily mean equality, although one way to allocate the burdens of collective action is to divide the total costs by the number of units that comprise the polity, such as families, households or individuals. Two other bases for allocating the burden are the ability-to-pay and the benefits-received principles. Ability to pay holds that those with greater ability to pay should pay more; benefits received, on the other hand, holds that those who receive the benefits from collective action should bear the costs associated with providing those benefits, in order to parallel the operation of private markets. These two criteria would seem to compete, but Adam Smith was able to reconcile them in his 1776 classic *The Wealth of Nations*, with his observation that greater ability to pay is a measure of the benefits received from being a part of the collectivity.

Once ability to pay is accepted as the most suitable criterion, one must determine the relationship between relative ability and the burden assumed, as well as how to measure relative ability. Vertical equity refers to how much more of the burden is assumed by individuals at different levels of ability to pay. Ability to pay is usually and most conveniently measured by income, but the definition of income can also be problematic. Persons at the same level of income can pay the same percentage of their income, and the higher-income persons would pay more; this is a proportional tax. Or persons at higher levels can pay at higher rates; this is a progressive tax. When persons at lower levels pay at higher rates, the tax is said to be regressive and clearly violates the ability-to-pay criterion. Horizontal equity refers to the degree to which persons at the same level assume the same burden. Differences in the definition of income can compromise horizontal equity; for example, persons whose income comes from investments in municipal bonds pay no federal income tax, because such income is exempted.

Finance professionals should also consider the stability of the revenue source, as well as its capacity for growth. Unstable revenues can make the annual budget process unpredictable and chaotic, while a revenue structure exhibiting little growth will require continuous appeals to the citizenry for rate increases and additional levies. These are the more technical dimensions of revenue management, but it should be clear from the preceding discussion that the design and analysis of a local government's revenue structure requires a host of political judgments. Once again, the finance professional cannot function as a professional without addressing these issues, including informing the political debate and assuming responsibility for the identification and enunciation of the long-term impacts of alternative courses of action.

SELECTED LOCAL GOVERNMENT REVENUES

In this section we review the major revenue sources used by local governments. In practice, the revenue mixes of local governments vary widely, even within a single state. The manner in which similar revenues are administered and structured also varies. In this section, we describe the general characteristics of commonly employed revenue sources in an effort to summarize the issues that finance professionals must deal with in formulating revenue structures. The revenues reviewed are the property tax, sales taxes, the income tax, and user fees and enterprise charges.

Property Tax

The property tax is a tax on wealth rather than income or consumption. Local governments target two types of property. Real property consists of land and improvements on it, such as homes, businesses and other structures that are permanently affixed to the land. Personal property is divided into tangible and intangible property; the former includes moveable objects such as machinery, inventory and furniture, and the latter refers to personal property items that have no intrinsic value, but rather represent legal claims to wealth, such as stock certificates, bonds and mortgages. Real property can be further differentiated into use-based categories: residential property, commercial and industrial property, and agricultural property. The distinction between the various forms of real property is important, because different types may be taxed at different rates. In addition, property owned by governmental units, churches and educational institutions may not be taxed at all.

This section will focus on the tax on real property. This source remains a major source of revenue for local governments, although the relative dependency on the property tax by local governments has declined over the last three decades. Citizen surveys indicate that the property tax is also consistently ranked as one of the most unpopular taxes in the nation. Several reasons have been advanced for this finding: the property tax is a tax on unrealized capital gains in that the tax rises with the value of the property unless the rate is reduced, and this is perceived as unfair, because the gain in wealth is realized only when the property is sold but the tax is due annually; the tax is often used to balance the local budget when further expenditure reductions are deemed unfeasible; the tax is highly visible even if it is paid through mortgage escrow accounts, because a single large bill is received by the property owner each year; the assessment of the value of the property is viewed as being highly subjective, and the tax is perceived as arbitrary; and the tax is inflicted on the payer, because he or she does not participate in the collection process, as with the income tax.

The determination of the amount of revenue to be generated by the property tax consists of three basic operations: the assessment of the value of the property, the determination of the tax rate, and the collection of the tax. The assessment phase consists of the identification and classification of all real property in the jurisdiction, and this function is usually the responsibility of the elected or appointed tax appraiser. Actual assessment practices vary widely, and these will not be inventoried here. An important component of the assessment process is the determination of exemptions. These may include basic homestead exemptions for resident owners, and additional exemptions for widowers, the elderly, and handicapped persons. After the property is assessed and the tax toll is certified, a tax rate can be determined. The property tax is expressed in "mills," and one mill yields $1.00 of tax liability for every $1,000 of assessed value. A property tax rate of 10 mills applied to a $100,000 house valued at 100 percent of market value would yield $1,000 in taxes ($10 \times 100 \times 1 = 1,000$). A 10 mills rate on a $120,000 house assessed at 50 percent of market value would yield $600 ($10 \times 120 \times .5 = 600$). This assumes that the assessed valuation includes all available exemptions. The total amount collected is called the levy, and the calculation of the millage rate begins with the identification of the desired levy. If expenditures exceed projected revenues during the budget process, expenditures must be rolled back or the property tax levy must be increased, since the property tax is usually the most productive tax controlled at the local level. The property tax is a sure tax, because delinquent taxes can result in a lien of the property and be collected when it is sold, or delinquent accounts may be sold to private collectors at a discount. Annual delinquency rates are not likely to exceed 5 percent, because the monthly mortgage payments that include payments to tax escrow accounts remain a high priority even in times of economic distress.

The wake of the tax revolt found many local governments with severe restrictions on their capacity to increase property tax levies and/or millage rates. In some cases, levy increases are benchmarked to inflation indices. In others, voter approval is required for millage rate increases, or maximum increases in millage rates or assessments are limited to fixed percentages. Some local governments are required to adopt the roll-back rate, or the millage rate that will yield the same levy as the previous year after assessments have been increased to reflect increased value and new construction has been added to the rolls; additional millage requires voter approval. These limitations have constrained the capacity of the property tax to respond to the demands of inflation and increased growth.

Federal tax policy encourages home ownership by allowing deductions for property taxes and mortgage interest in the federal income tax. Given an income tax rate of 28 percent, local property owners in effect pay only 72 cents for every dollar of local government services funded from the property tax. This federal policy may distort private economic decisions in favor of home ownership, but this is not a direct effect of the property tax. The property tax is also a very stable source of revenue; the property does not go anywhere and will usually steadily appreciate in value. The rate of appreciation is tied to the regional economy, which must provide jobs for the homeowners. The tax is an expensive one to administer, however, even though very little is required from the payer. The requirements for periodic reassessment, record keeping, the monitoring of improvements to property, and collection and enforcement erode the efficiency of the tax, and this may be another reason for its unpopularity.

The property tax also reflects the benefits-received criterion for allocating the burdens of collective action, because quality local services and maintenance of public infrastructure add to the value of real property in the community. The percentage of one's income devoted to housing will eventually decline as income increases, however, and the property tax is probably regressive, particularly at high income levels. The tax may also encourage the development of homogeneous communities, because the owner of an expensive home in a community comprised largely of lower-cost homes will assume a greater percentage of a given tax burden than if he or she were located in a community comprised of similar homes. The durability of local property tax rests on the fact that it affords local governments a measure of autonomy from their states, and endows each community with a sense of shared enterprise.

Sales Tax

Compared to the property tax, the sales tax is a very efficient tax. It is tax on consumption levied at the retail transaction stage. Much of the administrative costs are borne by the retailers, who keep a small percentage for their trouble. The collected taxes are forwarded to the states, which usually share a percentage with the localities where the transactions took place. Centralized administration allows for the realization of economies of scale and avoids duplication of effort. The tax is virtually invisible to the payer, who pays it as a percentage of the retail charge. The sales tax produces abundant revenues at low rates—usually from 5 to 8 percent—and the low rates are unlikely to affect economic preferences. The tax is levied at the retail stage so that it does not affect production decisions. If the tax were also levied on purchases by firms for production processes, producers would have an incentive to internalize these costs and avoid the tax; that is, firms would expand to produce raw materials and provide necessary machinery within the firm in order to reduce external transactions, and the tax would distort normal business decisions.

The sales tax is also a regressive tax, because higher-income persons consume a smaller proportion of their incomes than persons with lower incomes, who may consume their entire incomes or save very little. A person who consumes half of his or her income would pay an effective rate that would be half the rate of a person who consumes his or her entire income. Exemptions for food, medicines and, less often, clothes serve to mitigate the degree of regressivity. However, the purchase of most personal services, such as those provided by attorneys, accountants, gardeners and pool cleaners—staples for some high-income persons—are also usually exempt from the sales tax, because such a tax would be viewed as a tax on the incomes of the providers.

In 1986, the federal income tax deduction for sales taxes paid to other units of government was eliminated, partly because reported payments were merely rough estimates based on income and state of residence. However, the sales tax does allow residents of the jurisdiction to export part of their tax burden to shoppers from other areas. Some states allow local governments to add an additional percent or two to the state sales tax, and those collections are reserved for the jurisdiction that levies the additional tax. This option generally requires approval through a local referendum. Communities considering this option should be made aware that substantial differences in rates between neighboring jurisdictions can erode the tax base of the one with the higher rate, as shoppers have an incentive to cross the border to reduce the costs of consumption. Sales tax collections are sensitive to business cycles, and hence less stable than property taxes. Yields will grow with inflationary spirals and shrink in times of recession. Collections are a function of the regional economy that provides disposable income, and they will also respond to growth in the economic base.

Excise taxes are applied to selected commodities, usually on a per-unit basis rather than as a percentage of price. These include "sin" or sumptuary taxes designed to curtail consumption of some commodities, such as cigarettes or liquor. The per-unit levy serves to enhance the regressivity of the tax, because consumers of a quart of expensive liquor pay the same tax as consumers of less expensive liquor. However, excise taxes are also levied on luxury items, such as yachts and large, "gas-guzzling" automobiles. Excise taxes are also collected by the state and they are often returned to the locality in which they were collected. In some cases, individual excise taxes are earmarked for specific purposes. For example, motor fuel and gasoline excise taxes might be earmarked for highway and road maintenance and construction. When used in this way, excise taxes function as benefits-based taxes, because those who pay the taxes are direct beneficiaries of the resulting expenditures based on their personal expenditure patterns. Excise taxes on hotel or motel rooms are usually levied as a percent of price, and they allow local governments to export a portion of their tax burden to tourists.

Income Tax

The federal income tax code defines income broadly, and it is structured as a progressive tax. States that "piggy-back" on the federal tax also employ its broad definition of income, but local governments that levy an income tax usually only target wages. The rate is usually 1 to 2 percent of the wages. The local income tax is proportional in design but regressive in effect, because high-income persons are more likely to have income from sources other than wages. Horizontal equity is also compromised, because persons with identical incomes are not taxed at the same rate, and some are not taxed at all. An income tax levied at the workplace makes it possible for local governments to tax commuters, and it allows central cities to pass some of the costs of maintaining their amenities to the suburban residents who take advantage of them.

The local income tax is administered in a variety of ways, but the focus on wages results in low administrative costs. The tax is collected by the employer and forwarded to the local government. Residents who work elsewhere are generally required to file, but they can claim credit for any income tax paid to another jurisdiction through their place of work. Other localities simply "piggy-back" on the state income tax. Some states allow local governments to also levy a corporate income tax, and this can be more costly and quite complex to administer. The local income tax is not universally adopted by the local governments in the states that make this revenue source available. It can be viewed as a tax on business when firms located in a jurisdiction that levies the tax must compete for employees with firms in neighboring jurisdictions with no income tax. In his review of the literature on the subject, Robert Bland (1989) concludes that the tax should be universally adopted in order to preclude any effects on the locational decisions of firms and individuals.

Income tax collections are clearly sensitive to the business cycle, and they are not as stable as property tax collections. But Bland's review (1989) suggests the income tax may tend to supplant the property tax in jurisdictions that have both, for two reasons: yields from the income tax grow faster than property tax collections when rates are held steady, and the presence of an income tax tends to lower property values, particularly when it is not universally adopted in the region or state. Thus, the jurisdiction becomes increasingly dependent on an unstable revenue source. However, the income tax helps local governments to recoup the revenues lost in property tax abatements implemented to attract capital investments. Like property taxes, local income taxes can be deducted from adjusted income in calculating federal tax liability.

User Fees and Enterprise Charges

The public sector provides certain goods and services when these goods and services cannot be divided into units suitable for pricing, as with police and fire services, or when market prices would put them out of reach for some despite the spillover benefits that accrue to society as a whole, as with public health and education. However, in the face of tax revolts and the loss of intergovernmental aid, local governments are under pressure to adopt market mechanisms to fund some basic services. User fees reflect the benefits-received principle for allocating the burden of collective action; rather than providing services through general taxes, those who desire the service pay a fee to fund its operation. Once again, this ignores the fact that spillover benefits associated with consumption of the service will be lost to society as a whole if some are unable to pay. Finance managers should identify services amenable to user fees, and then determine whether these services are used primarily by high- or low-income citizens. As we have seen, local government revenue structures are regressive, and income redistribution can be pursued only through providing services from general taxes that primarily benefit low-income persons. Access to available public services is a crucial factor in maximizing responsiveness to the needs of the public as a whole.

Most governmental services are not amenable to the imposition of a fee structure in any case, and, when they are, the fees may be costly to collect. The installation of meters or the implementation of cash register systems may be necessary. However, like private market exchanges, fees signal the actual demand for the service and contribute to allocative efficiency. They also encourage technological efficiency in delivering the service; managers seek to minimize costs in order to minimize the fee and maximize the customer base. Alternatively, user fees could be used to recoup only a part of the cost of providing a service. The collected user fees are general-fund revenues, and are not retained by the agency that imposes them, as is the case for enterprise-fund agencies. However, the fees can be accounted for in a manner that achieves the same end.

Enterprise charges, like user fees, allow local governments to collect revenues for services from institutions normally exempt from property taxes, such as churches, schools and government buildings. For example, if a jurisdiction opts to provide sanitation service through its general-fund allocations, these institutions would receive the service for free because they would pay no property tax, the main revenue source for most local governments. If the sanitation department is structured as an enterprise-fund agency, these exempt institutions would be required to pay the fee charged for the service, unless they were specifically exempted. Enterprise charges differ from user fees, because subscription to the enterprise service is required; persons volunteer to pay user fees because they want a particular service or program.

Enterprise fund revenues can be costly to collect. Meters must be read and/or bills prepared and mailed monthly or quarterly. The costs of administration are recovered through the enterprise charge, and the users of the service ultimately bear these costs. Enterprise charges are probably more regressive than the property tax they replace; in fact, high-volume users of such services as sanitation are charged at a lower per-unit rate. Franchise fees and utility charges collected from private utility companies and cable television companies operating in the jurisdiction have the same characteristic, in that they are usually calculated as a percentage of the retail charge.

Two additional significant revenue sources that are widely used are interest income and special assessments fees. Interest income represents earnings on investments. Many local government revenues, such as property tax collections, are made available during the first quarter of the fiscal year, and the funds would sit idle until needed if they were not invested. In the past, the investment of local government funds had been a somewhat mundane task, in that the emphasis was on the protection of the principal. Finance professionals have come under some pressure to increase yields from investments in recent years, and a host of investment vehicles have been developed by financial markets. This has become a potentially fruitful area for revenue management, requiring a range of technical skills and substantive knowledge. Special assessments represent collections resulting from compulsory levies against certain properties. They defray a portion or all of the cost of specific improvements or services presumed to be of general benefit to the public and special benefit to the assessed properties, as with the construction of sidewalks or the installation of street lights. If a majority of the property owners in an identifiable district vote to impose the assessment, it is levied against all the owners. Relative burdens are often calculated as a function of benefits received; for example, sidewalk assessments may be based on linear feet of property paralleling the sidewalk.

ENHANCING REVENUE CAPACITY

A local government that is delivering a mix of services, that is responsive to the needs of its citizens, seeks to develop a revenue structure that will allow it to maintain its service levels and provide for future growth. We have indicated that in the present environment, this end necessitates the aggressive and proactive management of current sources. The Advisory Commission on Intergovernmental Relations (ACIR, 1996) has identified three options available to local government managers seeking to balance service demands and revenues: broadening existing sources through rate increases or optimization strategies, developing new revenue sources, and reducing current service levels. Revenue optimization is the process of generating additional revenue from current sources, while revenue diversification involves the use of alternative revenue sources available under current law. The final component of the ACIR's recommendations is expenditure reduction; this option represents a failure of revenue enhancement efforts.

The first step in determining a jurisdiction's ability to increase its revenues is to measure its revenue capacity. Helen Ladd and John Yinger (1989) have developed a ratio that serves as an indicator of the relative fiscal health of local governments and includes a measure of revenue capacity. They apply the average tax rates levied on the major sources of revenue available to local governments (usually in a particular state in order to account for states' influence in this regard) to the relevant tax bases in the targeted local government; this yields the amount of revenue that can be collected in the jurisdiction if average rates are applied to available sources. The local cost of providing average service levels is subtracted from the revenue yield, and this is divided by the revenue yield to create a measure of fiscal health. Weak fiscal health can be attributed to the high cost of delivering average service levels, to the fact that low rates are applied to the relevant bases, or to weaknesses in those revenue bases (such as low income levels or low retail activity). The first may signal the need for expenditure reductions and the application of cost containment techniques, and the last for economic development efforts or the search for more productive revenue sources. If weak fiscal health is due to low rates, the jurisdiction has excess revenue capacity. However, political culture and local history can override and analytical definition of excess capacity.

Revenue optimization can be divided between those strategies that increase the local tax burden through tax base expansion, and those techniques that have no direct impact on local tax burdens. In regard to tax base expansion, a number of local governments have developed ways to make existing revenue sources more productive. For example, a local government may attempt to advance the property tax collection process by adopting a partial-year assessment process for new construction, based on substantial completion or acquisition. These collections are typically delayed until the year following completion. One of the most prominent methods of expanding the tax base is the growing dependency on user charges and fees.

There are a host of optimization strategies that increase yield without expanding the tax base. One of the more successful options available to local governments is establishing an effective cash management program. The primary purpose of any cash management system is to ensure that resources are on hand to satisfy current legal obligations (pay the bills) as well as to provide opportunities to invest any excess cash in income-producing activities. As discussed in Chapter 5, an integral component of cash management is cash flow forecasting. The peaks and valleys of revenue collections, primarily driven by property and income tax collections, produce periods during the year when excess revenues can be invested in income-producing activities. Moreover, encumbered and unencumbered fund balances can be scrutinized to determine if these items can be expedited for investment purposes. For example, resources for the purchase of equipment are typically encumbered once the purchase order is issued. However, delivery of the equipment may come two or three months later. In this case, cash often sits idle in a bank account drawing minimal interest, or a check is issued once the invoice is received.

The three components of cash management are collections, deposits and disbursements. The collection process seeks to expedite the receipt of cash. Some of the more common techniques currently utilized by local governments include lockbox, electronic transfers, and early payment incentive programs. A lockbox system, such as a post office box, assures timely deposit of funds, with the financial institution collecting and depositing the cash or check and forwarding the original documentation to the local government. The purpose of a lockbox system is to reduce the time lag between receipt of cash and recording of cash for investment purposes. Wire transfers, where deposits are made electronically, provide another means of expediting the collection of cash, and in many instances are quicker and less expensive than a lockbox. Early payment incentive programs offer discounts to individuals who pay their bills early, and normally represents the difference between the current interest rate on investments and the percentage decrease offered. The net effect is a given percentage increase in cash.

An efficient cash management program depends largely on the quality of banking services. Local governments should become knowledgeable about the array of services offered by banks. Standard banking services include the processing of deposits, checks and account reconciliation. But banks also offer several other services that can help reduce or minimize idle cash. Zero-balance accounts (concentration accounts) maintain no balance. As checks are presented for payment, funds are automatically transferred from a central account to the zero-balance account (ZBA). At the end of the day, the ZBA is overdrawn because funds are not transferred until the end of the business day, when the bank knows exactly how many checks have cleared the account. This service allows all funds to remain invested in a central account until the very last minute.

Disbursement programs are concerned with paying bills, and here local governments seek to delay payment for as long as possible. In some cases, local governments can slow payments through the use of warrants. A warrant is a draft payable through a bank. When a warrant is presented for payment, the bank does not pay it until it is accepted by the local government. The use of warrants reduces the amount of funds the municipality must have on deposit at any given time. Banks, however, do impose higher service charges for warrants than they do for checks, because of the greater amount of clerical work involved. Therefore the increased costs must be balanced against the earnings available to the local government on the funds retained. Consequently, effective cash management provides a vehicle to increase yields from investments at minimum cost, other than the administration and banking costs associated with the cash management activity.

Another area that has received increased attention from finance professionals is establishing a balanced and productive revenue system. Revenue diversification focuses on the problem of maximizing the effects of the positive characteristics of individual sources and minimizing the negative elements. Through the application of established portfolio management techniques, it may be possible to identify a growth-instability frontier for any given set of taxes, similar to the risk-return frontier for a set of financial securities. The portfolio approach can be used to improve revenue stability without adversely affecting long-run growth. A key to successful revenue diversification is recognizing that the effects of substituting revenues from one type of tax for those from another depend not only on the growth and variability characteristics of the two taxes, but also on their interactions with other taxes in the local government's portfolio.

The maintenance and enhancement of the revenue capacity of the local government is a core responsibility of finance professionals and professional public management in general. We have suggested that one way to stretch revenues is to enhance the allocative efficiency of the jurisdiction's service mix; political responsiveness of the allocation scheme reduces pressures for expenditures and preserves revenue capacity. We have described how finance professionals can apply their technical expertise to the management of the revenue structure. However, the identification of an optimal revenue structure also requires professional managers to make political judgments regarding equity, who should pay, and access to services. Technical expertise cannot be applied in a political vacuum. The legitimacy of such decisions are enhanced when they are made by the organization's managers as a whole, employing an organization-wide perspective. This perspective helps to ensure that the decisions reflect the needs of the jurisdiction as a whole. We have previously suggested that program managers are reluctant to take responsibility for the fiscal policies associated with their services; here again revenues are viewed as the product of a distant environment. The consensus-building process regarding the application of technical expertise in the area of revenue structures can help build the organizational culture necessary to support consensus-building efforts in the area of the expenditure mix, where the need for technical expertise is sometimes less obvious and where it is usually applied in fragmented, conflictual processes dominated by narrow self-interest. The sub-optimal allocation decisions that emerge ultimately strain revenue capacity.

REVENUE MANAGEMENT SUPPORT STRUCTURES

The data necessary to support revenue management efforts are often lacking. Even the managerial functions of finance professionals are not well supported by data when they are defined as something more than simple control. The revenue forecasting and cash management functions may not have access to monthly collections, or efforts to structure user fees and internal service-fund charges may lack accurate cost-of-service data. When revenues are viewed as the products of a distant environment that managers do not control or influence, information regarding their nature may not be viewed as particularly necessary.

We are familiar with a case in which a county government instituted an extensive revenue analysis project, because a strategic planning effort had revealed a lack of understanding regarding revenue bases. One source was a mobile home license fee that was collected by the state and returned to the localities where the mobile-homes were located. Fees from mobile homes located in the unincorporated area of the county were intended for the county government, but analysis indicated that in many cases the state revenue office was sending the funds to the city indicated on the post office address. The county had missed out on at least $100,000 in fees annually for the previous twenty years, because this source had been viewed as a gift from the state rather than as an asset to be closely managed. In another case, research indicated that in the early 1950s the state had frozen distributions of pari-mutuel wagering to the counties, because the counties had not been able to agree on an allocation plan that would reconcile the demands of those who actually housed the race tracks and those that had none. The total collections were to be re-allocated when an agreement was reached, but this arrangement had been lost in antiquity. The state had continued to distribute equal shares of 1950s pari-mutuel wagering funds to the counties, and had proceeded to divert the substantial growth that had occurred since then to the state's general fund.

Local governments can improve operations in these areas through the adoption of available computer technology. The manual recording of receivables and payables into the general journal inevitably results in posting errors that are difficult to detect and correct, and which complicate the preparation of the annual report. The adoption of geographical information systems facilitates the assessment of property values and the recording of plat information. Cash management that relies on bank reconciliations to determine cash position will result in lost investment interest. There are a host of software packages available to local governments that can aid in cash forecasts, and which provide a historical summary of actual versus forecasted receipts and disbursements. Other programs help evaluate the cost of bank services, and investment management software can calculate interest rates and yields and provide cash-balance reports. In smaller jurisdictions where payments are received by a clerk who often has other demanding responsibilities, the need for these technologies is particularly pressing, but the funds may prove elusive. The level of technical expertise necessary to implement a cost accounting system, for example, may call for the services of a consultant and the extensive training of personnel. These costs may simply outweigh the potential benefits received, for instance, from increased user charges at the local swimming pool.

Technology alone, however, cannot provide the support structure that is needed to develop a fully articulated revenue management system. Those individuals responsible for accounting, financial reporting and property assessment must be able and willing to provide the data that is needed in a timely manner. In many cases, accounting information is often backlogged for three or four months, and program managers often track their own expenditures; this practice can result in the proliferation of systems providing conflicting information. The modified accrual basis of accounting also allows considerable discretion in defining the "availability" of revenues and the "currency" of the financial resources that will be used to liquidate liabilities. Abuse of this discretion can mask revenue problems. Finance professionals must take responsibility for more than simply seeing that the annual budget is balanced; they should focus their expertise on the long-range financial viability of the jurisdiction. The sharing of financial information also has an interorganizational dimension. The municipal planning department should forward building permit data to the county property appraiser so that property assessments can be adjusted; this can be facilitated through the implementation of a distributed geographic information system. State and county professionals should share forecasting assumptions and actual collections with local governments. The cultivation of such an information network must be a priority of the local government finance professional.

The effectiveness of administrative support systems should also be evaluated periodically. We have suggested that program managers are loath to collect accounts receivables; user fees are deposited in the general fund for reallocation, and enterprise managers recoup losses through fee increases. In one jurisdiction we are aware of, the finance manager proposed to centralize the collection function in his department. This collection function would be funded through penalties on delinquent accounts; the collected receivable would be credited to the general fund or the enterprise agency owed the funds. Shortly after implementation, the collection function was recovering half its cost in penalties, and it had collected hundreds of thousands of dollars in outstanding receivables—often with no more effort than a simple telephone call. This system represents an innovative use of the internal service-fund mechanism to overcome an inherent weakness in the public organization.

It is important to stress that establishing the effectiveness of a revenue management system may require several years of operation. However, the entire effort is geared to managing the resources currently available to fund public policy preferences in the context of their long-term impact on the financial capacity of the organization. These efforts require technological investments, intraorganizational and interorganizational coordination and communication, and supporting administrative systems. Finance professionals seek to optimize current revenues as they explore alternative revenue sources, and they must do this in legal, political and economic environments that are constantly changing.

MANAGERIAL ISSUES

We have contended that one of the core functions of professional public management is to maintain the revenue base of the jurisdiction in order to provide for its long-term financial viability. Short-term expenditure and revenue decisions should be made in this context, because the continued funding of annual expenditures and the regular collection of the revenues to fund them both depend on the financial condition of the jurisdiction. Unfortunately, there is no general consensus regarding what the financial condition of a local government should look like, and very little normative theory has been developed to guide the actions of public managers in this area. This is in part of failure of practice, because theory tends to follow practice in public management, and public managers spend considerably more time attending to the annual budget than they do to its long-term implications for the financial health of their communities. But the fact that theory follows practice is a failure of theory builders.

Financial health refers to more than those crises that signal its absence, such as bond defaults or bankruptcy. The International City/County Management Association (Groves and Valente, 1994) has identified four distinct meanings of the term "financial condition." One is cash solvency, which refers to the ability of a local government to pay its bills in the very short term; another is budget solvency, which refers to the local government's capacity to balance the annual budget. Shortfalls in available cash can result from poor cash management, and may not signal any underlying financial problems. The fiscal problems associated with funding all identified service needs form the essence of the annual budget process, and shortfalls here are inevitable. The long-run balance between revenues and expenditures, including the pension costs and accumulated employee leave that may not appear in the annual budget document, constitutes the third aspect of financial condition, long-run solvency. Service-level solvency, the fourth component, refers to the capacity of a local government to provide for the health, safety and welfare of the citizens of the community. Thus, for the ICMA, financial condition refers to the government's ability to maintain existing service levels, withstand periodic local and regional economic disruptions, and meet the demands of normal growth and change. The political and cultural dimensions of this definition should be evident.

The ICMA's Financial Trend Monitoring System (Groves and Valente, 1994) is comprised of thirty-six indicators representing a variety of factors related to financial condition. Although favorable trends can be identified for most factors, the ICMA does not establish absolute standards for any of them. In fact, the relative importance of the indicators is a function of local history, politics and culture. The same contingencies limit the usefulness of types of financial ratios used in the private sector, where the financial health of most business entities can be summarized with six ratios and compared with the relative health of any other. Most of these ratios can also be constructed for local governments, but, just as in the case of the ICMA's indicators, there is no overarching theory to establish their relative importance. Idiosyncratic accounting practices also limit the comparability of financial ratios.

As described above, Ladd and Yinger (1989) compared the expenditure and revenue capacities of local governments on the bases of the costs of providing average service levels and the yields that could be realized from average rates. In an implicit criticism of the approach manifested by Ladd and Yinger, Robert Berne and Richard Schramm (1986) recommend that analysts evaluate cities via averages calculated from a reference group of ten or more similar cities, using a variety of indicators like those identified by the ICMA. The reference group cities should be in the same state as the target city, in order to minimize differences in functional responsibilities and available revenue sources. But it is on this point that an essential dilemma emerges: averages constructed from cities that are located closely together and share similar revenue structures and spending patterns, as well as a common economic base, may mask shared systemic problems or structural weaknesses, and the fact of being ''above average'' may lend decision makers a false sense of security; on the other hand, averages representing a more broadly based population of cities lose relevancy and substantive meaning. Political history and culture and the local demand for services can differ widely even among neighboring cities, and remain additional wild cards in these analyses. Berne and Schramm also summarize the research literature that suggests the credit ratings issued by bond-rating companies are often subjective, are based on many elements that are unrelated to financial condition, and are poor predictors of financial problems. James Howell and Charles Stamm (1979) employed a range of measures of financial stress on a variety of cities, and found that different measures led to different conclusions regarding financial condition; the same results were obtained in Pearl Kamer's study (1983).

In addition to conceptual and measurement problems associated with financial condition, the reasons why some local governments slip into crisis situations also seem to vary. Cleveland's 1978 default was related to Ohio's liberal laws regarding the assumption of short-term debt by municipalities, to misuse of short-term debt by a series of mayors, and to the political power that accrued to the local banks that held the debt. The technical default suffered by New York in 1975 was rooted in the power wielded by public employee unions in local politics. More recently, the budget crisis that evolved in Miami was largely the product of a casually corrupt political system and an enabling social culture. Cleveland was also dealing with sectoral shifts in the structure of the national economy that had eroded its industrial base, and with a noose of surrounding suburbs that prevented growth through annexation. The prominent role that New York played in financial markets encouraged the tacit conspiracy of state and local public officials and the financial establishment that allowed the city to pursue unsound financial management practices and budgetary policies; the uncertain ramifications of a default by such a large borrower caused these groups to foreclose an actual default. Miami had been subjected to waves of immigration that had exacerbated existing poverty and had strained the capacity of the city to meet the demands of diverse political groups. However, these external factors may have led to different results in different political and cultural contexts. The centrality of what are often highly idiosyncratic contextual factors complicates the development of theory regarding financial condition. The role of revenue structures in financial condition is even less well understood, particularly the interaction among revenue sources. Revenues combine in a variety of ways in a range of communities, and revenue management efforts must also focus on local context.

Financial condition is a multidimensional concept, but its meaning is ultimately defined by the political community. Professionalism in this area must reach beyond the application of accepted theory, because tested theory does not exist. In order to pursue their responsibilities in maintaining the financial viability of the communities they serve, therefore, professional public managers must engage that community. The premises and perspectives that drive decision-making in the public organization should be informed by knowledge of local political and cultural context. Public managers should seek to build such knowledge into the formal and informal archives of the public organization, and the regular use of this information into the culture of the public organization. Engagement efforts must extend beyond regular contacts with elected representatives, because these part-time officials are usually focused on short-term political ends. The maintenance of the revenue bases of the jurisdiction and the continued funding of the policy preferences of the community require a long-term perspective and a continuing dialogue between the citizens and the stewards of their public organization. Public managers seeking to fulfill basic professional responsibilities cannot escape politics.

REFERENCES

Advisory Commission on Intergovernmental Revenues (1996). *Significant Features of Fiscal Federalism.* Washington, D.C.: U.S. Government Printing Office.

Berne, Robert, and Schramm, Richard (1986). *The Financial Analysis of Governments.* Englewood Cliffs, N.J.: Prentice-Hall.

Bland, Robert L. (1989). *A Revenue Guide for Local Government.* Washington, D.C.: ICMA.

Colbert, J. B. (1684). Cited in H. L. Mencken, *New Dictionary of Quotations on Historical Principles from Ancient and Modern Sources.* New York: Knopf, 1942, 1178.

Groves, Sanford M., and Valente, Maureen Godsey (1994). *Evaluating Financial Condition: A Handbook for Local Government* (2nd ed.). Washington, D.C.: ICMA.

Howell, James M., and Stamm, Charles F. (1979). *Urban Fiscal Stress.* Lexington, Mass.: Lexington Books.

Kamer, Pearl M. (1983). *Crisis in Urban Public Finance: A Case Study of Thirty-eight Cities.* New York: Praeger.

Ladd, Helen F., and Yinger, John (1989). *America's Ailing Cities: Fiscal Health and the Design of Urban Policy.* Baltimore: Johns Hopkins University Press.

Rubin, Irene S. (1993). *The Politics of Public Budgeting* (2nd ed.). Chatham, N.J.: Chatham House.

Chapter 7

Capital Budgeting and Economic Development

No community can afford to sit on its assets.

Edward J. Blakely (1994)

The long-term economic vitality and fiscal health of a local government is at least partly a function of its current service levels and short-term capital investment decisions. Available data indicate that since the late 1960s local governments have decreased, in real terms, their commitment to capital spending, and the consequences of this general lack of capital investment are growing more apparent. Capital disinvestment ultimately manifests itself as higher costs for current public services because of inadequate or deteriorated facilities, higher repair and replacement costs for facilities and equipment that have not been maintained properly, the diversion of resources from current operations, increased indebtedness and pressures for increased taxes, and private-sector disinvestment.

Communities invest in capital facilities and infrastructure in order to support the delivery of current services, maintain and develop their tax bases, and encourage private investment and economic development. The required investment, even if the jurisdiction borrows funds for capital improvements, diverts revenues from current operations. In order to minimize costs and disruptions to current services, and make responsive investment decisions, the community should develop a long-range capital improvement plan (CIP). The adoption of a formal capital planning process helps elected officials, professional administrators, the business community and citizens make informed choices regarding trade-offs between current service levels (tactical spending decisions) and infrastructure investments for the future (strategic spending decisions). A CIP links strategic investments to the annual budget process, and the allocation of funds for strategic investments should be a part of the budget process. A capital facility's operational impacts, such as staffing, maintenance, and operational supplies, are often overlooked in the process of planning the financing and construction of the facility. A unified budget framework encourages decision makers to consider the impacts of capital investments on the annual budget. On the other hand, elected officials are often tempted to postpone major capital investments in favor of short-term operating needs, and a unified budget may make these tendencies more manifest.

In a strategic context, capital planning is linked to the economic, physical, environmental, social, organizational and political culture that undergirds local economic vitality and sustainable growth. Capital planning provides opportunities to evaluate the goals and assumptions of current taxing and spending policies. The capital planning process encourages policy makers to develop a strategic vision that can motivate and support economic activity that encourages growth, and it helps the annual budget process to adapt to shifting geographical and economic realities. By raising capital budgeting from a task that a government does each year to a process rooted in the long-term service delivery needs of the community, the economic vitality of the jurisdiction can be sustained. A capital budget that is the product of an integrated resource allocation and planning process also communicates to the private sector that the jurisdiction is professionally managed and will support private investment and economic development.

The recruitment of new businesses or the expansion of existing businesses creates a demand for additional labor and can result in higher incomes for residents. Higher incomes allow for greater economic vitality. The economic attractiveness of the community increases property values and real wealth. We have identified maintaining the economic viability of the local government jurisdiction as a core responsibility of the finance professional, and the capital planning processes described here are tools for achieving that end.

This chapter examines the role of capital budgeting and capital improvement planning as tools for integrating the long-term service delivery needs of the jurisdiction within the demands for current services. We describe the elements of the capital planning and capital budgeting processes, and we examine salient issues associated with these processes. The relationship between capital planning and economic development is reviewed as well. We also explore how managers throughout the organization are linked to the capital planning process, and to the economic vitality of the jurisdiction. We close with a short case study of an effort to finance infrastructure improvements and regional economic development through revenue sharing.

CAPITAL BUDGETING

Most local governments prepare separate capital budgets to allocate resources for the acquisition or construction of facilities or other items that have a long useful life, are very costly, and are not likely to be funded again in the short term. The term ''long useful life'' means that these items will not be consumed during a single budget year. These items are differentiated from operating capital items by the fact that their useful lives extend for several years, and their costs are high relative to the size of the general budget. Large jurisdictions may budget vehicles as operating capital items, while in other jurisdictions these may be major capital acquisitions. Lastly, governments often borrow funds for capital acquisitions, while operating capital is funded through current financial resources. The requirement that operating budgets must balance precludes the inclusion of capital items, because including them would cause wide fluctuations in budget levels and—if borrowing funds is not an option, and long-term savings prove infeasible—wildly changing tax rates would probably be unacceptable to the public.

Capital items are costly and they represent major investments for local governments. They require the deliberation, study, analysis and consideration of alternatives and their consequences that the time constraints associated with the annual operating budget process militate against. In contrast to the operating budget, the nonrecurring nature of capital expenditures means that decision makers cannot simply look to last year for guidance regarding these investment decisions. One-shot, very costly expenditures would also have a difficult time competing directly with the settled policy represented by the recurring expenditures of the operating budget, particularly in light of the fact that capital items promise future benefits. But capital items do compete with operating expenditures for resources, and their separate consideration should not obscure this reality. The separate financing of long-term projects through borrowing also enhances intergenerational equity in the allocation of tax burdens. The borrowed funds are repaid over the life of the funded item, and the citizens assume a repayment burden that is proportionate to the period of their use.

The hypothesized connection between public capital spending and economic development would seem to be an intuitively sensible proposition. Private individuals and private-sector businesses would seek to invest in communities with quality services, adequate supporting facilities, and sound infrastructure in order to protect the value of their own investments. Empirical research has developed some support for that proposition (Munnell and Cook, 1991). Alicia Munnell (1990), for example, establishes a positive relationship between investments in public infrastructure and growth of the private sector. Charles Hulten (1990) links the rapid economic growth in the U.S. during the 1960s to relatively high investments in infrastructure, and the gradual decline in productivity since the 1970s to lower spending in infrastructure development and maintenance. The economic development function on the local government level is reviewed more closely later in this chapter. First, we review elements of the process of identifying and funding capital facilities and infrastructure improvements: capital planning, analysis of capital projects, prioritizing capital projects, presenting the capital budget, and evaluating capital expenditures (Steiss, 1989). This section is followed with a brief note on financing capital projects, which is also the subject of Chapter 8.

Capital Planning

Investment in capital facilities without the benefit of rational planning can result in substantial monetary and service costs for citizens, government, and industrial activity (Moak and Killian, 1964). Failure to properly manage and invest in long-term public facilities can adversely impact the financial viability of the local government and current and future private-sector business activities. In order to maximize the benefits from capital investments, these decisions should be made in a strategic context rather than on an ad hoc basis. The capital improvement plan (CIP) is widely considered a key planning and management tool local governments utilize to link the long-range capital needs and economic development objectives of local governments. The adoption of a multiyear capital plan is a complex, time-consuming, and often frustrating and politically volatile process. The annual operating budget process tends to push policy decisions into the background by concentrating on incremental adjustments to prior-year expenditures. But capital investments commit current and future citizens to a pattern of expenditures and service levels, and by their very nature they focus attention on the future of the jurisdiction and the ends of collective action. At the same time, the size of the expenditures and their potential effects on the long-term financial viability of the jurisdiction call for careful analysis and the application of substantive expertise.

The primary purpose of capital planning is to identify and monitor proposed capital projects, and coordinate the financing and timing of their capital improvements in a way that maximizes their return to the public. Bradley Doss regards the CIP as a "comprehensive document that enables local governments to budget for immediate capital projects, evaluate the conditions of existing projects, and assess the future capital needs for either expansion, renovation or construction of new capital stock" (1993: 272). Douglas Shumavon describes the CIP as "the foundation for capital expenditures because it blends program and needs analyses with financial analysis. When properly developed and used, the CIP becomes a critical tool for anticipating large expenditure items, and determining when and how much money will be needed to keep up with infrastructure needs" (1992: 38). Doss' studies (1987, 1993) demonstrate that cities with a separate capital budget are more likely to have a CIP than those without a separate capital budget. Doss further determines that larger cities are more likely to have a CIP than smaller cities. In addition, professionally managed cities are more inclined to adopt a CIP than cities administered by mayors. Moreover, state and federal policies or mandates were found to influence local adoption of a CIP.

The CIP represents the immediate and detailed portions of the long-term capital facilities plans of local governments. It is at the same time a fiscal planning tool used to forecast future borrowing and to manage capital funds, and a tool for the orderly maintenance and replacement of capital facilities and equipment. The CIP can also serve as a mechanism for redesigning and coordinating local government subdivision ordinances, requirements for development permits, and annexation agreements (Government Finance Research Center, 1983). The CIP allows the local government to respond to as well as to guide private development in the jurisdiction by making supporting infrastructure available and by signaling developers where such investments will be made in the future.

The CIP generally groups projects by funding source, and it details the level of funding planned for the various stages—land acquisition, design, demolition, construction—of each project. Most studies suggest that the normal span of a CIP ranges between five and six years. According to Alan Steiss (1989), a period of six years is regarded as the most desirable and convenient for detail programming of capital expenditures, although in some jurisdictions shorter or longer time spans are considered appropriate. Longer time frames may encourage unrealistic planning and the inclusion of "pie-in-the-sky" projects; shorter time frames do not allow adequate planning, because many capital projects extend over several years.

The current year of the CIP is usually adopted as the capital budget for that year—that is, if the forecasted funds are actually available and the political winds have not changed significantly. The forecasting function is clearly important here; over-forecasting may result in the elimination of a politically popular project as it approaches the current year. The CIP does not bind policy makers until the funds for the identified projects are actually appropriated in the capital budget, but elected officials may be under some pressure not to disturb the flow of resources identified in the CIP. By tying real funds to capital planning projects, the CIP discourages the development of simple "wish lists," and is endowed with the aura of settled policy. Of course, political and economic forces do affect the design and implementation of the CIP, particularly when new leadership assumes responsibility. A CIP provides local officials a certain degree of protection from various interest groups in the decision context of capital planning, and a carefully designed program and schedule of priorities give officials a sound basis to resist ill-conceived or untimely action. Additionally, decision makers may include a project in the "out-years" of a CIP to mollify a particular group or divert political pressures, and such a project always seems to be pushed back when it approaches the third or second year.

Analyzing Capital Requests

Many local governments maintain neither an accurate inventory of their fixed assets, nor a list of the replacement costs or an estimate of the useful life span of their capital facilities and equipment. If a city hall was built in the 1970s at a cost of $1,000,000, this does not necessarily mean that the value of the asset in the 1990s is $1,000,000. The cost of construction, the value of the land, and a number of other cost factors have changed. Moreover, the fact that local governments do not normally depreciate their fixed assets severely limits their ability to accurately assess capital needs.

To complete an inventory of current fixed assets, a local government must identify and locate all the land, facilities, and equipment it currently owns. For each capital item the following information should be collected: the date of construction or acquisition; the original cost of the asset; improvements or modifications that have been made since acquisition; an assessment of the current condition of the asset; estimates of utilization levels; its depreciated value; its maintenance, repair and replacement costs; and the expected life-cycle or replacement date of the asset (Steiss, 1989). The next step is to evaluate the current condition of the asset. This task can be accomplished through various means, such as contracting an engineering study of the capital facility to analyze its current operating capacity, establishing performance benchmarks that track the number of malfunctions or breakdowns that have occurred over a given time period, and monitoring the number of complaints received from users of the facility. More analytically rigorous methods for determining the utilization rates of current capital items also exist, but in most cases these methods do not provide any more useful information than the experiences of the individual or individuals who are charged with the responsibility of maintaining the facility.

Replacement analysis is a technique that can be employed to evaluate the costs associated with repairing or replacing current assets. Although each capital facility calls for different technical considerations, a basic consideration in any facility is its depreciation rate, or depreciation costs. The cause of decline in service potential can be classified as either physical or functional. The physical causes of capital depreciation include such things as ordinary wear and tear from use, rust, the effects of wind and rain, and decay. The most important functional cause is obsolescence. Computers that are working well may be replaced because new, smaller computers that compute faster and more efficiently provide a more economical option. Changing demographic conditions may also be a functional cause of depreciation, such as when a larger waste water treatment plant must be built due to a growing consumer base. An understanding of the specific causes of depreciation can assist in estimating an asset's useful life. Oftentimes, a decision must be made whether to replace or repair a fixed asset. For example, should a local government repair an existing jail, build a new facility, contract with another jurisdiction, or follow the trend to privatization in this area?

The calculation of the depreciation of capital investments is a necessary step in determining replacement schedules, repair costs and salvage value, and a variety of methods exist for this purpose. We are not suggesting, however, that local governments should record these charges on the asset side of their general ledger. Depreciation information helps local governments to maximize the useful life of a capital asset, minimize the costs of replacement, and optimize the mix of capital projects in their CIPs. This information can inform the decision-making process and help to dissipate political demands for sub-optimal investment schemes. Ultimately, one's level support for a particular capital facility is a function of one's perceived need for the service it supports; this is to say that the analysis of the relative condition of capital facilities and the need for repair or replacement (or the need for different facilities) is very much a subjective process.

Finance professionals should also be aware of depreciation in order to meet their responsibilities in regard to the long-term financial viability of the jurisdiction. The capital planning and budgeting processes are highly political, but they also call for the expertise of finance and planning professionals, engineers and substantive service managers. The local government organization's professional managers should seek to develop a capital investment scheme based on available data regarding the condition of existing facilities and projections of future needs as indicated by demographic trends and economic development goals. The organization should engage the political process with a consensus plan based on the range of professional expertise that it houses.

Ranking Capital Projects

In Chapter 5 we outlined the elements of the benefit-cost model, and we identified a method for ranking capital projects that maximized net benefits in light of a budget constraint. We reiterate the point that rankings based on analytical techniques are subject to the vagaries of politics. If all of the top-ranked projects are police department projects, or all of them are in one councilperson's district, or a politically popular project does not make the final cut, the rankings will invariably be revised. Projects that mitigate potential liability to lawsuits, those that correct current deficiencies, and those required by the comprehensive plan (if the jurisdiction is required to prepare such a document) are usually ranked highest in importance. The service impacts and revenue-generating capacities of projects are also closely examined. Ideally, these issues are quantified and built into the benefit-cost analysis in order to facilitate comparisons, but these criteria may be dispositive regardless of the benefit-cost analysis.

Once again, the value of correcting service deficiencies or enhancing service levels is a function of the value of the service. The fact that professional management's pursuit of economy, efficiency, and effectiveness in the delivery of public services is constrained by political and fiscal realities does not relieve them of responsibility for those ends. Once again, the culture of the local government public organization should support the rational pursuit of these ends and the employment of decision criteria that reflect the needs of the community as a whole. The most formidable constraint on fulfilling these responsibilities comes from managers who pursue narrow political interests defined from the perspective of their particular agencies. The public organization should engage the political community as a unified professional entity. However, this unity cannot be imposed. The judgment of agency managers in the selection process is a crucial one, given that the projects being considered represent a range of substantive areas. Even the data required by the benefit-cost models come from the agency managers, as do estimates of factors that cannot be quantified. Thus, the accuracy of the models is also a function of the knowledge of substantive area managers, because the data provided will be products of the decision-making perspectives they employ. Top management must seek to develop a consensus ranking of projects by the organization as a whole. Over the not-too-long run, this approach fosters the very organization-wide decision-making perspective that it requires.

Presenting the Capital Budget

The consensus-building approach means that the organization's rankings will be based on more and better data, and the analyses will be less vulnerable to political winds. We have indicated that the capital budgeting process is often a contentious one, but the common citizen is usually interested only if a particular project affects him or her in some direct way. The technical and financial aspects of the projects tend to be the focus of discussions, and these are less accessible to the general public. Conflicts seem to settle around special interests—such as developers, contractors, architects and engineers, and the financial establishment—who often take a keen interest in the CIP development process as well as the deliberations regarding the capital budget. A consensus budget provides less access for these special interests.

The projects incorporated into the capital budget are usually arranged based on priority ranking, and normally range from urgent to deferrable. Although there is no standard form that a capital budget should take, and the GASB has established no guidelines for local government capital budgets, there are some baseline items that should be included: a detailed description of each capital project to be considered in the current budget year; a statement of the purpose of each project; a description of the method for financing each project and the sources of funds; and a schedule for the completion of multiyear projects. If the proposed capital budget does not simply mirror the second year of the previous CIP, management should anticipate questions regarding why some projects were pushed back or why others that may not have even been in the CIP were included in the proposed capital budget. The construction of capital projects is subject to delays, and forecasts of funds are sometimes incorrect, so some changes should always be expected in the CIP, particularly in the out-years. The less local government managers abuse this characteristic of the CIP to mollify supporters of "pie-in-the-sky" projects, the less likely it is that elected officials will look askance at legitimate changes.

In addition to the technical and financial information that must be included in a capital budget, local government managers should also outline linkages between each capital item and other planning processes, such as land use, comprehensive planning and economic development. The nature of the connection between public investments in capital facilities and economic development is reviewed below.

The Evaluation Phase

The final element of the capital budgeting process is the postcompletion evaluation or audit. Most capital facilities are evaluated periodically during their lifetimes, and we have suggested that depreciation data should be regularly collected and monitored. But the formal evaluation of the effectiveness of these individual facilities does not provide feedback regarding the effectiveness of the process through which they were selected for funding. The first formal evaluation may occur several years after the facility has been operational, and the particulars of its selection process may be lost in antiquity.

One of the purposes of the postcompletion evaluation is to assess the extent to which established goals and objectives were met during the construction phase. We have indicated that large construction projects can be affected by a variety of factors, and delays are inevitable; many of these delays can be managed, however, and many others can be avoided with proper management. Thus, the performance of contractors and suppliers is evaluated, as is the contribution of the local government's project management team. The evaluation effort also encompasses the planning phase, because any problems that occurred in the project may have been a function of poor or misleading data that led to the establishment of unrealistic targets. This evaluation information helps enhance the rationality, objectivity and integrity of the planning process.

Each project identified in the capital budget should be evaluated annually, whether it is completed or not. Often, interim reports provide useful indicators of potential problems, such as environmental problems that result in delays in engineering studies, or manufacturing problems over which the project managers or contractors have no control. In addition, formal project evaluations should be undertaken several years after a project has been completed to determine whether it is yielding the benefits projected in the analyses that supported the decision to undertake the project. Of particular interest here are the impacts of the capital project on the annual operating budget. Auditors should determine if staffing, operational needs, and maintenance costs were estimated accurately.

The goal of these efforts is to ensure that capital funds are managed efficiently. Thus, the efforts focus on both the individual projects and the decision-making process that created them. Oftentimes there is very little that can be done to correct existing deficiencies, but the data can improve the decision-making process. Lastly, the CIP process itself should be periodically subject to a formal program evaluation effort to assess the extent to which funds are being managed and budgeted efficiently and to ensure that the integrity of the process is being maintained.

FINANCING CAPITAL PROJECTS

We have indicated that local governments have the option of funding capital projects on a pay-as-you-go basis or by borrowing; the latter option is the subject of Chapter 8. Governments may also employ both of these methods depending on the nature of the project under consideration. With pay-as-you-go funding, policy makers set aside a certain amount of funds each year until enough are available to begin the project. Alternatively, the jurisdiction may raise taxes for a limited number of years in order to raise the necessary funds; this option may not be feasible unless the project has widespread support, because citizens tend to resist or move away from "spikes" in tax rates.

The set-aside option may be a feasible approach for small projects, but the funds may be vulnerable to the demands for other more immediate needs. For example, a jurisdiction may decide to set aside general revenues for the construction of a neighborhood pool. The funding required to begin construction may not be available for several years, because the set-asides must be small in order not to disrupt the flow of resources to regular operations. In the interim, a large fire may precipitate large amounts of unanticipated and unbudgeted overtime in the budgets of the police and fire departments. Funds deposited into the general-fund capital improvements account may be reprogrammed for this purpose. The pool will then still be in the out-years of the CIP, with no funds having been appropriated. This option can also be abused: general funds can be accumulated for a politically popular project that always seems to stay in the out-years of the CIP, because policy makers have other uses in mind for the funds. Many local governments, however, maintain a section of the CIP for projects funded from general revenues that are set aside each year.

We have suggested that the pay-as-you-go option compromises intergenerational equity, because those who pay for the projects may not be those who receive the benefits from the projects. Borrowing allows the project to be constructed immediately, and those who receive the benefits pay off the bonds over the life of the project. This is one reason why the set-aside option is used only for relatively small projects. The borrowing option also allows policy makers to manage the flow of resources to current operations and capital projects more effectively. The debt assumed to fund the project is serviced from current resources, and debt service diverts resources from current operations. This issue reflects the two basic responsibilities of professional public managers: the efficient provision of responsive services, and the long-term economic viability of the jurisdiction. Managers must balance these two responsibilities; here they must balance the flow of resources to current operations and the flow of resources to the capital facilities that will support services and economic viability. Some of the tools available to manage the effects of debt service on current operations are outlined in Chapter 8.

Impact fees can fund the construction of new capital facilities, or the expansion of existing facilities, made necessary by growth. For example, a large, new residential development may strain existing recreational facilities, road capacity, emergency medical and fire response times, and waste water treatment and potable water capacities. Impact fees can be collected from the builder, usually at the time a certificate of occupancy is issued, and the funds used to construct a nearby recreation center, to improve surrounding intersections and widen major arterial roads, to build a nearby fire station, and to enhance potable water and wastewater treatment infrastructure. The jurisdiction may have more pressing capital needs elsewhere, but impact fees must be earmarked for projects that are connected to the development from which they were collected. Projects funded through impact fees should be segregated in the CIP, although some of these projects may have additional sources of funds. Impact fees have also been levied to cover the costs of police, school, and mass transit facilities, as well as solid waste disposal and storm water drainage infrastructure.

Intergovernmental grants are an additional source of funds for capital facility construction and infrastructure development. The benefits of local government capital investments spill over to other jurisdictions, and the states and the federal government provide grant programs to encourage local governments to build such capital facilities. For example, a local government that discharges partially treated wastewater into a river has little incentive to build a better wastewater treatment plant, because the prime beneficiaries of this investment would be the jurisdictions located downriver from it. Grants help local governments with some of the costs of these facilities, and provide financial assistance to local governments with weak tax bases. However, these programs can serve to distort local priorities regarding the relative importance of alternative capital investments. A project that is perceived as "free" will rise in the local priority list. The grantor agencies often require local governments to fund a portion of these projects with their own resources in order to ensure that they really need the project. Requirements for matching funds can drain financial resources and managerial capacity from projects that could meet more pressing needs.

A final issue is the funding of projects involving the repair or renovation of capital facilities. These projects are usually too small or not suitable for funding through bond sales, but they are too large to be included as a capital outlay item in the operating budget of the agency that operates the facility. These projects may include the renovation of the roof of the library facility, the conversion of an old jail to office space for the police department, or the expansion of the public organization's warehouse. Rather than having the agencies compete for funding for these projects during the regular budget process, the legislative body should appropriate a given level of funds for such projects to a non-departmental account. This account could be managed by the top executives from the various departments that comprise the public organization, who would prioritize the projects as a team. This approach encourages the development of a wider perspective regarding the service needs of the jurisdiction, as well as the assumption of collective managerial responsibility for the long-term needs of the jurisdiction.

ECONOMIC DEVELOPMENT

The potential political and economic benefits of an economic development program are witnessed by the fact that approximately 20,000 state and local economic development organizations, spending approximately $30 billion in incentives, compete for roughly 700 industrial locations each year (Bahl, Weist and Schulman, 1987). However, the use of the traditional tax abatements by local governments to lure private enterprises has come under considerable criticism. For most segments of the economy, taxes constitute only a small part of the cost of doing business, and abatements are usually well down on the list of factors that private companies consider when making location decisions. However, once the decision is made, private enterprises will ask for abatements and tout them as one of the reasons why they chose to locate in the community. Many jurisdictions even use abatements to entice companies located in neighboring jurisdictions to relocate; in light of the regional nature of local economies, these tactics result in a net loss to the regional tax base and yield no net gain for the regional economy. Obviously, local governments are not capitalists, and economic development is "an activity tightly bound to the core institutions of capital and sensitive to, even dependent upon, those who control the flow of investment" (Beauregard, 1993: 280). Local government finance professionals must come to understand this dependence in order to manage it.

Local government professionals cannot escape their responsibility for the long-term economic viability of their jurisdictions. Edward Blakely has observed that "[l]ocal government and community organizations are realizing that *all* public-sector actions have an impact on private decisions. Even the most narrow local governments . . . have affected economic development in their communities, if only through their passivity" (1994: 52). We have indicated that this responsibility is rooted in the obligation of the finance professional to maintain the revenue bases of the local government organization. The selection and funding of capital facilities in particular are public-sector actions that directly affect private-sector investment decisions.

It is well understood that the factor driving private-sector investments is profit maximization, but the role of local government in local economic development is less well understood (Blair and Premus, 1993). Blakely (1994) describes entrepreneurial, coordinative, facilitative, and stimulative roles for the local government, as well as overall strategies that focus on business development (demand-side strategies), human resource development (supply-side strategies), high-technology development, and community-based employment and development. Economic development goals can focus on preservation and social justice as well as growth. It is clear that a local government cannot simply import a tested model that has been successfully implemented in other jurisdictions. Blakely (1994) also describes a variety of organizational arrangements that house local government economic development programs, featuring various public-private arrangements, degrees of independence, and funding sources. On the regional level, cooperative arrangements and formal institutions will also reflect local issues and politics and will be even more idiosyncratic (Savitch and Vogel, 1996).

The research literature has offered up a variety of substantive economic development strategies, but a consensus seems to be emerging that strategies focusing on enriching the region's infrastructure rather than on attempting to revitalize specific manufacturing industries will probably be more successful (Beyers, 1992; Schoonhaven and Eisenhardt, 1992). These infrastructure factors include a skilled work force, the presence of production support services, and access to communication and transportation facilities, as well as traditional infrastructure facilities such as potable water plants, wastewater treatment and sewer service, and power sources. Capital has become as mobile as people, but local governments must make certain that they also provide the quality services and supporting capital facilities that will attract skilled individuals to the community; private capital will follow skilled labor as well as seek to attract it. Thus, current operations are as crucial to long-term economic viability as capital improvements and economic development programs.

For Blakely (1994), the most effective strategies to attract jobs and increase the wealth of a jurisdiction are developed locally. We have suggested that there is no real political constituency for the long-term financial viability of the local government organization. Paul Peterson has suggested that economic development planning tends to be the product of "highly centralized decision-making processes involving prestigious businessmen and professionals" (1981: 132). These groups are likely to be pursuing narrow ends tied to the development of the jurisdiction's economic base, and this points to the need to expand participation to include the general public so that the interests represented are more broadly based. However, in her research involving eight cities, Susan Clarke (1995) found that the loose coupling of the economic development policy-making process manifested by most cities is often overcome by arrangements that limit participation and veto points in order to build consensus and provide for stability. In short, the rationality and efficiency demanded by what can be a very technical process require that participation be limited, and the short-term focus of the general public facilitates its exclusion. However, Michael Pagano and Ann Bowman (1995) found that the enunciation of a strategic vision is crucial to economic growth, and in his study of enterprise zones, Ronald Erickson (1992) found that these kinds of economic development tools are more effective when they are part of a larger strategic plan for development. A strategic plan for the growth and development of the jurisdiction will have more legitimacy if it is the product of an open process. The decision-making process should deal with the conflict during the development phase, even though this may compromise the rationality and cohesiveness of the plan, in order to ensure long-term acceptability. Policy makers can employ the "not-in-my-backyard" concerns of the general public, which could ultimately scuttle the best-laid plans to encourage participation.

In order to minimize the deleterious effects of these trade-offs, the local government's professional managers should acknowledge their responsibility for the long-term economic viability of their jurisdiction and seek to develop a consensus economic development plan that reflects their collective expertise. The public organization can identify potential conflicts and work to resolve them through this internal development process while maintaining the rationality and cogency of the plan. Once again, expertise in this area means knowing the jurisdiction and appreciating the centrality of context rather than in simply importing accepted theories and tested programs. We are not suggesting, however, that the plan can simply be imposed in the public. The expertise housed in the local government public organization should seek to frame complex political issues so that they can be open to meaningful public discourse. Without this effort the questions will be framed by those with narrow and vested interests, and the abrogation of the responsibility to provide a general framework would constitute tacit support of vested interests. The public managers must set aside their own parochial interests, and participation in the development process would build their capacities to do so by encouraging them to adopt an organization-wide perspective regarding the long-term financial viability of the supporting jurisdiction.

Public managers are connected to the long-term economic health of their jurisdictions through their responsibility for the allocative efficiency of the capital budget and for the promulgation of a long-term economic development plan, as well as through their responsibility for the quality, efficiency, economy and responsiveness of service delivery systems. Their involvement in capital planning and economic development planning will instill a long-term, organization-wide perspective that can carry over to the annual budget process. Their proactive, substantive involvement in these political processes is legitimized if they engage the political community as a collectivity of professionals. This political involvement is unavoidable in any case, and the organizational development and managerial capacity–building goals outlined here merely seek to optimize the results of this political role in terms of the jurisdiction as a whole. The presence of a viable, integrated organization on the local government level makes the attainment of these goals feasible.

MANAGERIAL ISSUES

In 1985, the mayor of the city of Akron, Ohio emerged from a legislative hearing on annexation thinking that there had to be a better way. Over the previous few years, Akron had waged a series of costly and contentious annexation battles with the four townships (subcounty governments that administer basic services largely in the unincorporated areas of the county) that surrounded it, but these had not yielded any real economic gains for the city. The annexed areas had agreed to be annexed, but they had, of course, expected a higher level of services from Akron. But Akron's population base had been shrinking; since

1950, the city had annexed almost twenty-eight square miles, increasing its size by 52 percent while its total population had dropped by 20 percent. At the same time, the townships lacked the funds to develop the infrastructure necessary to attract new development and provide the service levels that would make Akron's services less attractive to neighboring businesses and residents. A particularly significant issue was access to potable water and wastewater treatment facilities. Stringent federal environmental and water quality statutes had made these facilities very costly and had limited the expansion of septic tanks. Recognizing its growing dependence on and the increasing promise of the water-intensive nascent rubber industry, Akron had acquired rights to, or purchased outright, most of the potable water sources in the area shortly after the turn of the century, and the city was selling water to nearby municipalities—those with the necessary infrastructure—at Akron rates plus a surcharge of as much as 50 percent.

Legend has it that two township representatives overheard the mayor muttering to himself after the hearing, and talks were scheduled. Five years latter, legislation enabling the creation of Joint Economic Development Districts (JEDDs) between municipalities and their contiguous township in charter counties (Akron's Summit County was the only one in Ohio, but the statute has since been extended to other counties) was approved by the Ohio state legislature. The City of Akron began negotiations with its four townships, and in November of 1994 voters in three approved JEDD contracts. Akron would provide water and sewer services to businesses in the designated JEDD areas (each initially limited to 2,000 acres by the enabling legislation) at Akron rates plus 10 percent, and the city would not annex any of the townships' land without their permission. The townships would retain the property taxes from the JEDD areas, and the city would receive any income taxes from businesses located within the JEDDs.

Ohio townships cannot levy an income tax, and Akron's ability to use of its substantial enterprise fees for non-enterprise-related expenditures is constrained. Akron exchanges some of its water and sewer fees for income taxes that will eventually find their way into its general fund, and the townships realize the additional property taxes that come with development. The income tax collections were initially earmarked to fund the extension of the necessary infrastructure into the townships. The periods of the contracts would extend for ninety-nine years with provisions for two fifty-year renewals. Townships residents would also be allowed to petition for water and sewer services as the pipes approached, at Akron rates plus 22.5 percent with the tap-in fees prorated over ten years. The townships would assume the cost of providing additional services to their JEDDs, and a joint city-township board of directors would oversee the routine operations of each JEDD.

The residents of one township rejected a JEDD agreement with Akron on two occasions, primarily because the majority did not want development. The agreements with the other three townships have been put on hold because two of them would have required Akron to take water from the Great Lakes watershed, which would have been released into the Mississippi Basin. The eight states that border the Great Lakes must approve any plan that results in a net loss to the Great Lakes watershed. As of this writing, seven states have approved, largely because the State of Ohio agreed to release water from a state-owned source to make up for any Great Lakes water that ends up in the Gulf of Mexico. This plan is opposed by a city to the south of Akron that is developing its own JEDD agreements with two of Akron's four partners. The contentiousness surrounding annexation processes has been replaced by new areas of conflict.

David Rusk (1993) studied the histories of 522 cities in 320 metropolitan areas between 1950 and 1990, and he found that cities with lower initial population densities in 1950 and higher levels of geographic expansion since that time had achieved higher levels of economic development. He termed these "elastic cites," and he found that elasticity in a city's borders yielded benefits for the entire metropolitan area. In his influential book *Cities Without Suburbs* (1993), Rusk recommends that metropolitan areas should develop area-wide governance structures that can mobilize the resources of the area and coordinate regional economic development efforts. In a 1996 address at the University of Akron attended by one of the authors, Rusk endorsed the JEDD concept, and he suggested that it held promise as a mechanism for area-wide coordination. The JEDDs put the city in a position to drive private development efforts by controlling the location of supporting infrastructure, but the city is likely to follow the market in order to protect its investment and maximize income tax collections. The fiscal borders of the city have certainly become more elastic.

In the Summit County area, however, the JEDD has become a vehicle for the traditional competition between cities in Ohio for economic development and the income tax it brings. Cities with income taxes are able to recoup the property tax abatements they give to private enterprises to locate within their boundaries. Because school districts have no income tax, they have been fiscally stressed by this practice, and the Ohio state legislature has recently limited municipal property tax abatement programs. The model tax-base sharing program was implemented in the Minneapolis–St. Paul metro region in 1971. In this plan 40 percent of revenue increases in the commercial-industrial property tax base for a seven-county area is placed into a single fund, and then redistributed to the communities in the area based on population and a need factor that reflects disparities in the per-capita market value of all real property. The rationale of the plan reflects the assumption that communities will reduce competition for economic investment if they share the benefits from development in the area wherever it occurs. However, the Twin Cities area had had a fifteen-year history of metro planning and governance structures before the plan was implemented. The Akron area had not had similar experiences.

The case of the Akron JEDDs illustrates the regional dimension of economic development. The development in suburban areas often would not occur without the presence of the central city, but the benefits of such development are often out of the reach of the city. If mechanisms exist that allow jurisdictions to share in the benefits of regional economic development, the jurisdictions are less likely to engage in destructive competition for it. Formal annexation is one method that cities can employ to reap the benefits of contiguous development, but this option is costly and equally contentious. The JEDD mechanism allows Akron to accrue some of the benefits of development in its surrounding townships, and to share in the costs of providing supporting infrastructure. We have suggested that substantive service managers must rise above parochial interests and view the role of their agencies from the perspective of the jurisdiction as a whole; the same can be said for the jurisdictions in an economic region. However, the governance structure manifested by the local government's public organization—as torn by centrifugal forces as it is—is usually not available to the region, nor does the region operate an integrative budget process that can serve as a vehicle for the recognition and communication of common goals.

The case also illustrates the relationship between private economic development and public investment in supporting infrastructure. The JEDD mechanism could potentially be a tool for directing private investment and managing growth in the region. This would allow decision makers to plan for the provision of supporting services, maintain existing service levels, and balance the needs for growth with the demands for current services. We have identified the maintenance of the long-term financial viability of the jurisdiction as a core responsibility of the finance professional, and here we suggest that this responsibility cannot be effectively pursued without a regional perspective on decision-making regarding economic development. Additional elements of the intergovernmental context of economic development are also evident in the Akron case: the state legislative action to authorize the JEDD concept, the impact of federal environmental statutes on the cost of infrastructure, and the interstate agreement regarding the use of water from the Great Lakes. In the absence of a strong, clearly enunciated urban policy at the federal level, state and local governments must become adept at managing horizontal relationships among one another.

Lastly, the case illustrates the importance of understanding the political, cultural, social and legal contexts in which one's jurisdiction exists. Ohio has a very fragmented system comprised of what are often fiercely independent local governments; compared to the rest of the nation, Ohio is a local government–dominated state, in that a clear majority of the state's total public-sector expenditures have historically been made at the local level (Bahl, Weist and Schulman, 1987). Thus, unlike the Minneapolis–St. Paul region, the Summit County region had had no history of regional governance. Contexts define opportunities for and constraints on action, as well as long-term goals to develop and alter contexts. Theories of economic development cannot simply be imported and implemented without consideration of their interactions with contexts. Once again, local government managers should build such knowledge into their organizations and see that it informs their decision-making processes.

REFERENCES

Bahl, Roy, Weist, D., and Schulman, Wanda (1987). "The Fiscal Implications of Industrial Restructuring: The Case of Northeastern Ohio." In David L. McKee and Richard E. Bennet, eds., *Structural Change in an Urban Region: The Northeastern Ohio Case*. New York: Praeger, 155–202.

Beauregard, Robert A. (1993). "Constituting Economic Development: A Theoretical Perspective." In Richard D. Bingham and Robert Mier, eds., *Theories of Local Economic Development*. Thousand Oaks, Calif.: Sage, 267–283.

Beyers, William (1992). "Producer Services and Metropolitan Growth and Development." In Edwin S. Mills and John F. McDonald, eds., *Sources of Metropolitan Growth*. New Brunswick, N.J.: Rutgers University Center for Urban Policy Research, 125–146.

Blair, John P., and Premus, Robert (1993). "Location Theory." In Richard D. Bingham and Robert Mier, eds., *Theories of Local Economic Development*. Thousand Oaks, Calif.: Sage, 2–26.

Blakely, Edward J. (1994). *Planning Local Economic Development* (2nd ed.). Thousand Oaks, Calif.: Sage.

Clarke, Susan E. (1995). "Institutional Logics and Local Economic Development: A Comparative Analysis of Eight American Cities." *International Journal of Urban and Regional Research*, 19 (4): 513–534.

Doss, Bradley C. (1993. "Capital Budgeting Practices." In Thomas D. Lynch and Lawrence L. Martin, eds., *Handbook of Comparative Public Budgeting and Financial Management*. New York: Marcel Dekker, 225–264.

Doss, Bradley C. (1987). "The Role of Capital Budgeting and Related Fiscal Management Tools in Municipal Governments." *State and Local Government Review*, 18 (Fall): 101–108.

Erickson, Ronald A. (1992). "Enterprise Zones: Lessons from State Government Experience." In Edwin S. Mills and John F. McDonald, eds., *Sources of Metropolitan Growth*. New Brunswick, N.J.: Rutgers University Center for Urban Policy Research, 161–182.

Government Finance Research Center (1983). *Building Prosperity: Financing Public Infrastructure for Economic Development*. Washington, D.C.: Municipal Finance Officers Association.

Hulten, Charles R. (1990). "Infrastructure: Productivity Growth, and Competitiveness." In *Infrastructure Needs Assessments and Financing Alternatives*. Subcommittee on Policy Research, United States Congress. Washington, D.C.: U.S. Government Printing Office.

Moak, Lennox L., and Killian, Kathryn (1964). *A Manual of Suggested Practice for the Preparation and Adoption of Capital Programs and Capital Budgets by Local Governments*. Chicago: Municipal Finance Association of the United States and Canada.

Munnell, Alicia H. (1990). "Why Has Productivity Growth Declined? Productivity and Public Investments." *New England Economic Review* (January/February): 2–22.

Munnell, Alicia H., and Cook, Leah K. (1991). "Financing Capital Expenditures in Massachusetts." *New England Economic Review* (March/April): 52–79.

Pagano, Michael A., and Bowman, Ann O. (1995). *Urban Revitalization: Policies and Programs*. Baltimore: Johns Hopkins University Press.

Peterson, Paul (1981). *City Limits*. Chicago: University of Chicago Press.

Rusk, David (1993). *Cities Without Suburbs*. Baltimore, Md.: Johns Hopkins University Press/Woodrow Wilson Center Press.

Savitch, Hank V., and Vogel, Robert K. (1996). "Perspectives for the Present and Lessons for the Future." In Hank V. Savitch and Robert K. Vogel, eds., *Regional Politics: America in a Post-City Age*. Thousand Oaks, Calif.: Sage, 275–302.

Schoonhaven, Carol B., and Eisenhardt, Karen M. (1992). "Regions as Industrial Incubators of Technology-Based Ventures." In Edwin S. Mills and John F. McDonald, eds., *Sources of Metropolitan Growth*. New Brunswick, N.J.: Rutgers University Center for Urban Policy Research, 210–252.

Schweke, William (1987). "Why Local Governments Need an Entrepreneurial Policy." In Jeffrey I. Chapman, ed., *Long-term Financial Planning: Creative Strategies for Local Government*. Washington, D.C.: ICMA, 36–42.

Shumavon, Douglas H. (1992). "Financing Infrastructure Development in Local Government." *The Municipal Yearbook*. Washington, D.C.: ICMA.

Steiss, Alan W. (1989). *Financial Management in Public Organizations*. Pacific Grove, Calif.: Brooks/Cole Publishing Co.

Chapter 8

Debt Management

Much attention has been focused on the assessment and selection of capital projects while much less effort has been applied to an analysis of how best to pay for them.

Government Finance Research Center (1985)

The market for local government securities has changed dramatically since the mid-1980s. On the consumption side, there has been a significant change in the purchasing patterns of individuals, insurance companies, commercial banks, mutual funds and other institutional investors—driven in part by changes in tax treatment of municipal securities, and in part by the rapid growth that has taken place in the capital markets since 1984. On the supply side, there has been an increase in the use of negotiated sales, a higher reliance on revenue bonds compared to general obligation bonds, new restrictions on the uses of tax-exempt bond proceeds, and the availability of more complex bond structures and bond packages (for example, put and call options, capital appreciation bonds, double-barreled bonds, and interest-rate swaps). Despite these substantive changes, relatively little attention has been paid by academicians and practitioners to debt management.

This lack of attention is especially troubling when considered in light of the fact that the volume of local government long-term debt has increased over 320 percent between 1980 and 1994, from $213.6 billion ($943 per capita) to $663.7 billion ($2,549 per capita). In addition, short-term borrowing (usually retired within the same fiscal year, or within a three- to five-year period in some states), in the form of tax anticipation notes (TANs), bond anticipation notes (BANs), revenue anticipation notes (RANs), variable rate demand notes (VRDNs) and tax-exempt commercial papers (TECPs), has also witnessed dramatic growth, rising from $8,546 million in 1980 to $17,332 million in 1994. In sum, local governments are using more than $650 billion in long-term debt and $1.7 billion in short-term debt to finance their service development and delivery systems and associated capital projects.

One reason why debt has become so popular, both politically and economically, is that it is viewed as a relatively "painless" method for generating resources in a fiscally conservative environment. From a political advantage, debt allows current taxpayers to receive additional public services without bearing the total costs. Elected officials may see debt as a means of postponing the payment of highly visible capital acquisitions—that is, passing the cost on to a future generation of taxpayers. In communities characterized by increasing mobility, incurring debt to enhance service levels can become an attractive political option, or investment in capital facilities may be viewed as altogether unnecessary. However, the alternatives to borrowing in order to finance the construction of capital facilities also have unattractive characteristics. Savings for the costs of the project would mean that the citizens bearing the costs may never realize any of the benefits of the project. Additionally, the funds would be vulnerable to the need to fund emergency spending and new programs demanded by citizens during the savings phase. Huge increases in taxes in order to collect the necessary funds in one or two fiscal years would disrupt current services and probably precipitate a mass exodus of businesses and residents from the jurisdiction. Borrowing for the project and paying back the funds over the life of the project allows more of those who actually pay for the project to share in its benefits, so intergenerational equity in the provision of these facilities is enhanced. The funding, planning and equity issues associated with the construction of capital facilities illustrate our contention that there is really no constituency for the long-term financial condition of the local government jurisdiction.

The determination of whether a government should borrow, and how much should be borrowed, is essentially a benefit-cost question: an immediate gain in financial resources should be evaluated in the context of future real cost of principal and interest on debt service, and the maturation schedule of debt repayment. Ideally, a decision to borrow should be made deliberately, after careful appraisal of benefits and costs. In practice a great deal of borrowing occurs as a result of emergencies, miscalculations or weak debt policies, with little or no systematic comparison of benefits to costs. In order to avoid these untimely and costly occurrences, financial professionals must evaluate debt practices in the context of a fully articulated debt management program.

In this chapter the concepts of debt management will be explored with a view to the financial condition of local governments. The financial crises experienced by Cleveland and New York in the 1970s, briefly described in Chapter 6, were both precipitated by inability to service debt. States establish legal limits on the amount of debt that may be outstanding at a given time, and the credit analyses of bond-rating agencies also constrain the capacity of local governments to issue debt. We contend that effective debt management must be rooted in the management of the organization as a whole, and debt management must become more than a function conducted by finance professionals. This chapter concludes with an examination of the managerial issues associated with establishing internal debt policies. We suggest that these policies should be the products of an organization-wide process, and that participation in this process can enhance the decision-making perspectives of substantive service managers.

LOCAL GOVERNMENT BONDS

Effective debt management involves several goals: ensuring that bondholders are paid on time and in full, without jeopardizing the provision of essential public services; avoiding excessive tax burdens for community members and businesses; maintaining a flexible debt structure in order to be able to meet unanticipated revenue shortfalls and emergency expenditure needs; and structuring debt in a manner that facilitates long-term financial stability and growth. Debt is normally incurred in order to finance capital facilities, so the debt management function must seek to balance the needs for current services with the long-term needs for these facilities. Debt-service demands often compete for funds directly with current services, but they usually enjoy legal priority. In order not to disrupt the flow of resources to current operations, debt managers should structure the overall debt so that a level flow of funds can service the debt, regardless of its relative size.

Local governments have historically relied on two borrowing options: general obligation bonds and revenue bonds. General obligation (G.O.) bonds are backed by the "full faith and credit," or full taxing capacity, of a local government; G.O. bonds are considered to be debt of the primary unit as a whole and not of any individual fund or component unit. Although G.O. bonds are guaranteed by the full taxing power of the issuing government, they are ordinarily serviced by the property tax, and the sale of these bonds must be ratified through a vote of the citizens of the issuing jurisdiction. Revenue bonds, however, are usually issued without a popular vote. Ordinarily the local government simply pledges to use debt backed by a specific portion of a certain tax or revenue—for example, 1 percent of a 6 percent sales tax (called tax increment debt)—or it pledges to use a certain portion of the revenue generated by some municipal facility for debt retirement. The facilities are often structured as enterprise funds, and the revenue bond issue is reported as a debt of the enterprise fund that services the debt.

Revenue bonds may be issued with covenants that give them the status of tax-supported debt, although the intent is that the debt be serviced from the resources of the enterprise. Under these circumstances, debt is treated as a long-term obligation of the enterprise fund, and a contingent liability is levied against the general fund. In some states, debt of an enterprise fund is not counted against the debt margin, while in other states it is. Debt backed by special assessments against property deemed to be particularly benefited by a capital project for which the debt was incurred is called special assessment debt. Special assessment debt is considered a general debt of the entity if the local government is obligated to assume payment of debt service should collections of special assessments be insufficient to cover the debt and the interest thereon. A number of local governments have attempted to spark economic development by providing the financial resources "up front" to provide infrastructure improvements in certain areas of a community. Under these arrangements local governments have issued tax increment bonds, which are secured by the taxes collected on the growth in assessed value of real property in the identified area.

The advantage of the G.O. bonds is that they usually carry a lower interest rate than revenue bonds, and a G.O. issue is less costly to prepare. The lower interest rate charged for G.O. bonds is directly related to the fact that these bonds are backed by a local government's full taxing power and creditworthiness. A small reduction in the interest rate will yield substantial savings over the life of the issue; for example, a 1 percent difference in a $10 million G.O. bond issued for twenty years results in a decrease of approximately $840,000 over the life of the issue. A disadvantage of G.O. bonds is that they require voter approval, and the costs of such referenda can be substantial. Requiring local governments to place G.O. bonds on the ballot may increase the accountability of local governments, but the requirement for voter approval may delay the issuing of bonds; this may be costly to an issue if favorable market conditions are lost. Revenue bonds avoid the referendum process, and can be issued on a more timely basis. Revenue bonds may be offered during favorable market conditions in order to reduce overall costs, but taxpayers are often unaware of such actions.

General obligation bonds are typically sold in serial form, where each bond issue has more than a single maturity period. Serial bonds are generally classified based on the repayment of principal. When the total principal of an issue is repayable in a specific number of equal installments over the life of the issue, it is called a *regular* serial bond. When the first installment is delayed for a period longer than a year after the date of issuance, but thereafter installments fall due on a regular basis, the bonds are knows as *deferred* serial bonds. When the amount of annual principal repayments is scheduled to increase each year by approximately the same amount that interest payments decrease, so that the total debt service remains reasonably level over the term of the issue, the bonds are called *annuity* serial bonds. *Irregular* serial bonds may have a customized pattern of repayment that does not fit the other three categories.

Revenue bonds are normally sold as "term" bonds, in which the payment of principal falls on the date of maturity. Often, to reduce costs of revenue bonds, a covenant is established mandating the utilization of a sinking fund to retire a fixed amount of principal each year. In effect, this "mandatory" sinking fund effectively converts a term bond structure into a serial structure. In an alternative form of sinking fund, an "invested" sinking fund, the issuer makes annual or semiannual payments to a third party bond trustee; the third party then invests the funds so that there are sufficient resources to retire the term bonds at the maturity date. Current U.S. Treasury regulations prohibit the investment of sinking fund monies in taxable securities, so arbitrage opportunities do not exist. In any case, if local governments earn interest by investing borrowed funds at a higher rate than the borrowing rate, the resulting income is subject to income taxes. If borrowed funds sit idle for extended periods of time, the interest earned is, once again, subject to federal income taxes.

A fundamental difference between G.O. bonds and revenue bonds is the cost associated with issuance. Cost is a function of the risk associated with the bond issue. Since G.O. bonds are backed by the full faith and creditworthiness of the local government, while revenue bonds are backed by the revenue potential of a given project, investors require additional return (in terms of higher interest rates) for the riskier investments. Investment risk, historically, has been based on the possibility of default by the issuer. If a local government goes bankrupt, it may not repay the principal and interest. However, different types of bonds have different types of risks associated with them. Eight risk dimensions of local government bonds are listed on Table 1. It should be noted that several of the identified risks are not mutually exclusive, since they involve the loss or change in value of the bond's principal, or the loss or change in value of its interest payment.

Local governments in general have experienced a long-term trend toward greater reliance on revenue bonds, due to caps on outstanding G.O. debt and widespread resistance to tax increases. More recently, local governments have explored a number of creative ways to finance long-term capital projects. These financing arrangements include different types of bonds, leases, and bonds secured by leases. A primary objective in many of these efforts is to increase the marketability of local government bonds, specifically revenue bonds. Like their private-sector counterparts, these innovative methods have been designed to protect investors against large deterioration in capital value, providing them with ongoing tax-exempt income in exchange for lower interest rates, and generating additional investment opportunities in the tax-exempt bond market. Although the array of options has grown exponentially, each variant has different implications for debt management. The following discussion focuses on the more common techniques utilized by local governments.

Put and Call Options

Under the put option, the bondholders can "tender" bonds back to the local government issuer and require the issuer or designated party (usually a bank or underwriter) acting on behalf of the local government to purchase the bonds at a specified time and price prior to the scheduled maturity. This option in a bond structure provides for greater liquidity for investors by allowing bondholders the option of tendering the bonds back to the issuer during times of increasing

Table 1
Risks Associated with Investing in Local Government Bonds

Risk Dimensions	Description of Risk
Default risk	If a local government goes bankrupt, it may not pay back the principal and interest on its bonds.
Delayed or delinquent payments	Although technically this is a form of default, if payment resumes, it is not a full-scale default.
Loss resulting from rating change	This is the risk of changing credit quality—typically bond downgrade.
Liquidity	This risk stems from an investor's possible inability to obtain cash immediately or quickly for the bonds.
Marketability	There may not be any buyers.
Call	Loss may result when bonds are "called" or paid back long before their maturity or expiration date.
Loss of asset value	This occurs when the inherent value of the bonds' principal falls. A bond's price goes down when the yields on current prevailing bonds go up.
Loss of interest	If investors have to sell during periods of lower interest rates, and if they cannot reinvest principal at as high an interest rate as previously, they lose interest. It is the same as the risk of call except that the investor, not the issuer, initiates the sale.

interest rates or falling bond prices. There are several variants in the design of a put bond. A "European" option allows bondholders to exercise a put once during a defined period, much like the closed-window provisions of certain early-retirement buyout plans. In contrast, the "American" option allows bondholders to exercise a put option periodically, usually annually, and usually after five or ten years. In both cases, the put option allows bondholders to avoid exposure to market risk, and should lead to lower rates of interest. Local governments utilizing this feature must ensure that an adequate reserve is maintained to cover the possibility that a substantial number of options are exercised during any given period.

The call provision identified in a bond covenant provides for payment of an outstanding obligation at a specified price prior to the obligation's scheduled maturity. The call or redemption provision may be either mandatory or optional. Mandatory "sinking fund" features identified in the call option require the local government to redeem a specified quantity of bonds at a specified date. Optional redemption occurs at the limited discretion of the local government. Extraordinary mandatory redemption is triggered by a major occurrence such as the abandonment of project plans. Call provisions provide the opportunity to refinance bonds when interest rates drop; it then may become economically feasible to ease the pressures on debt ceilings, and to lower overall debt service costs. However, investors prefer a higher interest rate or a premium on par for callable bonds because of the possible deterioration of capital that results when bonds are matured early.

Adjustable Rate Bonds

Adjustable rate bonds (ARBs), commonly referred to as variable or floating-rate bonds, can be used to attract investors who want to hedge against market rate increases and maintain their investment yield during these cycles. An ARB is a fluctuating amount of interest, adjusted at specified intervals and usually referenced to some standard measurement scale (such as U.S. treasury bonds or bills). There are various ways that ARBs can be structured, ranging from a floating-rate bond to an adjustable floating-rate bond.

A floating-rate bond bears a "floating" or varying interest rate. They are typically issued by local governments that want to take advantage of current tax-exempt interest expenses compared to long-term rates. A floating fixed-rate bond is similar to the floating-rate bond, with the additional stipulation that the issuer has the option at a given time to fix the rate, typically during more favorable interest rates. An adjustable floating-rate bond, which functions like the put-option bond, allows the issuer to adjust the interest rate during put periods to potentially minimize the amount of outstanding put options that will be tendered. Although ARBs have lower interest costs, they may result in uncertain debt service requirements, and local governments should plan accordingly.

Super Premium Bonds and Original Discount Bonds

Other innovations in the tax-exempt municipal securities market are the super premium bonds (SPB) and original discount bonds (ODB). In the private capital markets, an original discount bond is called a discount bond, where the stated value of the bond is sold at a discount. In contrast, a super premium bond is sold above par value, with a stated interest rate less than that of other similar issues. As a result, the bond is sold for a price considerably less than its par or stated value. Accordingly, much of the return to the investor holding a SPB will be enjoyed through the accretion in the price as the bond approaches maturity. The holders of ODBs realize a higher return early in the life cycle of the bond. One limitation of SPBs is that debt limitations may be exceeded because the value of the bonds at redemption is much greater than the proceeds received from the discount.

This brief review was undertaken to demonstrate that there are a variety of tools available to finance professionals to manage overall debt and the debt service stream. The appropriate mix of debt service and current expenditures is a policy decision subject to the constraints of state law and the standards of the financial establishment. It is certainly an area in which the local government finance professional should take an active leadership role. But once this mix is established, the identified tools allow local government finance professionals to minimize the costs of borrowing and still maintain a steady level of debt service payments. This approach minimizes disruptions to the stream of revenues available to fund current services. We have witnessed more than one case in which a local government was forced to cut back operating expenditures—with no small cost in term of service quality and employee morale—because the jurisdiction faced an increase in debt service payments over a period of several years. The short- and long-term responsibilities of local government professional managers should not have compete for attention within the public organization. As we have suggested, the long-term financial condition of the jurisdiction is partly a function of the capacity of the public organization to meet the short-term service needs of the community, and these needs cannot long be met without attending to the long-term financial condition of the jurisdiction in the short term.

THE DEBT PROCESS

Regardless of the form of the bond, the sale of public debt involves three basic phases: origination, underwriting and distribution. The origination process includes all activities necessary to prepare a new issue for sale. In most cases, local governments do not have the knowledge and expertise to prepare an issue, nor do they have the time and resources to market the bonds to investors. Local governments, therefore, often turn to an underwriting syndicate to perform these functions. The underwriting syndicate purchases the bonds from the local government at a predetermined price, and sells and distributes the securities to the investor. Each of the three phases associated with the issuance of local government debt is discussed in more detail below.

Prior to initiating a formal bond process, a determination needs to be made confirming that the local government is willing and able to borrow money from the private markets. Deciding to borrow, and how much to borrow, are both technical and managerial questions. The technical dimension centers on the capacity of the organization to service debt. This requires a determination of the debt capacity of the local government. The managerial dimension includes an examination of debt capacity in light of the long-term economic viability of the organization; the identification of the various stakeholders that must be involved in the process to ensure that debt can be serviced, and the determination that the taxpayers will not be burdened with untimely debt. All decisions to borrow are contingent upon political environment, difficulties in issuing debt, and costs, and the bond process can be stopped up until the date of sale.

Determining the amount of long-term debt that can be issued by a local unit

Table 2
Determination of Direct and Overlapping Debt, City Anywhere, FY 1998–1999

	Gross Debt Less Debt Service Assets	Percentage of Debt Applicable	Amount of Debt Applicable
Total Debt	$121,695,000		
Less debt service assets	13,665,319		
Direct Net Debt	$108,029,681	100.00%	$108,029,681[a]
Overlapping debt:			
Water and sewer fund	$20,553,000	56.23	$11,556,952
Road and bridge fund:			
General obligation	57,000	56.23	32,051
State gasoline	60,000	33.41	20,046
Bridge construction	2,200,000	56.23	1,237,060
Total	$22,870,000	56.17	$12,846,109
School Board Commission	$25,285,000	56.23	$14,217,755
Hospital Board	2,665,000	56.23	1,498,829
Total Overlapping Debt	$50,820,000	56.20	$28,563,393[b]
Total Direct and Overlapping Debt	$158,849,681	86.99%	$136,592,074[c]

a. Direct net debt, 15.56 percent of assessed value of real property; $541.64 per capita
b. Overlapping debt, 4.11 percent of assessed value of real property; $143.23 per capita
c. Direct and overlapping debt, 19.68 percent of assessed value of real property; $684.98 per capita

is a function of legal restrictions (such as state statutes, local ordinances, current debt policies or bond covenants) on the amount of debt that can be outstanding at any one point in time as well as the type of debt that can be issued. Economic factors (such as the revenue and tax base) and market conditions (such as current interest rates and market saturation) also affect the amount of debt that can be issued. Further, if a local government's credit rating is not high enough to be competitive with other issues at a given interest rate, a market may not exist to purchase bonds, or the demanded rate of interest may make the sale uneconomical.

State statutes establish limits that may not be exceeded by the governmental units that share a tax base. A given parcel of real estate may be the basis of the taxing capacity of several jurisdictions; for example, a county, a city and a school system may levy property taxes on the same parcel of land. When this situation occurs, the total debt resting on the property is referred to as "overlapping debt." The total amount of long-term debt against property located within a given local government is provided on Table 2. Analysis of this type begins with the direct debt, which is that owed by the reporting entity. To this direct debt are added amounts owed by other units and authorities that levy taxes against the same property on which the direct debt is based. Notes included as a part of Table 2 disclose the relation of direct debt and overlapping debt to assessed valuation of real property, and also reveal the amount of direct and overlapping debt borne by each resident. Another matter of importance in relation to long-term debt is the legal limitation upon the amount of long-term debt that may be outstanding at a given time, in proportion to the assessed value of property within the jurisdiction represented. This type of restriction protects taxpayers from potentially confiscatory tax rates, which would encourage citizens to exit the jurisdiction and ultimately compromise its ability to service the debt. Even though tax-rate limitation laws may be in effect for a governmental unit, an additional limitation upon bonded debt is usually needed because the prevailing practice is to exempt the claims of bond-holders from the barrier of tax-rate restrictions.

The debt margin is also an important concept. Debt limit refers to the total amount of specified kinds of debt that is allowed by law to be outstanding at any one time. The limitation is likely to be stated as a stipulated percentage of the assessed valuation of property within the government's tax boundaries. It may relate to either a gross or net valuation. A local government's debt margin refers to its borrowing power, and is the difference between the amount of debt limit calculated and the net amount of outstanding indebtedness subject to the limitation. Total general long-term debt must, in some local governments, include debt serviced by enterprise funds, if such debt was issued with covenants that give the debt tax-supported status in the event resources of the issuing fund are insufficient to meet required interest or principal payments. Although it would be in keeping with the purpose of establishing a legal debt limit to include the present value of capital lease obligations along with bonded debt in the computation of legal debt margin, state statues generally do not specify that the liability for capital leases is subject to the legal debt limit. Table 3 provides the computations of legal debt limit and legal margin.

The Origination Process

Once a decision has been made to borrow money and a determination made that the local entity has the capacity to service the debt, the next step is to start the bonding process. When the origination process for bond issues is conducted "in house," it is often completed under the guidance of an independent financial advisor, a bond counsel, and a technical advisor, such as a consulting engineer. During this phase all the necessary documents to conduct the sale of the bonds are completed. These include the official statement, the bond resolution, the bond indenture, and the notice of sale (if competitive bidding is used) or a request for proposals (if a negotiated sale is used). The official statement (OS) identifies the details concerning the bond contracts and information about the issuer, and is the primary legal document which summarizes all the salient features of the underlying documents and agreements supporting the offering. As

Table 3
Computation of Legal Debt Margin, City Anywhere, FY 1998–1999

Assessed value of real property		$831,747,280
Assessed value of personal property		72,946,720
Total Assessed Value of Real and Personal Property		$904,694,000
Debt limit, 20% of assessed value		$180,938,800
Amount of debt applicable to debt limit:		
General obligation bonds and warrants	$167,050,000	
Notes and mortgages payable	375,200	
Other	5,747,981	
	$173,173,181	
Less:		
Net assets in Debt Service Funds applicable to bonds and warrants included in legal debt limit	$10,556,755	
Items excluded from legal debt limit:		
General Obligation Warrants applicable to sewer improvements	$33,119,000	
General obligation lease with Public Building Authority	3,900,000	
	$80,575,755	
Total amount of debt applicable to debt limit		92,597,426
Legal Debt Margin		$88,341,374

a legal document, the OS is considered the primary disclosure document presenting information that is material to the offering and that is to be used by investors in determining the creditworthiness of the issuer.

Unlike a corporate prospectus, the local government's OS is not required to be registered nor is it reviewed by the Securities and Exchange Commission (SEC), although the SEC requires that the underwriter review the OS prior to purchasing the issue. To assist local governments in developing an OS that complies with SEC antifraud provisions and discloses all material information, the Government Finance Officers Association (1995) has prepared the following list of items that should included:

1. Cover page, including the name of the issuer, the date, and other pertinent information.

2. Introduction, describing all the key features of the issue and issuer.

3. The name, location, and type of government unit issuing the bonds.

4. A description of the debt structure.

5. Relevant legal matters regarding the issue.

6. The bond resolutions and bond indenture.

7. Financial information about the issuer.

The OS usually includes a reference to the bond counsel, and the opinion of the bond counsel is rendered within the statement. The role of the bond counsel is not to render an opinion as to the creditworthiness of the issue or the issuer, but to state categorically that the interest on the issue is tax-exempt according to federal income tax laws, state laws and local laws. In addition, the opinion verifies that the issue is legal, valid, and binding upon the issuer. The bond opinion is often a required component in any official statement. This opinion may be the only legal opinion contained in the official statement. The following information is commonly attested to or contained in the bond opinion:

1. The issuer possesses the power and authority to issue and sell bonds.

2. The ordinance has been duly adopted by the local authority, and it is valid, binding and enforceable.

3. The bonds that have been authorized by ordinance are executable.

4. The liens on revenues being pledged are valid, and first lien and security interests are maintained.

5. The issues are tax exempt under local, state and federal laws.

No underwriter will release an offering until a bond counsel has provided a "clean" opinion. These opinions are normally quite complex since the financing arrangements have to comply with the IRS code and regulations, rate covenants and other statutory provisions.

In addition to the bond counsel opinion, the bond indenture of trust (the bond resolution, or the contract), which is made between the borrower (the issuer) and the lender (the trustee representing the interests of the bondholder), is provided. The trust indenture establishes the exact nature of the security of the bonds and the trust provisions. For G.O. issues, a trust indenture is not normally provided, and instead the state and local statutes identifying the provisions of the revenue and security terms are identified. For revenue bonds, the trust indenture is the primary document that defines the terms of the security and financing structure of the issue, outlines the type of revenue to be pledged to pay the principal and interests (including a flow of funds), and establishes the security terms. The bond indenture must be carefully and completely defined, because this is where bondholders will look for satisfaction in the case of default. The bond indenture also includes the amount of bonds to be issued, the maturity schedule, the security pledged to pay the bonds, provisions for advanced retirement of the bonds (either refunding call or sinking fund), conditions under which additional bonds may be issued, a commitment as to the maintenance of rates so that income covers debt service, and a description of the project to be undertaken.

The Underwriting Phase

As stated previously, the sale of local government bonds involves three different activities: origination, underwriting and distribution. While both negotiated and competitive bidding involve all three activities, they differ in how these activities are combined, how the underwriting syndicate is selected, and how prices are determined. In a negotiated sale, the issuer selects a firm to serve as the managing underwriter. The selection process often involves the use of a request for qualifications or a request for proposals. Applications from potential underwriters are evaluated using a set of criteria that include the underwriter's expertise, financial resources, compatibility and experience, as well as other significant criteria. The local government issuer, together with the firm selected to serve as the senior management underwriter, then assembles an underwriting team to structure, underwrite and distribute the bonds. The terms and conditions of the offering, including the underwriter spread and planned reoffering yields, are established through a process of negotiation between the issuer and the underwriter prior to the date of issuance.

In a competitive sale, the issuer and/or its independent financial adviser will conduct the origination activities; these tasks include structuring the bond, preparing the official statement, obtaining a rating and scheduling the sale date. Once the terms of the offering are established, the sale of the bonds is advertised through a notice of sale consistent with state or local statutes. The notice of sale (NOS) should include, at a minimum, the total par value of the bonds to be sold; the maturity structure and dates; bond restrictions and covenants; interest costs; minimum amount of purchase; the time, date and place for receipt of bids; the criteria on which the issue will be awarded; the size of the good-faith deposit; the name of the bond counsel; and the name of a contact person. On the sale date, sealed bids are accepted and opened simultaneously, and the bonds are awarded to the syndicate bidding the lowest cost to the issuer. The underwriting syndicate then resells the bonds to investors.

The procedural differences between the two methods of sale, especially the manner in which underwriter compensation and planned reoffering yields are established, may lead to differences in the total borrowing cost to local governments. In addition, cost differences may depend on a number of other factors, such as front loading, true interest costs versus net interest costs, and value to market of underwriting services. The provision of services by a private underwriting syndicate is paid for by the difference between the gross proceeds received by the underwriter from the sale of the bonds on the market and the price paid to the issuer for the right to sell the bonds, and is usually denoted in terms of dollars per $1,000 par value.

The gross underwriter spread consists of four primary expense categories: takedown, management fees, underwriting risk and expenses. The largest component of the spread is the sales commission (takedown). It represents the compensation to the underwriting syndicate for selling the bonds. The charge for management services includes fees for origination and advisory services. The underwriting risk is compensation paid to the syndicate for the market risk in a fixed-price underwriting, while the expense category represents the charges for such services as printing, legal counsel, rating-agency services and the like. When a negotiated sale is used, local government managers must be careful that the relative costs of the underwriter are consistent with the issue being proposed.

The Distribution Phase

The market for local government bonds consists of a primary and secondary market. The primary market, or new-issue market, is where bonds are initially sold. Changes in federal income tax laws have altered the traditional mix of buyers of municipal bonds, but such bonds still appeal primarily to individuals and enterprises seeking to shelter assets in tax-free income streams. Investors are willing to accept lower interests rates than those offered by corporate bonds, because the federal government continues to exempt income from local government bonds from the income tax. Exemptions are filtered through tax brackets, and hence their value increases with income. For example, $10,000 in interest from a municipal bond is worth $3,500 in avoided taxes to someone in the 35 percent tax bracket, but only $2,200 for someone in the 22 percent bracket; the same persons may have received more interest by investing in a private-sector issue, but the interest income would have been subject to federal income tax.

The secondary market, or trading market, in local government bonds refers to the market in which older issues are bought and sold before their final maturity. This nationwide market consists of dealers who typically trade bonds over the counter. The existence of the secondary market also provides investors the chance to alter their portfolios in terms of the types of bonds they own, their maturities and their ratings (risk levels), and to time losses and gains in order to minimize exposure to capital gains taxes. Secondary markets give bonds the quality of liquidity, and this makes them a more attractive investment.

BOND RATINGS

Rating services, such as Moody's, Standard & Poor's, and Fitch Investors Service, contend that the rating level issued for a particular issue (or government) is not a definitive statement of the creditworthiness of the issuing entity, but is merely a product of "rules of thumb" regarding relative risk. However, investors use ratings to determine which bonds to purchase. Underwriters tend to favor investment-grade bonds, and syndicates are sometimes difficult to assemble for speculative-grade bonds. In addition, the federal government uses the ratings of these services as the benchmark for bank portfolio audits; these audits establish legal categories regarding what bonds banks, other financial institutions, and legal fiduciaries may invest in for trusts and other portfolios. The investment-grade rating is taken as an indication that issuers are highly unlikely to default on these bonds, and the federal government therefore allows the bonds to be counted at cost (rather that at market value) during day-to-day trading, when computing the solvency of a particular bank or financial institution.

A rating downgrade can severely impact the financial position of a local government, and could potentially place the entity into receivership. Bond ratings also impact the costs of marketing a bond issue, because an underwriting firm's profits are tied to bonds ratings. John Petersen (1975) concluded that an Aaa bond's average cost for an underwriting is $3.10 less per bond than the cost for a Baa. Thus the higher the rating, the lower the profit; the riskier the bond, the higher the charge for underwriting. This is virtually a self-fulfilling prophecy, for far more underwriters tend to bid on Aaa securities, and the lack of competition among underwriters also raises the price that must be paid to obtain underwriters, and so, ultimately, to sell the bonds.

Bond-rating agencies consider a variety of factors in assessing the creditworthiness of a jurisdiction. Obviously, debt policy, debt structure, debt burden and history, and potential future borrowing needs are prominent factors; however, the jurisdiction's revenue systems and budgetary history, as well as its organizational structure and managerial capacity, are also considered. The agencies look for evidence of professionalism and financial responsibility in account structures, reporting procedures, budgetary and financial planning processes, and financial control mechanisms. The finance establishment can exert considerable influence with regard to the internal structures, procedures and decision-making processes of local governments seeking to minimize their borrowing costs. The underlying economic base of the jurisdiction and the region in which it is located are critical elements; long-term trends in this area determine the jurisdiction's capacity to collect the revenues required to retire the bonds. Each rating agency weights these elements differently, and this is further evidence that normative theory in this area is weak; the details regarding specific procedures employed for particular types of issues are closely guarded by the agencies. Clearly, however, the relationships among managerial capacity, organizational development, capital planning, and economic development efforts become manifest when the long-term borrowing capacity of the public organization is formally assessed.

Local governments attempting to receive a higher rating from the rating organizations can accomplish the task by utilizing credit enhancements to back a particular issue, and/or by creating a financial environment that is conducive to higher ratings. The first approach, and perhaps the quickest, is bond insurance. Bond insurance is purchased by the local government from the bond insurance company, which guarantees payment of principal and interest in the event that the local government defaults. The premiums for this type of insurance range from .25 to 1.5 percent of the total value of the issue (including both principal and interest). A second method to receive a higher rating is through a letter of credit or line of credit issued by a bank or savings institution. A letter of credit is fundamentally a surrogate for bond insurance, with the bank pledging its creditworthiness that the local government will make the payments; if the local government does not, the bank will extend the credit necessary to make the payments. The costs of this type of arrangement to the local government are normally charged annually. A number of states also provide local governments the opportunity to participate in state credit guarantee programs. Some states have established credit funds that ensure that if a local government defaults on a bond, the state will step in and make payments to the bondholders. This type of arrangement can range from full guarantee to partial guarantee, and in both cases local governments pay a sizable premium to enter the credit program.

The efforts of local governments to fund their long-term capital development needs are clearly dependent on private investors, the expertise of private-sector finance professionals and the markets of the financial establishment. Some observers have called for states to build on their credit guarantee programs by providing funds from which their local governments can borrow, and a few states have made some progress in this direction. Local governments and the state would contribute to this revolving fund, and the funds could be borrowed at very low rates of interest. However, other observers feel that political criteria for the selection of projects to be funded would replace the financial discipline imposed by private markets and bond-rating agencies, and this would lead to the funding of financially questionable projects and a poor allocation of the funds available for capital investment. Local government financial managers should seek to increase their own knowledge regarding borrowing options, as well as the knowledge of the organization's substantive service managers. After reviewing of highly publicized municipal financial crises, Gerald Miller concluded that ''[t]he problem common to these instances of scandal, default, and waste is one of information poverty and undue deference to those who seem to help make up for it'' (1996: 384).

ALTERNATIVE LONG-TERM FINANCING METHODS

To avoid the complexities and costs associated with the bond process, a number of local governments have turned to nondebt methods for financing capital projects. One method that has gained widespread interest and use is leasing. Frequently, this method of financing is simply an agreement between the local government and the vendor who is providing the asset, such as a computer, vehicle or building. For certain items, the vendor may not want to provide the financing, and a leasing company may become involved. A leasing company acts as an intermediary in the agreement and will identify investors who are willing to provide funding for the asset in exchange for the pledge of the government's lease payments. The leasing company may sell certificates of participation (COPs) to investors for a share of the tax-free income stream. Leasing is an attractive alternative because in most cases it is not considered debt; leasing agreements are not applied to the debt ceilings, and voter approval is not required to enter into the agreement.

The determination of whether to lease or purchase an asset involves a number of important considerations. One factor that should be considered is how long the local government plans to keep the asset. Those items that will be kept for a long period would be good candidates for acquisition through debt. On the other hand, if the item is only going to be kept for a short period, it may be possible to save money through a lease arrangement, especially if the asset depreciates quickly. The second factor to be considered is the technological obsolescence of the asset. Those items, such as computers, that traditionally have a short obsolescence horizon may be more appropriate candidates for lease arrangements. However, one area that has manifested dramatic growth in capital leasing is buildings. A third factor to consider is the buy-back option that normally accompanies lease arrangements. If the lease offers a bargain price for the asset upon termination of the lease payment cycle, leasing becomes an attractive option. However, if no market exists for the resale of the leased asset, then leasing may not be a promising approach.

Local governments can use several varieties of lease arrangements to obtain all or a portion of the necessary capital. For present purposes, leases can be classified as either operating or capital leases. The most common type of lease is the operating lease, which is generally used to provide office equipment and other moderately priced capital items without having to purchase them directly. An operating lease becomes a capital lease if the terms of the lease meets any of the following criteria:

1. The lease transfers ownership of the asset to the lessee by the end of the lease term.

2. The lease contains an option to purchase the leased asset at a ''bargain'' price.

3. The lease term is equal to or greater than 75 percent of the estimated economic life of the leased asset.

4. The present value of rental or other minimum lease payments equals or exceeds 90 percent of the fair value of the leased property less any investment tax credit retained by the lessor.

In many cases the lease agreement will contain a cancellation or ''fiscal funding'' clause, which permits the governmental lessee to terminate the agreement on an annual basis if budgetary funds are not appropriated to make the required payments. Cancellation clauses are normally a matter of legal form rather than substance, because a local government could seriously damage its creditworthiness if it failed to honor its lease commitments. If the application of the funding clause is judged to be remote, the lease should be classified as a capital lease.

More recently, tax-exempt lease purchases and sale-leaseback arrangements have been used successfully by local governments. As a special type of lease purchase agreement, the tax-exempt lease provides the lessor with tax-exempt interest on the lease payment made by the local government. In a sale-leaseback arrangement, the capital asset is sold to a private investor or investment group, and some or all of it is then leased back for use by the local government. If the lease is structured as an operating lease (subject to the annual budget process), it allows the private investors the advantage of federal tax laws for depreciating fixed assets, investment incentives, and possibly investment tax credits (for renovation projects, such as buildings owned by the government and sold to an investment group, then leased back). Under this arrangement, the local government may realize a lower cost than debt service costs, because of the tax advantages realized by the investors.

MANAGERIAL ISSUES

Debt management is a vital element of the long-term financial health of local governments. Debt commits a government's revenue-generating capacity several years into the future, and a debt structure that is not managed properly may negatively impact the government's flexibility to respond to changing service priorities, local emergencies, revenue flows and cost structures. How a bond issue is sold has implications for the yields, spreads, total interest costs and ultimately the financial position of the issuing entity. Capital budgeting and debt management are concerned with the provision of the capital facilities and infrastructure necessary to support the delivery of current services and the long-term financial condition of the community. We have indicated on several occasions that positive outcomes in these two areas are core responsibilities of the public finance professional.

We have reviewed the desirability of receiving a favorable credit rating in this chapter, and have outlined the influence of bond-rating agencies in this regard. Unlike that of private corporations, the creditworthiness of local government bonds and other forms of government debt depends on a wide array of factors: the outstanding debt of the issuing entity and possible demands for additional debt, budgetary procedures employed, legal restrictions on revenues and debt levels, and managerial capacity, as well as principles of finance solvency. The knowledge necessary to assess the wide range of public offerings is difficult to acquire, and hence a relatively small group of municipal specialists strongly influences the credit rating of local governments, and ultimately the costs of capital acquisition and construction. The power of rating agencies thus extends well beyond their obvious role in the bond market. However, the histories of the financial fiascoes in New York and Cleveland in the 1970s, and more recently the investment debacle in Orange County, California, have provided clear evidence that the financial establishment puts other considerations before the financial viability of any particular local government. Local government finance professionals must learn to be much more than passive participants in the borrowing process.

In response to the identified responsibilities of the public finance professional and the suggested overdependence on private-sector influence and expertise in the borrowing process, we have attempted to outline some of the "nuts and bolts'' of borrowing. What emerges is evidence of a very arcane field that demands a high level of expertise, and this would seem to ratify the dependence on the finance establishment. However, our brief review suggests that the local government finance professional has a range of borrowing options available to him or her, and each has important implications for immediate costs and long-term obligations, as well as for the revenue stream to support current services and the financial viability of the jurisdiction. If borrowing issues are left to private-sector expertise, those experts make policy in these areas. We have indicated that a jurisdiction's debt policies are closely reviewed by bond-rating agencies, and it is in the area of debt policies that local government finance professionals can respond to the needs of the jurisdiction and also meet the criteria of the finance establishment.

We have continuously stressed that the contexts in which local government managers operate are highly idiosyncratic, and debt policies should be based on a thorough understanding of the local political culture, service history and value preferences. However, the following is a list of areas in which policies may be formulated:

1. Ratio of G.O. debt to assessed valuation of real property.
2. Ratio of total overlapping debt to assessed valuation of real property.
3. Maximum length of average weighted G.O. bond maturities.
4. Ratio of G.O. debt service to total own-source, nonenterprise revenues.
5. Per capita G.O. debt as a percent of local per-capita income.
6. Reasons for issuing G.O. debt.
7. The use of Tax Increment Financing (TIF) and special assessments.
8. Factors to be considered regarding competitive versus negotiated sale of bonds.
9. Factors regarding advance refunding of bond issues.
10. Factors for merit-based selection of underwriters in order to eliminate political awards.
11. Debt-monitoring procedures.
12. Percent of enterprise fees supporting debt service.

Obviously, the policy development process must operate within the constraints of state statutes and mandated debt policies. Debt policies should not, however, become so burdensome or be followed so tightly that they inhibit the government's legitimate efforts to provide public services and facilities.

Debt policies should be developed as part of a comprehensive package of financial management policies. This would include policies regarding taxes, fees and other revenues; fund reserves; investment goals; and budget policies. The development of these policies, including the complicated debt policies, should be a product of the management staff of the organization as a whole, including the range of substantive service managers. This enables more knowledge of the community and the value preferences of the citizens to be brought to bear on the development process. The service managers also speak for the public organization, and they can help citizens understand the need for investment in capital facilities and service infrastructure. This educative role is essential given that there is no political constituency for the long-term financial condition of the jurisdiction, and service managers are more likely to fulfill this role if they understand the policies that drove the decision-making process; they are more likely to understand if they played a part in the policies' development.

Lastly, substantive service managers must develop some level of financial knowledge in order to function effectively in their service areas. Local governments are becoming increasingly reliant on their own-source revenues, and this trend has been coupled with taxpayer resistance to increasing taxes. This means that whatever funds are available for new programs or service expansions to meet growing demands will be funds that the jurisdiction already has; reallocation of the existing pie has generally replaced the traditional allocation of a growing pie. Local government managers must become more aware of where funds are located and what is being done with them. They must learn to read Consolidated Annual Financial Reports, expenditure reports and revenue reports and they must become more knowledgeable in regard to debt policies and investment strategies. A substantive service manager who considers fiscal and financial issues solely the province of the finance professional will be a weak manager regardless of the level of his substantive knowledge.

One could conclude that if substantive service managers were armed with this knowledge they would be able to compete for funds more effectively, thus increasing the centrifugal forces that usually characterize the annual budget process. But participation in the development of policies to guide decision-making in areas such as long-term capital planning and debt serves to enhance the decision-making perspectives of service managers: it places their decision-making premises regarding their own service areas in a long-term and organization-wide context. We have contended that professional financial management broadly defined is a core element of all professional public management positions. Professionals are hired to achieve the economies associated with technological and allocative efficiencies. In order to pursue these ends effectively across the range of service areas, substantive area managers must view their services from the perspective of the community (and its economic viability) as a whole. If service managers are expected to assume this responsibility, they should participate in the development of the policies that establish the parameters for resource allocation decision-making processes in the public organization. Financial management should not be something that is done to them. Participation in the development of debt policies in particular encourages the long-term, organization-wide perspective that is also an essential element of professional public management.

The common management focus is on effective and efficient service delivery, both current and long-term, and the latter requires attention be given to the long-term financial viability of the jurisdiction. But long-term considerations often conflict with short-term needs—just as debt service diverts revenue from current services—unless they are approached from the perspective of what is best for the jurisdiction as a whole. Participation in policy development processes may help service managers integrate these perspectives, and this integrated perspective may be transferred to the annual budget process. De facto multiyear budgeting is achieved not through administrative fiat or bureaucratic mechanisms, but rather through the decision-making premises of the people involved. Decision-making clusters are integrated most effectively through people, not administrative mechanisms.

REFERENCES

Government Finance Officers Association (1995). *Development of a Debt Policy*. Washington, D.C.: GFOA.

Government Finance Research Center (1985). *Public/Private Partnerships: Financing a Common Wealth*. Washington, D.C.: GFOA.

Miller, Gerald J. (1996). "Stability and Turnover in Self-Serving Debt Networks." In Gerald J. Miller, ed., *Handbook of Debt Management*. New York: Marcel Dekker.

Petersen, John E. (1975). *The Rating Game*. Washington, D.C.: The Twentieth Century Fund.

Chapter 9

Summary and Synthesis

Of particular concern is that state budget practitioners have little useful theory to undergird their actions. . . . [P]ractitioners live in a world very much not of their own choosing and with concepts and tools that are consistently inadequate for the job expected of them. Nevertheless, it is a world in which the success of the enterprise is very much dependent upon the skills, talents, and judgment of the practitioner. It is a world of action that demands better supporting theory.

Merl M. Hackbart and Ronald J. Carson (1993)

This book is, in part, a polemic on the future of budget theory. The approach to budget theory outlined here is based on the assumption that, as an applied field, public administration should seek to develop theories that have utility for public administrators—that is, practical theories that identify possibilities for action or illuminate the nature of the practitioner's action environment. If the field is to produce practical budget theories, it must view the budget process from the perspective of practitioners. Local government practitioners practice in public organizations, and they experience budgeting as the resource allocation process of their organizations. The public organization's structure, culture, internal processes and administrative procedures, and network of external relationships define the local government practitioner's action environment. Thus, this book calls for the development of budget theory for local government grounded in the operation of public organizations and built with concepts from organization theory.

In short, public budgeting is conceptualized herein as an organizational process through which resources are ultimately allocated to the various components that comprise the organization, rather than as a formal political process through which a community decides who gets what, how much they get, and who pays for it. The boundaries of the local government organization are highly permeable, particularly during the formal budget process. The highly differentiated nature of the multiservice local government organization has enormous implications for budgeting. The various agencies that comprise the organization are typically united under a single executive, however, and this makes our organizational approach a tenable one. This approach points to a normative theory of local government budgeting, can provide a unique budgetary focus for public administration, and serves to align budgeting with theory building in public management in general. In this chapter we review past efforts at integrating organization theory and budgeting, and we explore possible avenues for achieving this synthesis. But first we review the normative implications of our framework and the connections between resource allocation and public management.

THE ROLE OF THE FINANCE PROFESSIONAL

The finance professional as economic analyst becomes irrelevant when theorists approach budgeting as a purely political process, and as a political actor his or her professional identity is lost. Rational analysis will never drive the policy-making process, so the finance professional is reduced to expertise on tap. On the other hand, the finance professional's claim to expertise carries no weight if he or she is just another politician. In this scenario, the finance professional becomes the technician who designs budget processes and tracks public expenditures. But if one approaches budgeting as an organizational process, the finance professional is cast in a new light. In a private-sector organization, the role of the finance professional is to provide for the long-term financial viability of the organization. The nature of the private-sector firm allows the finance professional to exercise this responsibility through the executive team in a top-down fashion. We contend that local government finance professionals have the same responsibility as their private-sector counterparts. However, the highly differentiated nature of the local government organization means that this responsibility must be pursued through the annual budget process. The budget process is the only organization-wide process or administrative system that integrates all of the agencies that comprise the local government organization, and the budget is a legal document through which the necessary authority can be exercised. The second characteristic that differentiates the private and the public finance professional is that the latter must attend to the long-term financial viability of the political jurisdiction in order to exercise his or her professional responsibility to the organization. A normative theory of public budgeting for public administration should be grounded in the organizational roles of the professionals involved, rather than in the formal budget process as a stand-alone, decontextualized phenomenon. Hence, our first proposition in a normative theory of local government budgeting is:

1. The local government finance professional should seek to protect the long-term financial viability of the jurisdiction during the annual budget process.

This is not to say that there is one best way, discoverable through structured analysis, to provide for long-term financial viability. Neither should the finance professional be given unfettered ability to implement any optimal solution on the basis of his or her expertise. The maintenance of the long-term financial viability of the jurisdiction is not simply a technical exercise, just as the viability of the private firm can be pursued in a variety of ways. The finance professional's role in the public organization and the public nature of the issue mandate that he or she bring the issue to the annual budget process. The lack of a political constituency dedicated to maintaining the financial viability of the jurisdiction augments the seriousness of this obligation, and serves to legitimize the professional's participation in the political process of determining the nature of that viability. This is essentially a political end, but it cannot be effectively pursued without the conscious involvement of the finance professional.

The finance professional spotlights the overall issue as a professional responsibility, illuminates options with structured analyses in his or her role as an expert, and inevitably champions policy alternatives as a political actor. The values that guide the managerial decisions that inevitably affect substantive policies lie in the professional's responsibility to the public organization and the political jurisdiction which it serves. These values reflect core professional responsibilities that are exercised through the organization. These values must ultimately manifest themselves in policies, not simply in processes. The professional provides processes for the articulation of alternatives, informs the policy-making process with structured analyses, and participates in the bargaining process. It is time for the city manager to quit when he or she must implement a substantive policy that will seriously compromise the capacity of the local government organization to provide for the general welfare of the citizens of the jurisdiction or will endanger the long-term financial viability of the jurisdiction. This decision will be based on the manager's evaluation of substantive policy in light of his or her professional responsibility. The focus on the public organization leads to our second proposition:

2. The finance professional should use the budget process to enhance the managerial capacity of the local government organization to meet the short-term needs of the citizens.

The technological efficiency of substantive service delivery systems is primarily the responsibility of the managers that drive them. However, the allocative efficiency of the mix of services is partly the responsibility of the finance professional. This follows from the first proposition, in that a jurisdiction that does not meet the short-term needs of its citizens will not be able to long maintain its financial viability. Any technological efficiencies achieved by the police department, for example, are blunted if the allocation scheme is inefficient of if they come at the expense of overall allocative efficiency. The capacity to make decisions that reflect a concern for the jurisdiction as a whole is a function of organizational culture, values, communication and trust, as well as the structure of the organization and its administrative systems. Thus, finance professionals have an organizational development responsibility, because they exercise their professional obligations through the public organization. The finance professional should employ the budget process—which, once again, is the only system that ties together the multiple service areas that comprise the local government organization—to enhance the capacity of the organization's managers to make allocation decisions that reflect the need to meet overall short-term service needs and long-term viability requirements.

We have used the term finance professional to refer to budgeters and financial analysts, but financial professionalism is an element in the job description of all public managers. All professional public managers are responsible for the efficient, effective and economical delivery of public services. But the traditional budget process does not encourage public managers to make short-term decisions from the perspective of long-term financial viability or overall allocative efficiency. Obviously, both of these ends are ultimately a matter of political philosophy, but the professional managers should appreciate that they must make decisions from this perspective. They usually do not, because the traditional budget process encourages self-serving behavior and mindless budget maximization. The finance professional should guide the application of these decision criteria within the public organization, and the budget process should be used as a vehicle for their development and application.

There is no body of knowledge that tells the finance professional exactly how to ensure long-term financial viability, what-short term needs should be met at what levels, or how to balance the two. Important factors and salient variables are woven into local context, and the identification of the optimal service mix and appropriate long-term goals is ultimately a product of the political process. However, the finance professional should inform the resource allocation process with knowledge of local context. Hence, our third proposition is:

3. The finance professional should systematically build knowledge of local context into the public organization, and see that it is applied during the budget process.

The short-term allocative scheme will not be responsive to local needs unless these are monitored and understood. The electoral process is not very precise in this regard and, in the short-term that is usually its focus, the political process may produce an allocation plan that is not very responsive to the jurisdiction's overall needs. As indicated above, there is no real political constituency for long-term financial viability. However, it is the responsibility of the finance professional to inform the budget process regarding the relationship of any proposed resource allocation scheme to meet the community's service needs, and regarding the implications that plan holds for long-term financial viability. The local government organization can provide the institutional memory and continuity needed to learn from contextual data and trends.

These three propositions, rooted in the organizational role of the finance professional, point to a normative theory of local government budgeting, or what budgeting "should be" on the local level. Budgeting should be responsive to short-term needs, should provide for long-term financial viability, should enhance managerial capacity to make decisions consistent with these ends, and should be based on knowledge of the context in which these ends will be pursued. We are less sure about how these ends can be pursued, partly because of the idiosyncratic nature of local government organizations and partly because so little budgeting research has been conducted from an organizational perspective. The remainder of the chapter will explore possible remedies for the latter point, but first we offer the following advice in summary of the book. We hesitate to cast these as prescriptions, because different local government organizations will manifest different needs and capacities, and, once again, many are little more than hypotheses to be tested at this point.

1. Local governments should adopt budget formats that provide for the explicit consideration of public policy outcomes.

This option can mitigate the centrifugal forces generated by the highly differentiated local government organization by providing a common focus on the general welfare of the community. The focus on policy outcomes signals the various agencies that they are working as a single organization. However, an organization that has achieved a satisfactory level of allocative efficiency in a mix of services supported by a strong political consensus may not have to expend the energy required by these formats. On the other hand, a community torn by political divisiveness regarding these issues may not be able to get through a budget process that focuses on policy outcomes. We recommend a target-base format that takes advantage of the capacity of the organization to compare alternative service levels at the margin. Some jurisdictions may need a true zero-base format with in-depth analysis of programs over a four-year cycle, as described in Chapter 2. Others may have to settle for an outcome-monitoring system as a first step toward building political consensus. Professional public administration promises efficiency, effectiveness and economy in the delivery of public services, and this cannot be accomplished without a focus on policy outcomes.

2. Local government organizations should develop an analytical capacity connected to the budget process.

A focus on policy outcomes will inevitably generate political conflict that must be informed by structured analysis of policy options. Internally, the connection to the budget process will give a "stick" to the analytical capacity and also provide potential "carrots" to encourage meaningful participation. We have suggested that the typical multiservice local government organization probably houses a broad range of analytical skills, substantive experience and practical knowledge that can be brought to bear on identified organizational, managerial and operational problems. Personnel with relevant skills can be brought together in temporary ad hoc groups to address specific issues. These "focus groups" also help to develop the organizational perspective described in #1 above. The focus on policy outcomes and the use of analytical techniques, and not simply the overnight adoption of canned management programs, must be the goals of a continuous organizational development processes.

3. Local government organizations should regularly measure and monitor the outcomes of their public programs.

These data support policy-making and analysis, but they also provide communication within the organization and between the organization and the community. We contend that the process of constructing a performance measurement system can also help develop the organizational perspective required in #1 above. The performance measurement system itself, however, should be continuously monitored and adjusted in light of the still primitive state of the art of performance measurement and the potential for generating perverse behaviors. There is also the problem of meeting the informational needs of operating managers, top management and the public with one system; once again, however, the effort can serve to enhance communication among these groups.

4. The budget process should occur within the context of long-term policy planning and concern for the long-term financial viability of the jurisdiction.

Annual budgets and short electoral cycles militate against a long-term perspective in the budget process. The local government organization should have the memory and continuity necessary to extend the budget process in light of the legal constraints on real multiyear budgeting and the policy changes often precipitated by elections. Rational policy-making and attention to long-term financial viability require a multiyear perspective. Such a perspective is precluded when agencies act as individual political actors and the organization sees its role as simply mediating among conflicting political demands. The local government organization must acknowledge and provide for its consensus-building role. Long-term financial viability and allocative efficiency cannot be achieved in a piecemeal fashion. This is not to say that the necessary consensus will not evolve and change, but only that short-term decisions should be made in some long-term context. The implementation of long-term finance monitoring systems, such as the ICMA's Financial Trend Monitoring System, should also be considered.

5. Economic development programs, debt administration and capital budgeting should be closely coordinated with the budget process.

The need to staff and maintain capital facilities should not place a burden on current service levels. The capital budget process should identify the impacts of each project on the operating budget. Debt policies should be set and payments leveled so that debt service does not disrupt the flow of funds to operating expenditures. Capital projects and debt should support economic development efforts. The need to adopt a regional perspective in economic development programs does not obviate the need to consider local impacts. The relationship between economic development programs and long-term financial viability, as well as the jurisdiction's capacity to maintain service levels, is self-evident. This relationship should be attended to even if the viability strategy consists of the no-growth maintenance of the status quo. The bases of individual revenues must be monitored even with a no-growth policy regarding the economic base of the jurisdiction in order to identify potential revenue gaps. The top managers of the various substantive service delivery systems should be involved in these long-term planning efforts. This participation can develop a long-term decision-making perspective that can carry over to the annual budget process and enhance the capacity of the organization to produce rational allocative schemes.

6. *Revenue systems are as crucial as expenditure patterns in determining the efficiency of the resource allocation scheme and long-term financial viability.*

Revenue systems effect economic development and access to current services. Finance professionals should not simply view the jurisdiction's revenue structure as a constraint within which expenditure demands must be met. The nature of the revenue structure expresses political values in the same manner as expenditure patterns. The widespread adoption of user fees may constrain any capacity to redistribute income at the local government level and meet community needs, while the adoption of progressive tax systems may hamper economic development efforts. The implementation of special taxing districts can fragment the policy-making process. The revenue structure of the local jurisdiction should be explored as a variable for achieving allocative efficiency and pursuing long-term financial viability.

In the first chapter of this book we suggested that resource allocation decisions and decisions that affect the nature of the formal budget process are always taking place within the local government organization. This is why research efforts that focus exclusively on the formal process cannot produce descriptive theory that is accessible to, or normative theory that is useful to, local government managers. Thus we must acknowledge the political role of the professional public administrator. This role is based on the administrator's professional role in the public organization, which is created by the political process and thus enables and legitimizes the administrator's political responsibilities. The professional public administrator is not cast as an atomistic political actor seeking to maximize his or her own self-interest, which clearly puts the unelected professional at odds with the values of the democratic process. Neither is the issue avoided by casting the professional as a value-free technician, in which case researchers can only provide instrumental theories regarding the application of management and analytical techniques. Democracy created professional public management, and enabled public managers to exercise professional expertise in public organizations; responsive theory-building efforts should approach public management through its organizational environment.

ISSUES IN BUDGET THEORY

In this section we examine some of the reasons why budget theory has not been responsive to the needs of public managers. According to Naomi Caiden (1990), public budgeting has been studied from three (usually divergent) perspectives: economics, management, and political science. In Chapter 1, we suggested that the fact that federal, state and local governments all do something called budgeting does not necessarily mean that they all do the same thing. Here we suggest that the fact that economists, political scientists and public administrators all study something called budgeting does not necessarily mean that they are all studying the same thing.

Budgeting studies rooted in economics tend to focus on the nature of public goods and the allocative efficiency of the mix of goods and services provided by government. Budgeting is approached as a subset of the larger problems of the efficient utilization of societal resources, and decision rules and allocation processes, including markets, are examined for their relative utilities in this regard. Recent efforts have also sought to construct models of public-sector decision making using concepts from microeconomics. The specter of the public administrator as budget maximizer is a central element in these scenarios. Economic models offer compelling logic, mathematical elegance, and simple forms that sidestep value issues, but Caiden concludes that "these theoretical excursions . . . [offer] remarkably little guidance to the budgeter in the practical world" (1990: 233).

Political scientists, of course, highlight the political dimensions of the resource allocation process and the budget's role in the policy-making process. The political perspective has been dominated by the theory of incrementalism, which began as a descriptive theory but achieved normative status in some circles. Incrementalism holds that public budgets were the products of a bottom-up, fragmented process that deferred to substantive expertise and previous allocation decisions; its normative manifestation holds that public policies should be made through such a piecemeal process in a pluralistic society, given the nature of the problems addressed and the dearth of causal knowledge. Political scientists characterize public agencies as atomistic actors in this political process. Lance LeLoup (1988) has questioned whether the incrementalist model was ever an accurate description of public budgeting as a whole, and maintains that it certainly ignores the role of the executive. LeLoup concludes that a top-down approach centered on overall fiscal policy began to gain a foothold at the federal level with the Budget and Impoundment Control Act of 1974. At the local level, this top-down approach, centered on the chief executive officer (given the part-time nature of legislative bodies), has always been a more accurate description of budgeting.

The economist studies economics and the political scientist studies political systems, and each naturally perceives and arranges reality to meet their needs. The less ambitious management school focuses on the relative strengths and weaknesses of various budget formats, and on the place of analytical techniques and formal policy planning in the budget process. It approaches budgeting as a technical process, and the prescriptions written from the management orientation are only accidentally based on descriptive or explanatory studies associated with any of the three perspectives. The management perspective is the one most obviously associated with public administration, and the utility of its prescriptions for enhancing the efficiency and rationality of the budgetary process is constrained by the same question that has dogged the field as a whole: efficiency for what? The management perspective focuses on professional administrators as technicians apart from the organizations in which they work and the political environments in which these organizations function. By separating the manager from the organization, the management perspective can avoid value issues. It also fails to address the allocative efficiency concerns of the economists, the budget maximizer of the public-choice model, the political issues of distributional equity and popular participation, or the challenge to the relevancy of analysis posed by the incrementalist model.

Another reason that budget theory prescriptions have been divorced from budget theory descriptions is that most of the latter have been based on studies of the federal budget process, and adoption of the former has been more widespread at the state and local levels. The substance of the dominant incrementalist description of the national budget process obviously limits the relevancy of management tools, but any descriptive theory of budgeting derived from analysis of the federal process will be of limited relevance on the local level. On the other hand, local government budget processes differ widely, and hence that area is a less fertile one for the development of a single theory of public budgeting than is the national budget process. The "grandness" of the theory derived from a focus on the federal government, however, is ultimately dimmed by its limited generalizability to other levels of government. The management perspective has left practitioners with an impressive array of tools for action, but no general guides to action.

The conceptual confusion and substantive fragmentation that characterize budget theory reflect the multidimensional nature of the subject, the variety of approaches brought to bear on it, and the fragmented structure of the field of public administration in general. The perspectives and findings of a range of related disciplines regarding a variety of relevant phenomena are imported by public administration but never synthesized to form a theoretical perspective that the field can call its own. The public organization focus of this book addresses shortcomings within the field of public administration that prevent it from establishing itself as a stand-alone discipline. It allows the field to plat the area between political science and economics as its own turf for budget theorizing. A multidisciplinary "borrowing field" such as public administration should reformulate and synthesize in order to stamp its borrowing as something more than simple duplication. The public organization and its environment can also function as the framework for a comparative approach to budgeting and financial management, one that can generate theories rooted in alternative organizational arrangements. Possible contingencies include organizational structure, form of government, degree of internal differentiation, political culture, financial condition and the nature of the intergovernmental network. The approach will also allow the public resource allocation process to be examined in the context of other organizational systems and processes, thus overcoming the constraints and limitations on theory building imposed by the fragmentation of public administration into compartmentalized subfields.

PREVIOUS ORGANIZATION-BASED STUDIES

Resource allocation issues dominate the organizational environments of local government managers. From their perspective, the formal budget process has the potential to continuously re-create the public organization. The appropriateness of the goals and technologies that define the organization is always in question, due to differences in political values and the general lack of cause-and-effect knowledge regarding many public issues. These goals and technologies are manifested in resource allocation schemes, and the budget process can potentially change organizational goals, enable new technologies that have resource allocation implications, and legitimize alternative organizational arrangements. The nature of these processes and the bases on which these decisions are made constitute the basic stuff of public management, describe the environment of the practicing administrator, and delineate the theoretical turf of public administration.

But few studies have approached budgeting from an organizational perspective. The most fully developed model is provided by Gerald Miller (1991) in his theory of government financial management. In Miller's theory of financial management, the financial manager must deal with the ambiguity and uncertainty precipitated by the social construction of an organizational reality by a variety of actors. These actors manifest a range of perspectives on and interpretations of organizational mechanisms, processes and other phenomena, such as the budget process. For Miller, traditional financial management theory is based on the assumption that there is considerable consensus about organization goals and technologies in public organizations, but this assumption may not hold for most governmental organizations. In this scenario, budget managers manipulate symbols and produce rituals centered on the common element of resource constraints. These serve to bridge the range of alternative visions of the organization's enterprise made possible by the absence of ''the widespread notion of 'making a profit' '' (Miller, 1991: 101). The budget office becomes a salient organizational actor and a unifying metaphor in an environment characterized by resource scarcity. Miller works from an interpretive paradigm, but the need for contextual analysis does not necessarily preclude positivist approaches.

Donald Gerwin (1969) developed a simulation model of the factors that influence the budget-making process in the administration of a public school system. Organizational structure, however, was not an explicit component of the model. Studies in this vein illustrate a core problem in building theories of budgeting: effective theory building requires a common focus for the examination of the multitude of elements that comprise the resource allocation process. The public organization can provide such a focus on the local government level. Irene Rubin (1979) examined the responses of five state universities to budget

cutbacks in an effort to determine the relationship between resource reductions
and the organizational concept of "loose coupling." This study was weakened
by conceptual confusion regarding the nature of "loose coupling." Conceptual
confusion is not uncommon in organization theory, and the need to develop a
certain level of facility in the fields of both organization theory and budgeting
can be daunting.

Rubin (1990, 1993) has also indicated that budget theorists must begin look-
ing inside operating departments for evidence of nonincremental policy outcomes, but this agency role is often manifested outside of the formal budget
process. Witness the police agency that reorganizes itself from a hierarchically
structured, legalistic organization to a decentralized agency featuring community-based policing. Although this change represents a major re-allocation of
resources and reorientation of substantive policy, it may not affect the agency's
operating budget. This example demonstrates the need for a broader definition
of budgeting rooted in the public organization. Tom Lynch developed an approach to public budgeting that focuses on

explaining those aspects of public budgeting involving policy-making, management, and
the interrelationship of policy and management. With a better theoretical knowledge of
that phenomenon, one can use that understanding to argue for change in the way that
activities are conducted in a bureaucracy. (1989: 325)

However, his model rests at an abstracted "systems" level, which he recognizes
may not be intuitively accessible to practitioners. Many theories of organizations
tend to reify their subject, and conceptual abstraction may become an issue with
any organization-based approach to budget theory.

Other studies have examined organizational dimensions of specific budgeting
processes, such as forecasting (Klay, 1985), decision sequencing (Whicker and
Sigelman, 1991), the adoption of budget reforms (Rubin, 1992), the supplemental budget process (Forrester and Mullins, 1992), and budget analyst behavior
(Thurmaier, 1995; Willoughby, 1993). These studies indicate that an important
link exists between the structure of the public organization and the nature of the
jurisdiction's budget process, and they highlight some of the areas in which
organization theory may be able to illuminate that relationship. The works of
Thurmaier and Willoughby are particularly relevant here; they focus on the
decision-making criteria of budget analysts and how these influence the budget
process. A natural next step is to trace the source of these criteria, which will
inevitably be influenced by organizational culture and structure.

None of the above studies manifests the approach to the building of budget
theory outlined in this book. Most employ specific concepts from organization
theory to examine individual components of the budget process. None proposes
to form a new basis for the development of budget theory by casting the formal
budget process as a part of the organization's resource allocation system. Miller's (1991) approach is the most fully developed in that it focuses on the highly

differentiated nature of the multiservice public organization and the potential for an integrative role for the budgetary process. In the following section, we outline some potential theoretical bridges between organization theory and budgeting.

PUBLIC BUDGETING AND ORGANIZATION THEORY

The concepts of differentiation and integration that have been featured in this book were first employed in an organizational context by Paul Lawrence and Jay Lorsch (1967). They describe how a complex environment requires an organization to become more differentiated in order to deal with the variety of demands emanating from its environment. Responses to demands for differentiation generate the problem of integration—that is, resolving the inevitable conflicts that arise from multiple perspectives and thus maintaining the identity of the organization. These researchers pinpoint the need for the emergence of conflict regulators in such an organization. Lawrence and Lorsch held that the ability of certain persons to resolve conflicts may be based on their perceived expertise rather than on the formal authority attached to their positions in the organization. However, we may want to explore the capacity of the centralized budget office to serve in a conflict regulation mode. Additionally, we may want to know how the centrifugal forces in multiservice local government organizations are affected by internal service funds and other fund structures, the earmarking of funds to certain services, the adoption of user fees, performance measurement systems, and other finance related systems. These centrifugal forces militate against the promise of professional public management, and studies of the efficiency, economy and effectiveness of public service delivery systems (and hence the allocative and technological efficiency of the resource allocation scheme) should be carried out in this context.

James Thompson (1967) has constructed a three-core theory of organizational structure, representing an attempt to reconcile the ideas that organizations can be opened to influences from their environments and yet function as rational tools to achieve a given end. He separates the boundary-spanning and the operational technologies of the organization (conceptually if not physically), and he identifies the managerial core as the one that mediates potential conflicts between the two and buffers the latter from possible shocks from the environment. The central point here is that organizations act to shield their core technologies from external influences. Thompson's framework may be serve for studies of agency behavior in the budget process. For example, zero-base budgeting was designed to encourage managers to reexamine and remake their core technologies; researchers can approach the local government organization as the environment of the individual agencies, and the efforts of the latter to protect their core technologies from environmental shocks in order to preserve their internal identities can be examined in this context.

Another approach to the idea that organizations are at once closed and open systems is the concept of loose coupling (Orton and Weick, 1990; Weick, 1979).

Interdependent elements of an organization are linked to form its identity and technology. These closed, rational aspects of organizational functioning are described by the term "coupled"; the fact that these elements are independent to some degree and their functioning open to other influences is captured by the adverb "loosely." Douglas Orten and Karl Weick (1990) point out that the concept allows organization theorists to approach organizations as simultaneously open and closed systems, exhibiting rationality and indeterminacy without identifying distinct locations for these properties. We have identified the resource allocation process as a dimension of organizational functioning, serving to couple the various service delivery systems that comprise the local government organization. The budget process can function as a tool for local government managers to establish the degree of coupling that optimizes the outcomes of the resource allocation process. The relationships among the budgeting process, loose coupling, and managerial decision-making perspectives are possible targets of explanatory theory building. The definition of the necessary optimal outcomes in an organizational context must be a product of normative theory building. In the view espoused here, optimal outcomes are those that provide for the long-term financial viability of the jurisdiction, including the efficient, effective and economical delivery of services to meet immediate needs.

The public organization is also coupled to its external environment, and this dimension is characterized by the exercise of political power. The concept of power and its effects on organizational structure, functions and development are prominently featured in organization theory (Perrow, 1986; Pfeffer, 1981; Salancik and Pfeffer, 1977). Terry Moe contends that

[t]he great challenge for public administration is to integrate politics and organization. The fact is, bureaucracy arises out of politics. Decisions about where agencies are located or how they are structured, staffed, and controlled are not made in some objective fashion by organizational theorists dedicated to the public good but by politicians and groups who are well aware that the details of organization are often crucial determinants of who gets what in politics. (1994: 18)

Gerald Salancik and Jeffrey Pfeffer (1977) make the point that one must look to environmental relationships in order to understand how power is exercised within an organization, and they demonstrate that power is dependent on how the critical issues, uncertainties and problems facing the organization are defined. Power will gravitate to those in a position to address these criticalities. Salancik and Pfeffer also warn that those with power are in a position to define those criticalities, and they may do so in terms that are conducive to continuing their exercise of power, rather than in terms that will provide an effective organization response to the actual demands of the environment. Public-sector practitioners experience power as a function of a variety of relationships with multiple constituencies, and they are certainly familiar with how these relationships can distort resource allocation priorities. The power approach also points to the necessity for finance professionals to establish the long-term financial viability of the jurisdiction as a critical organizational issue.

Organization theory can also provide a context and theoretical framework for theorizing about microlevel budgetary processes. The work of Thurmaier (1995) and Willoughby (1993) on the decision-making processes of budget analysts reflects the unobtrusive controls on decision-making outlined in Herbert Simon's classic work on the subject (1976). Theories regarding the substance of such criteria must also account for their source, and this suggests a marriage of budgeting and organization theory. Simon would contend that the organization defines rationality in the budget process. What has come to be called "garbage can theory" (March and Olsen, 1979) indicates that an element of control can be maintained even in an organization characterized by the absence of clear-cut preferences, a poor cause-and-effect knowledge base, questionable technologies and ambiguous environments, as is often the case in the local government organization. An exclusive focus on individual discretion in decision making overlooking organizational context may overstate the significance of the former. An organization approach would allow researchers to examine the application of technical, political and economic criteria by budget analysts in a common framework housing multiple realities.

Organization theory can also provide budget theorists access to macrolevel organizational functioning. J. Kenneth Benson (1975, 1982) constructs a political economy of interorganizational relationships that centers on the properties of the network in which the organization functions. These include both internal dependencies and network linkages to the larger pattern of social organizations. This model also encompasses management action within the individual organizations. Organizations pursue money and authority, and managers are oriented to extending and defending the organization's definition of its tasks and technologies, maintaining an orderly flow of resources, establishing a clear domain of high social importance, and fulfilling the organization's program requirements. Todd LaPorte (1996) contends that public organizations are encountering networks at a growing pace. Horizontal and vertical intergovernmental relationships, as well as private-public partnerships and contract management, can be approached by researchers as networks of organizations. Gage (1990) has characterized the present federalist structure as "budget-driven federalism," and public-sector management in this system is cast as the management of interdependencies. The intergovernmental and organizational network aspects of the resource allocation process are often overlooked by budget theorists, and are treated as separate subjects, partly because budget researchers do not have a common locus from which to examine them. When budgeting is cast as an organizational process, the environment of the organization can be conceptually linked to the budget process. Budget theorists can also focus on the resource issues that run through the various levels of Benson's model, and can illuminate the nature and role of fiscal relationships in LaPorte's approach to the structure of public-sector service delivery systems.

In the organization approach outlined here, budget researchers would also have a locus to apply postmodern approaches (Farmer, 1994; Fox and Miller, 1995) to budget theory building. Postmodernism encompasses a range of philosophical thought and social analyses, and it is not possible to summarize this rich literature here. Miller (1991) employs concepts from this school in his study of the organizational roles of budgeting and financial management. For postmodernists, organizations are simply socially constructed abstractions, rather than objective realities to which people react. Organizations are products of a field of social forces, and public organizations are produced through forces that bear on public concerns. In order for these organizations to reflect democratic values, they must be the product of open, authentic social discourse; otherwise they and their processes, including the budget process, are coercive. For some, the principal role of the professional public administrator is to facilitate such social discourse. By reifying public organizations and treating processes such as budgeting as purely technical endeavors, practitioners and theorists subvert true discourse.

Postmodernists are concerned with the nature of the language in which social discourse is conducted. Language should be authentic, sincere and clear, and discourse should be undertaken willingly, in the context of the public interest, and by making a substantive contribution to the process. In the approach outlined here, the substantive contribution of the finance professional is his or her professional expertise, but this must be contributed in a nonauthoritarian manner. This is particularly true in discourses regarding the long-term financial condition of the jurisdiction, and regarding the capacity of the public organization, rightly understood, to respond to and meet the service demands of the public. Neither can be discovered without noncoercive discourse. Social discourse is a continuous process, and any claim to ultimate knowledge is subversive and authoritarian; hence, institutions and the language through which they are created must be continuously deconstructed. For example, David Farmer (1994) outlines the many meanings of budgeting in history, and he demonstrates that these meanings are continuously evolving. Peter Manning (1992) describes how the categories that police agencies employ to define calls for service influence service outcomes. The role of the budget process as an internal and environmental communication process is highlighted here.

Another relatively new approach to public management is chaos theory (Kiel, 1994; Overman, 1996). In this view, order emerges from chaos rather than from a cycle or process through which management seeks to exercise control. Managers tend to tighten controls when chaos is at hand, but instability, disorder and variation can be approached as opportunities for change, learning and innovation. Following the prescriptions of the "self-organizing organization" school, chaos theorists hold that work processes and interaction systems will find their own points of equilibrium. Here, too, the reified organization and its control systems are characterized as inhibitors of natural processes. L. Douglas Kiel specifically cites the budget process as an external source of imposed order and a constraint on the capacity of public managers to perform effectively. Chaos theory encourages budget theorists and practitioners to view the resource allocation process as more than a series of linear events that comprise the budget cycle.

The public sector is only beginning to recognize the implications of the simultaneous pursuit of control and managerial effectiveness. Creativity, commitment and ownership cannot be commanded through administrative control systems and organizational hierarchies. These are the products of a supporting organizational culture that can be developed through the budget process in the local government organization, and can also serve an unobstrusive control function. The popular management literature on building new forms of "learning" organizations (Morgan, 1993; Senge, 1994) is relevant here.

The "reinventing government" movement (Osborne and Gaebler, 1992) also offers challenges for budget theorists, if for no other reason than that it is driven by practitioners and centers on budgeting. A tenet of the "reinventing" platform is that controls on the use of inputs by public managers should be removed, and managers should be held accountable for achieving policy outcomes. This movement directly addresses the control-effectiveness paradox that characterizes public management. Practitioners clearly connect budgeting to public management and organizational functioning in ways not considered by traditional budget theory. The gap between public management theory and budget theory has been partially filled by researchers employing principal-agent models and transaction cost analysis (Garvey, 1993; Williamson, 1994). These market-based theories undergird the privatization and contracting-out movements, rather than informing and supporting public managers. The public administration literature, manifesting the segregation of budgeting from public management in general, has had very little to say in the face of the market-based challenge, and hence little to say in support of public managers.

As a field of study, organization theory has been plagued by its own fragmentation, conceptual confusion and paradigmatic debates. W. Graham Astley and Andrew Van de Ven (1983) have identified six core theoretical debates in the field, but they contend that integration of these apparently incompatible perspectives is possible if they are approached as presenting different pictures of the same phenomenon. Gareth Morgan (1993) reached similar conclusions in his characterization of organizational life as inherently a paradoxical arena, where multiple perspectives must be brought to bear in order to diagnose, understand and act. The reality of organizational life, particularly life in public organizations, is suggestive of Aaron Wildavsky's (1961) "twilight zone" metaphor that opened this book. Organization theory is not presented here as the promised land for budget theory, but practitioners are generally more receptive to theoretical abstractions when those abstractions deal with the real world of practice.

CONCLUSION

The authors of this book do not seek to identify a single theory of local government budgeting and resource allocation processes and structures, organizationally based or otherwise. We have sought to demonstrate the potential of grounding budget theory in organizational functioning. We did not seek to identify the range of hypotheses possible in light of the myriad theoretical perspectives, but three preliminary testable hypotheses are presented here in order to illuminate the nature of the posited relationship between budgeting and organizational functioning. First, the range of alternative budgeting systems available to a given jurisdiction is determined to a great extent by the degree of integration manifested by the public organization. Second, in a reciprocal relationship the type of budget process employed also helps to establish the extent of organizational integration. Third, effective integration enhances management's capacity to provide a responsive mix of services more efficiently.

Traditional budget theory has given practitioners theories of political processes in which they can take little more than a layman's interest and management tools that are divorced from their action environments. If, as Irene Rubin (1990) contends, the field of budgeting is to become less restrictive in regard to what is important to budget theory, then it must find a locus to center its new foci. Organization theory should be one of those foci, and the public organization can serve as that locus. Organization-based budget theory will allow researchers to communicate with practitioners using a language, symbols, concepts and contexts that have meaning for practicing public administrators.

John Gargan (1993) suggests that a profession is a relationship among three areas of activity: theory generation, theory translation and advocacy, and theory implementation and routinization. Public administration researchers function in the first and second areas—at the very least the second: translating, reforming and synthesizing theories that may have been generated in other disciplines. Practitioners are responsible for the implementation and routinization of these operationalized theories. However, practicing public administrators cannot meet this responsibility if they are not provided with theories grounded in their action environments. Organization-based budget theory not only provides a common locus for a variety of theoretical perspectives on budgeting, it can also serve as a common focus for theorizing about the variety of functions that comprise public management. Practitioners are not simply budgeters or personnel managers, nor are they budgeters one moment and personnel managers the next; they are budgeters, personnel managers, program evaluators, organization theorists, etc., all at once. They need theories that reflect the reality of public management in order to educate the public about public management and meet the challenges of privatization, reinvention and coproduction.

Microlevel research in budgeting systems, strategies and tools need not be cast as untheoretical studies of analytical techniques, and macrolevel budgeting theories need not be limited to generalizing about political processes and economic impacts. Organization-based budget theory also points to a normative theory of budgeting rooted in the profession of public finance. Wildavsky (1961) contended that the development of a single normative theory of budgeting is a utopian dream in that it would signify the end of political conflict over the government's role in society. This assessment reflects the view that budgeting is virtually synonymous with politics. Normative budget theory for the public administrator would be focused somewhere between Wildavsky's macrolevel of societal values and the purely instrumental level manifested by the traditional management school. Normative budget theory would focus on the interrelationship between resource allocation systems and organizational structures and processes. Those structures and processes which enhance the capacity of the organization to identify resource allocation schemes that provide for the long-term economic viability of the organization are normatively superior, as are the short-term allocations that meet the broad range of immediate demands for services and that are designed in the context of long-term viability. This normative stance is based on the implied fiduciary relationship between the public finance professional and the public organization. These basic values should be considered in any mix of goods and services produced through the competition of political philosophies—indeed, this is a requirement for continued competition. The goal of professional public management is to increase the capacity of the local government organization to pursue these ends efficiently, effectively and economically, and the goal of public administration research is to provide theories that support public management.

REFERENCES

Astley, W. Graham, and Van de Ven, Andrew H. (1983). "Central Perspectives and Debates in Organization Theory." *Administrative Science Quarterly*, 28 (1): 245–273.

Benson, J. Kenneth (1982). "Networks and Policy Sectors." In David L. Rogers and David A. Whetton, eds., *Intergovernmental Coordination*. Ames: Iowa State University Press, 223–267.

Benson, J. Kenneth (1975). "The Interorganizational Network as a Political Economy." *Administrative Science Quarterly*, 20 (1): 229–249.

Caiden, Naomi (1990). "Public Budgeting in the United States: The State of the Discipline." In Naomi B. Lynn and Aaron Wildavsky, eds., *Public Administration: The State of the Discipline*. Chatham, N.J.: Chatham House, 228–255.

Farmer, David J. (1994). *The Language of Public Administration*. Tuscaloosa: University of Alabama Press.

Forrester, John P., and Mullins, Daniel R. (1992). "Rebudgeting: The Serial Nature of Municipal Budgetary Processes." *Public Administration Review*, 52 (5): 467–473.

Fox, Charles J., and Miller, Hugh T. (1995). *Post Modern Public Administration*. Thousand Oaks, Calif.: Sage.

Gage, Robert W. (1990). "Key Intergovernmental Issues and Strategy: An Assessment and Prognosis.'' In Robert W. Gage and Myrna P. Mandell, eds., *Strategies For Managing Intergovernmental Policies and Networks*. Westport, Conn.: Praeger, 127–150.

Gargan, John J. (1993). ''Specifying the Elements of Professionalism and the Process of Professionalization.'' *International Journal of Public Administration*, 16 (12): 1861–1884.

Garvey, Gerald (1993). *Facing the Bureaucracy*. San Francisco: Jossey-Bass.

Gerwin, Donald (1969). ''A Process Model of Budgeting in a Public School System.'' *Management Science*, 15 (7): 338–361.

Hackbart, Merl M., and Carson, Ronald J. (1993). ''Budget Theory and State Budget Practice: Analysis and Perspective.'' *Public Budgeting and Financial Management* 5 (1): 115–130.

Kiel, L. Douglas (1994). *Managing Chaos and Complexity in Government*. San Francisco: Jossey-Bass.

Klay, William Earle (1985). ''The Organizational Dimension of Budgetary Forecasting: Suggestions from Revenue Forecasting in the States.'' *International Journal of Public Administration*, 7 (3): 241–265.

LaPorte, Todd R. (1996). ''Shifting Vantage and Conceptual Puzzles in Understanding Public Organization Networks.'' *Journal of Public Administration Research and Theory*, 6 (1): 49–74.

Lawrence, Paul, and Lorsch, Jay (1967). *Organization and Environment*. Cambridge, Mass.: Harvard University Press.

LeLoup, Lance T. (1988). ''From Microbudgeting to Macrobudgeting: Evolution in Theory and Practice.'' In Irene S. Rubin, ed., *New Directions in Budget Theory*. Albany: SUNY Press, 41–65.

Lynch, Thomas D. (1989). ''Budget Systems Approach.'' *Public Administration Quarterly*, 13 (3): 321–341.

Manning, Peter K. (1992). *Organizational Communication*. New York: Aldine De Gruyter.

March, James, and Olsen, Johan (1979). ''Organizational Choice Under Ambiguity.'' In James March and Johan Olsen, eds., *Ambiguity and Choice in Organizations*. Bergen, Norway: Universitetsforlaget, 10–23.

Miller, Gerald J. (1991). *Government Financial Management*. New York: Marcel Dekker.

Moe, Terry M. (1994). ''Integrating Politics and Organizations: Positive Theory and Public Administration.'' *Journal of Public Administration Research and Theory*, 4 (1): 17–25.

Morgan, Gareth (1993). *Imaginization: The Art of Creative Management*. Newbury Park, Calif.: Sage.

Orton, J. Douglas, and Weick, Karl E. (1990). ''Loosely Coupled Systems: A Reconceptualization.'' *Academy of Management Review*, 15 (2): 203–223.

Osborne, David, and Gaebler, Ted (1992). *Reinventing Government*. Reading, Mass.: Addison-Wesley.

Overman, E. Sam (1996). ''The New Science of Management: Chaos and Quantum Theory and Method.'' *Journal of Public Administration Research and Theory*, 6 (1): 71–89.

Perrow, Charles (1986). *Complex Organizations* (3rd ed.). New York: Random House.

Pfeffer, Jeffrey (1981). *Power in Organizations*. Marshfield, Mass.: Pitman.

Rubin, Irene S. (1992). "Budget Reform and Political Reform: Conclusions from Six Cities." *Public Administration Review*, 52 (5): 454–466.

Rubin, Irene S. (1993). *The Politics of Public Budgeting* (2nd ed.). Chatham, N.J.: Chatham House.

Rubin, Irene S. (1990). "Budget Theory and Budget Practice: How Good the Fit?" *Public Administration Review*, 50 (2): 222–236.

Rubin, Irene S. (1979). "Retrenchment, Loose Structure, and Adaptability in the University." *Sociology of Education*, 52 (October): 211–222.

Salancik, Gerald R., and Pfeffer, Jeffrey (1977). "Who Gets Power—and How They Hold on to It: A Strategic Contingency Model of Power." *Organizational Dynamics* (Winter): 287–302.

Senge, Peter M. (1994). *Fifth Discipline: The Art and Practice of the Learning Organization*. New York: Doubleday.

Simon, Herbert A. (1976). *Administrative Behavior* (3rd ed.). New York: Free Press.

Thompson, James D. (1967). *Organizations in Action*. New York: McGraw-Hill.

Thurmaier, Kurt (1995). "Decisive Decision-making in the Executive Budget Process: Analyzing the Political and Economic Propensities of Central Budget Bureau Analysts." *Public Administration Review*, 55 (5): 448–467.

Weick, Karl (1979). *The Social Psychology of Organizing* (2nd ed.). Reading, Mass.: Addison-Wesley.

Whicker, Marcia Lynn, and Sigelman, Lee (1991). "Decision Sequencing and Budgetary Outcomes: A Simulation Model." *Public Budgeting and Financial Management*, 3 (1): 7–34.

Wildavsky, Aaron (1961). "Political Implications of Budgetary Reform." *Public Administration Review*, 21 (Autumn): 183–190.

Williamson, Oliver E. (1994). *Comparative Economic Organization*. New York: New York University Press.

Willoughby, Katherine G. (1993). "Decision-making Orientations of State Government Analysts: Rationalists or Incrementalists?" *Public Budgeting and Financial Management*, 5 (1): 67–104.

Index

About the Authors

GERASIMOS A. GIANAKIS is Assistant Professor in the Department of Public Administration, College of Health and Public Affairs, at the University of Central Florida. The author of numerous journal articles and book chapters, he is a member of the American Society for Public Administration. He was previously a budget manager with the city of St. Petersburg, Florida, and he began his public service career as a Management Analyst with the St. Petersburg Police Department.

CLIFFORD P. McCUE is Assistant Professor at the School of Public Administration, College of Architecture, Urban and Public Affairs, Florida Atlantic University. The author of numerous journal articles, book chapters, and monographs, including *Immigration and Its Impact on American Cities* (Praeger, 1996), he is a member of the American Society for Public Administration, The Government Finance Officers Association, and the International City/County Managers Association. He has served as Finance Director for the City of South Miami, Senior Budget Director for the City of Hialeah, and Assistant Finance Director/Budget Coordinator of Frederick County, Virginia.